Classical Indian Thought and the English Language

Classical Indian Thought and the English Language

Perspectives and Problems

Editors

Mohini Mullick
Madhuri Santanam Sondhi

Indian Council of Philosophical Research
New Delhi

D.K. PRINTWORLD
Publishers of Indian Traditions

Cataloging in Publication Data – DK

[Courtesy: D.K. Agencies (P) Ltd. <docinfo@dkagencies.com>]

Rendering of the Categories of Classical Indian Thought in the English Language: Perspectives and Problems (Workshop) (2011 : New Delhi, India)

Classical Indian thought and the English language : perspectives and problems / editors, Mohini Mullick, Madhuri Santanam Sondhi.

pages cm

Includes bibliographical references.

ISBN 13: 9788124608272

1. Philosophy, Indic — Congresses. 2. Sanskrit language — Influence on English — Congresses. 3. Sanskrit literature — Translations into English — History and criticism — Congresses. I. Mullick, Mohini, editor. II. Sondhi, Madhuri, 1935-, editor. III. Indian Council of Philosophical Research.issuing body. IV. India International Centre.host institution. V. Title.

DDC 181.4 23

ISBN 13: 978-81-246-0827-2

First published in India, 2015 Print run : 550 copies

Published by:
INDIAN COUNCIL OF PHILOSOPHICAL RESEARCH
Darshan Bhawan, 36 Tughlakabad Institutional Area
Mehrauli Badarpur Road, New Delhi - 110 062

and

D.K. PRINTWORLD (P) LTD.
Regd. Office: "Vedaśrī", F-395, Sudarshan Park
(Metro Station: Ramesh Nagar), New Delhi – 110 015
Phones: (011) 2545 3975, 2546 6019; *Fax*: (011) 2546 5926
e-mail: indology@dkprintworld.com; *Website*: www.dkprintworld.com

Printed by : D.K. Printworld (P) Ltd. New Delhi

Contents

Part II

Acknowledgements

THE papers, responses and discussions published in this volume are from the proceedings of a Workshop convened by Dr. Mohini Mullick and Madhuri Santanam Sondhi on *Rendering of the Categories of Classical Indian Thought in the English Language: Perspectives and Problems* held at the India International Centre, New Delhi, in December 2011. This highly interesting interdisciplinary gathering of scholars from India and abroad came to debate this reasonably new – new to the seminar circuit – topic which was facilitated primarily by the Indian Council of Philosophical Research. ICPR Chairman Prof. Ramakrishna Rao readily responded to our request to sponsor the Workshop, and it is to him we owe our primary thanks. We also owe thanks to successor Chairman Prof. Mrinal Miri and Member-Secretary Dr. Manenda Pratap Singh for enabling this project to be published by the ICPR. Other institutions equally forthcoming with their support were the Ministry of Culture, Government of India, the Indian Council of Cultural Relations, Ministry of External Affairs under the direction of Dr. Karan Singh, which undertook to sponsor the travel of participants from the USA, Canada and Belgium; the India International Centre which, with the support of Dr. Kapila Vatsayan, Director of the Asia Project, hosted and provided the venue, and last but not least,'Manana', The Devahuti-Damodar Svaraj Trust and its trustee, Veena Sachdev, which shouldered the onerous responsibilities of administering the Workshop.

Mohini Mullick
Madhuri Santanam Sondhi

Introduction

THE essays we have assembled for this volume were presented at a workshop organized in Delhi in December 2011.

Their themes centre on a proposal that initiated the process of setting up this event, and which is reproduced below:

> **Proposal for a Workshop on the Rendering of the Categories of Classical Indian Thought in the English Language: Perspectives and Problems.**
>
> The problem of translation – especially that involving technical vocabulary – has now received wide recognition the world over. Translation studies are a well-established discipline and the literature continues to grow.
>
> Scientific texts appear to have successfully solved the problem by standardizing technical terms that are then absorbed by all languages of instruction and communication. But this vocabulary has been developed largely in the West and in Western languages and has been absorbed into almost all non-Western languages.
>
> The problem becomes acute when we are dealing with vocabularies of long standing belonging to ancient cultures, hence well established in their own spheres of discourse. Despite this, not nearly enough attention has been paid in this country to the dangers and pitfalls of rendering ancient and not so ancient Indian texts – largely written in Sanskrit, as also in Pāli and the Draviḍian languages – in the English language, a language that has come to acquire the status of near monopoly as the

medium of instruction and the communication of research.

This workshop aims at bringing into collective focus what we believe each individual scholar grappling with Indian categorial thought has some time or other encountered: the problem of conveying ideas, concepts and indeed entire categories that are embedded in their own unique world-view, a view, we might add, that is very much still with us.

Ceaseless talk of multiculturalism and lip service to pluralism and the like have failed in altering this fact, predicated as it is on a hierarchy of the languages of 'power'. The extent to which this dominance has led to a fundamental misconstrual, not to say, suppression of the deepest intuitions and insights of non-Western cultures – the present focus is on India – is a matter that requires urgent probing and examination.

There is a growing literature – unfortunately emanating largely from the West itself – that has been drawing attention to anomalies, contradictions and outright distortions in the writings of scholars of Indian thought who use the English language.

The view that philosophy is a universal enterprise and that place and time are irrelevant as coordinates in its practice, has been advanced by a number of scholars. These scholars also believe that we should engage 'creatively' with the texts of the past. Those seeking to return to some unalloyed, pristine meanings are falling prey to the myth of origins. This view should find place in these deliberations as it is an influential post-modern view generated in the West. Inter alia it may be noted that a distinction could be made between an 'organic' evolution of concepts, something which certainly happened in the course of Indian intellectual history, and the conscious imposition of terminology that belongs to languages that are 'in power'. (Even if this is a spurious distinction, it requires airing.)

A counterset of considerations stems from the fact that unlike the Greek civilization, the thought worlds of ancient and medieval India are still very much alive and with us in contemporary India. In this perspective, to even begin to understand contemporary India and its dilemmas and crises, it is essential to come to grips with the foundational concerns, wisdom and follies of a civilization that has refused to die.

In practical terms this workshop could serve as a setting out of guidelines for scholars who are either forced to take a Procrustean approach or do so quite willingly in order to fall in line with what some see as 'universal' philosophy.

Numerous Greek, Latin, German and French words have been absorbed over the years, perhaps centuries, into the English language, precisely because scholars became aware of the fact that no accurate translations are available in English. A smattering of Indian language terms now is also freely used by speakers of English: one immediately thinks of *avatāra, paṇḍit* and *guru*; there are others. But when it comes to serious discussion of ancient Indian thought categories – *jñāna, pramāṇa, anumāna, darśana* and a host of others, terms in the English language are almost invariably used in academic publications even after it is noted that the target term is not an exact one. Thus, Western categories are implanted into non-Western discourses. The term 'religion', it has been argued, is just such an implant.

These matters are in need of in-depth discussion if we are to avoid travesties such as the rendering of the Sanskrit term *dharma* as 'religion' and *śabda* as 'letter'. (We emphasize 'Sanskrit' here because in the Hindi language,

> *dharma* appears to have taken on this meaning in quite an irrevocable manner – Hindi is very much a language in evolution.)
>
> In practical terms, scholars will be invited to present their thoughts and suggestions on this subject. To take an example: the notion of 'the secular' being a corollary of 'the religious' has been the subject of serious and unresolved debate in India. It is also of urgent importance to achieve clarity on the subject. Political philosophers, scholars in the field of jurisprudence and social scientists must come together and discuss these issues. Similarly, scholars of moral philosophy, ontology and theory of knowledge, to give only some examples, will make presentations in the field of their interest and specialization.
>
> Finally, this cannot remain a piecemeal exercise. Deliberations will necessarily result in a more fundamental examination of where the problems lie.

Along with the foregoing guidelines, for most papers, respondents were invited to identify the main issues presented and to initiate further discussion. Since the proceedings were recorded, we finally had the benefit in each session not only of the presentation of arguments and counter-arguments, but also of a prepared analysis of the main thesis and then a general drawing out of issues as the discussion was thrown open to the floor. We felt that the ideas and controversies generated and the sheer weight of scholarship presented, should not remain lost to the general reading public who did not attend these proceedings. The new generation of students, the editors feel, might particularly benefit from exposure to the fresh perspectives presented in the course of the three-day workshop which critically examined the assumption (that has come to be unquestioningly accepted amongst academics, namely, that all learning must in today's 'globalized' world, take place in the English language.

The Indian educational system is facing (though not always facing up to) a crisis, the reasons for which it is not the present task to expatiate. It must nevertheless be stressed that the parasitical nature of our intellectual pursuits is not the least of these reasons.

When it comes to the understanding of our own classical traditions, their rendering into the English language has only served to obscure the great cultural divide between the history of Western thought and the history (followed by stagnation) of our own ways of looking at the world. That a substantial part of this project was completed during a period of India's colonial history, and was not preceded by (indeed did not permit) considered debate on the new ways of learning initiated by our colonial masters, reflects the effects of domination and intellectual hegemony with which we continue to grapple even today.

This collection of papers is divided in two parts. Part I consists of those papers that dealt with the broader, theoretical and methodological issues that form the background to the more specific predicaments that scholars face today. Part II consists of papers that have carried out an analysis of concrete concepts/categories in translated works which have now coloured the understanding of contemporary readers who have no direct access to original texts written in our classical languages.

Each contribution to the proceedings has brought fresh, even unique, insights into the debate in light of its author's convictions and preoccupations.

Sudipta Kaviraj raises a fundamental question that few have raised: what is the need to translate at all? How should this be done?

S.N. Balagangadhara takes up the question of cultural difference and the need for serious comparative work in this context. Our present understanding of ourselves is based on categories employed by the social sciences that are clearly alien to the thought-life of Indian culture and civilization. He traces the genesis of these problems.

D. Prahlada Char the eminent Sanskritist who has lived with the problem of the translation of Sanskrit texts into English, brings concrete examples of distortion to bear on the proceedings.

Claus Oetke takes an opposing stance, arguing forcefully that there is nothing unique in the translational problem faced across cultures – at least not in terms of the Western and Indian world-views.

Vivek Dhareshwar seeks a more radical frame in which to place the predicament of contemporary Indian scholarship. Our cognitive enslavement cannot be accounted for in terms of the translation problem, he argues. The mismatch is between the way we experience the world in our day-to-day lives and the theoretical vocabularies we employ to illuminate this experience.

In Part II, K.D. Tripathi examines the historical fortunes of the *Abhinavabhāratī* with special reference to the treatment given to key concepts in Indian 'aesthetics'.

P.K. Mukhopadhyay writes on the seminal problem of the availability of ethics in our tradition. Inevitably, the focus is on the notion of *dharma.* He further examines the very nature of the problem that is under the scanner and solutions offered in contemporary literature.

Wagish Shukla's contribution is unique in that it appears to underpin the entire controversy of the nature of the Sanskrit corpus. His thesis is that the very conception of language in the Indian classical tradition differs from that found in Western literature: it is performative and not referential. This must alter, in his view, our understanding of the meaning and purpose of the questions that have been raised in classical literature.

Aloka Parasher Sen throws historical light on the course taken by the notions of *varṇa* and *jāti* in Indian society. Bringing a great deal of scholarship to bear on the subject, she explains the foreigner's understanding of these very complex categories in terms of 'caste', against the background of this country's colonization by the West.

Ramkrishna Bhattacharya traces the history of Indian materialism but interrogates the term's applicability to the literature. Are the Cārvākas just materialists, he asks?

It seems to us, the editors of this volume, that further debates on the issues raised in these pages should now not be delayed. This book seeks to ignite this larger debate.

Mohini Mullick
Madhuri S. Sondhi

Part I

1

Why and How Should We Read Ancient Texts?

Sudipta Kaviraj

> I know it will be said: what can be the use of Sanskrit at the present day? Is not Sanskrit a dead language? And are not the Hindus themselves ashamed of their ancient literature? Do they not learn English, and do they not prefer Locke and Hume and Mill to their ancient poets and philosophers?
>
> – Max Müller 2000 (1883): 71

> India is well on the way to losing its memory, and not just losing it – since the past never passes away – but surrendering it to the abusers of memory.
>
> – Sheldon Pollock 2011: 38

THIS workshop is primarily focused on the challenges in the translation of ancient texts. Translation can mean several different things: rendering a word into a word, but also rendering one language into another, and this raises the question of rendering one conceptual language into another and the questions of its possibility if we lack non-ostensive reference. But I decided to focus on a question which I think stands behind this question. The way the question is set up for our workshop presupposes the idea that it is useful and important to read ancient texts in Sanskrit; the primary hurdle is translation – the fact that they are in Sanskrit and we cannot read them easily, and further, because Sanskrit constitutes a unique linguistic world, it is hard to render its ideas adequately into English. I think we have a prior question to resolve. Translation is required only if we resolve to read; and it seems that the primary question in India about our classical thought is, increasingly: why should we read classical thought at all?

What Is Involved in the Basic Historicity of Texts

In our encounter with classical Sanskrit texts, we must submit to the double historicity of reading. The first act is to recognize the historicity of the text – the time-lapse and temporal interpretative deposits the text acquires through its historical existence; we must also reflexively record our own readerly historicity – the conditions under which we read. Historical reading is to bring these two historicities together. There is no other kind of reading: the only other way, which is not a sensible way really, is merely to forget these conditions.

I felt the need to make a few remarks on these two questions after reading Stephen Phillips's work (2008: 170-78) on translation. His criticisms of Patrick Olivelle's translation of the *Gītā* encourage us to think about several things. The major and crucial questions are about how we should read texts like the *Gītā* today. The primary objection he makes against Olivelle's translation is that it is too eager to persuade the contemporary reader to read the text and neglects and bypasses the distinguished traditions of *Gītā* interpretations in the long past of Hindu thinking.

The essential problem here is similar to one that was central to Western interpretation theory several decades ago. A vigorous debate began in the 1970s around the question of reading texts of Western political thought, in which, against the prevailing orthodoxy of the 1960s which regarded texts of political theory as philosophy, Cambridge School scholars pressed for a historical, contextualist reading practice. This theory suggested that successful reading of a text from the past depended entirely on the capture of the 'language' in which the text was composed and received by its intended original audience. Although contextualists implicitly acknowledged that textuality is a strange phenomenon which separated writing from the circumstances of its origin, they would have argued that it is incoherent to think that an author could write a text 'for posterity', i.e. for an audience about which he could have no conception. Successful reading of texts from the past which would avoid anachronistic presentist misreading depends crucially on 'bracketing' our present language and accurately accessing the language of the text.[1]

But this argument was not unchallenged. Against this kind of interpretative theory (which is identical to Dilthey's in the tradition of German hermeneutics and in major respects derived from it), H.G. Gadamer's work offered two forceful counter arguments. It is true that an author cannot conceive of the mental world of a future audience but the act of writing itself has a paradoxical quality based on the imminent 'absence' of the author; the textuality of the text consists in its strange placement between the linguistic horizon of the author and a separate horizon of the reader. A text therefore cannot be said to bear a meaning, only potentiality of meaningfulness (Gadamer[2] 1992). Textual meaning, strictly speaking, is like the intrinsic aurality of music. It is only when the text is 'played' – brought to a representation, in both senses of the term,[3] that it comes to acquire meaning. Thus the text is invariably singular, its meanings invariably plural. From this point of view, it is a false

[1] For the presentation of the case for the Cambridge school, see Skinner 2002.

[2] The discussion of a radical historicist position is based primarily on H.G. Gadamer 1992.

[3] That is, presented again under necessarily different circumstances, and more crucially, presented in a different mediun – like the musical signs transformed into aural sound, or the words of a play spoken in acting by a real actor.

temptation to infer a singularity of meaning from the singularity of the text.[4] Paradoxically, we can concede both claims: that in the author's mind the text must have borne a singular meaning which he intended to convey through writing or textualizing; but textualizing is always through the means of language, and it is in the nature of linguality that meaning cannot be intentionally controlled, that it comes to submit itself to the intentionality of others – readers, players, actors, interpreters – all the unknown characters the text is bound to encounter in its history. The text is poised necessarily between the two intentionalities of the author and the reader and it is always subject to a refraction of receptive intentionalities of numerous kinds.

Gadamer's second argument was that it is hard or impossible to 'bracket' our own language. Both Diltheyan romantic hermeneutics and English theories of historicist reading simply assume, without much examination, that we can. But clearly, that is an idea that ought to be examined critically.[5] It is impossible to get out of our language to access another – to keep these two languages impermeably separate. In language at least, there is no Archimedean point. All that we can do is to be reflexive about our own linguisticality and acknowledge that though we must try to capture the difference of the other language, it is captured within our own.[6] Instead of trying to

---

4 In some of his essays Roland Barthes (1974) tried to capture something similar by distinguishing between a text and a work.

5 There was of course no direct argument between Gadamer's form of radical historicism and the Cambridge school. But the argumentative connection is obvious; and in the debates about Skinner's work some scholars made this point: see for example, Joseph Femia 1984.

6 It seems that the position that historical languages are hermetically sealed is also mistaken: we can formulate strategies to capture other languages inside our own: but this is a problem rather than something that can be done without difficulty. However, this is not the place to develop this argument fully.

accomplish something impossible, we should submit to the demands of what is linguistically feasible. To return to the instance of the *Gītā*, we can derive several different positions among which we are invited to adjudicate. The first is the Skinnerian injunction that if we are reading a historical text, we must try to read it in its own language (language A), in the context of its own linguistic creation. The second option is to decide that recapture of that language is either impossible or problematic and we should try to present it in our own language of the present (say, language F) which was Olivelle's choice.[7] Phillips suggests a complex and interesting option: to convey to the reader reading a text in language F that it was composed in language A but was interpreted powerfully in languages B, C, D, E in intervening periods when significant linguistic and life-world changes occurred. This position of course implies the further difficulty of taking into account the fact that in each case of interpretative movement, readers faced their own version of the translation problem (A–F). A full understanding of the hardness and complexity of our task would mean that a particular text composed in language A would then be captured in each successive language. The task of the present interpreter would be to show in case of each significant transformation of conceptual languages what the nature of the change was and consequently what was significantly new in this process of historic translations–interpretations. In many of these cases, the readers may think that they are engaged in an interpretation but that might mask an underlying process of translation which they may not see so clearly, because unlike modern culture, they did not have such a highly developed vocabulary of the historical. In this question, my own sympathies are substantially

[7] This, of course, suspends a discussion of what the properties internal to a 'language' in this sense, are. A language is always a language adequated to a life-world, and if the language F is connected to a life-world that is utterly different, that raises significant questions of translatability.

with the historicist position. And I think the great salutary effect of a rigorous discussion of this question would allow us to perceive an inadequacy of Gadamer's own interpretation of the rule of historicity, just as he showed an inadequacy in Dilthey's (Gadamer 1992). Gadamer too, oversimplified the nature of the historicity of texts by turning it into a two-language process – of A and F. In cultures of great actual continuity, sometimes it is impossible to read a text like the *Gītā* from a temporal distance. This temporal distance is filled with interpretative readings of the *Gītā*; any reading in language F will involve reading the text through its earlier readings, rather than the text itself. The text's existence is always mediated by intermediate interpretative texts or commentaries. This shows that the enterprise of 'going back to the text itself' is not something that can be done 'naturally': rather it is a deliberate 'unnatural' strategy which seeks somehow to peel off the interpretative sheaths around the text and reveal the text itself.

There is a further complication to note in this process. Traditions continue for long periods; but they can also get radically ruptured for historical reasons. Through the prevalence of Sanskrit, a kind of continuity was maintained in Indian Hindu culture for a long time, just as Persian maintained it for the Islamicate part of Indian culture. To take an example in analysis of literary aesthetics, the emergence of the Kashmiri *rasa* aesthetics continued unruptured for a long time. Colonialism and the catastrophic decline of Sanskrit produced a radical rupture in this tradition. Similarly, the *Gītā* was read through an uninterrupted tradition of commentarial reception. Yet the startling truth about history is that with the 'death of Sanskrit' this easy intelligibility and Āgamic continuity was broken. When modern thinkers returned to the *Gītā* with a vengeance in the nineteenth century, to them this earlier commentarial history of reception was in large measure lost, and they went to an unhistorical, or rather unhistoricized text called the *Bhagavad*

Gītā, i.e. a text from which all these traces of prior reading had been cleansed.

Reading the interpretations of the *Gītā*, including the versions in the modern period by Bankim Chandra Chatterjee, Balgangadhar Tilak and Mohandas Karamchand Gandhi, and appreciating our own growing distance from these, gives us a much fuller and more complex understanding of the conditions of historicity. All this is about the question: how should we read an ancient Sanskrit text? Thinking about it, it appeared to me that Olivelle's choice was related to a desperate attempt to answer a more fundamental problem:[8] why should people read such texts at all? One powerful way of answering that sceptical thesis is to suggest that contemporary readers will gain something directly from the text, that it could speak to them directly, and say something valuable.[9] It appears to me undoubtedly true that this is a prior question to the other, and requires some thinking on our part about how we can answer it or can we answer it at all?

Therefore, we must try to confront this harder and more dismal question: why should we read the classics at all? 'We' belong to three categories whose cognitive interest in reading texts from Sanskrit is quite distinct. The first group consists of people like Phillips or Pollock who revived my interest in the Sanskrit that I knew and taught me much more besides, who come from a different culture, but developed a scholarly interest in the world of *devabhāṣā* and what it was doing in the world of men. For them, an answer to the question why we should read Sanskrit must be framed in a classically historicist fashion.[10] A

---

8 The desperation is not restricted to Olivelle: it is a desperation we commonly share.

9 Two significant examples of this attempt, from very different periods, are that of Max Müller and Pollock.

10 Indeed, in a recent lecture to the South Asia Institute Heidelberg, on its fiftieth anniversary, Pollock has presented an argument which is →

much harder question is whether people like us – Indians who do not have a special scholarly interest in Sanskrit texts – can have an untextual but serious intellectual interest in the Sanskrit tradition. Interest in antiquity must be specialized and belong to a small number of individuals with special cognitive interests and intellectual skills. But that does not mean, as the Western example shows, that interest in those arguments must be limited to them. Aristotle could hardly have been the figure he is in modern political theory, if using him required knowledge of the intricacies of ancient Greek. It is plausible to assert that for us Indians, knowing our 'traditions' – in Persian or Sanskrit – must constitute a part of self-understanding, a knowledge of what we are and where we have come from, or how we have become the way we are. This is a separate argument from the classical historicist one that all forms of human life are unique and valuable and therefore a worthy subject of investigation. My impression is that this line of reasoning is fraught with much trouble which we casually ignore. Curiously, if we think historically, it is much harder for an Indian to relate to his tradition than it is for a European to relate to his, despite the paradoxical fact that in some ways our society is far less modern than that of the Europeans.

To compare Western cultures with our own on this question is instructive, but also puzzling. Instructive because in contrast to the near disappearance of true Sanskrit scholarship from inside our university system, in the West classical scholarship occupies a relatively small, highly specialized but intellectually alive social space. Although pressure from barbaric Thatcherism occasionally asks why scarce resources should be spent on the teaching of Greek and Latin, and though undoubtedly these skills have shrunk alarmingly in their school system, which would produce the base for research, it is unlikely that Western

---

← strongly 'historicist' in the sense in which German hermeneuticists like Dilthey or Droysen used it.

universities would imminently abolish departments of classical learning. By contrast, in India we have successfully abolished serious classical learning in both sides of culture – Islamic and Hindu – or for those allergic to religious words, Persianate and Sanskritic: – from those places where serious research takes place – in our universities and institutes. Serious knowledge of Sanskrit still survives precariously in some endangered centres, like traditional Sanskrit schools and a few specialized universities. But if they do not have any contact with serious cognitive process of social life, they are likely to wither. Thus we observe a strange paradoxical contrast. In the West, tradition had entirely disappeared from social life, but its knowledge is securely cultivated in the specialized space of the university. In India, a great deal of tradition survives in social life, but knowledge about it is in serious danger of elimination.

Let us assume that we face a radical scepticism about what we do. Activity or enquiry such as ours – into esoteric arguments in texts of great complexity written in a dead language in a time long past, to give it the maximally disadvantageous description – must justify itself ordinarily by one of two different types of arguments which for the sake of simplicity I shall call historical and philosophical. But we can subdivide the historical itself into two types of concerns.

The first kind of historical curiosity is very specific. I can become, for reasons of pure biographic accident, interested in the intellectual history of Kashmir in the ninth-tenth centuries, which would require that I read texts from that period and also read about those texts. In that case, my cognitive relation to these texts will be quite similar to the interest taken by a Western scholar in some respects. It will be an antiquarian curiosity in a strict sense: it is a curiosity about a part of the past which does not bear a strong connection to my present. It is not present in my present in any significant way. Consequently, the knowledge that is produced about such matters could not play a significant role in my self-knowledge as a member of my specific historical society.

The second kind of historical enquiry is more general and could be called roughly a genealogical enquiry. Like family genealogy, we start from the present and ask 'where have I come from?', and the answer to that would lie in an accurate construction of a family tree. Several differences between these two types of question should be noted, though both are historical. The second enquiry is rooted in the present and in a sense, stems from a curiosity to understand the present itself. If we live on one side of a significant historical rupture like the coming of modernity or the entry of colonialism, it makes sense to say that we cannot understand social form B, which is precisely produced as a result of this rupture, if we also do not have some sense of social form A with which B is rupturally connected in the sense that they stand on two sides of a historical transformation. We cannot entirely understand the 'modern' in a self-enclosed way, indeed we cannot have a clear judgement about modernity's claims to novelty, if we do not have an understanding of what it is supposed to be different from.[11] That is what I want to call a ruptural connection or a ruptural contiguity. It is a contrast, but also an epistemic connection: without knowing A we cannot say we really know B, if B's claim to its self-identity is constituted by the claim that it is radically different from A. Crucially, the first kind of question is quite different: the tenth century in Kashmir is not rupturally contiguous with my present; and we cannot make a strong argument that without learning about tenth-century Kashmir, somehow my understanding of my own present would remain deficient.[12] We need a different justification. I now want

[11] Pollock has also made this argument forcefully. In my case, I came to this conviction by thinking primarily about questions of the state and forms of social power. See Kaviraj 2010.

[12] It may be that I put this too strongly for polemical reasons: but I would like to see a forceful counter-argument.

to explore the second form of historical questioning a bit more fully, because it produces several difficulties.

Short History and Long History: The Dismal Implications of the Concept of 'Effective History'

In a sense the historical argument appears at first sight, at least abstractly, very compelling. What can be a more forceful argument than saying that we must understand our past because that is where we have come from, that is what has shaped, and in a manner of speaking created, our present? But that is a compelling argument only at first sight. When we look closely we discern numerous difficulties. We must remember that all pasts are not similar. Time produces distance, like space. The time we want to study through these efforts at classical scholarship are often of a very distant past. One major insight of modern historical thought is that temporal distance and historical distance are not identical. Continuity is a structural, not a purely temporal quality: a culture can have continuity for centuries; and a relative short space of time can comprise a real rupture. The Sanskrit texts for which, for various reasons of biography we feel a deep attraction, were produced across an admittedly long time, but many of them are from the deep past.

Sanskrit intellectual life spanned a vast temporal span from the Vedic texts to vibrant poetic and textual production in the seventeenth century. Even if we accept Pollock's view about the 'death of Sanskrit' poetry after Panditraja Jagannath in Shah Jahan's court, which I think we must, it is a vast swathe of time which had centres of high creativity clustered in certain geographic regions at certain temporal points. After a sustained development of a high Sanskrit culture from the third century BCE to the tenth century CE, Sanskrit intellectual and poetic production continues in various centres down to the time of the Mughals. Critics of Pollock's thesis are right in a modified sense if they claim that knowledge and cultivation of the Sanskrit tradition continues much after the time of the Mughals. Even in the nineteenth century, Sanskrit scholars produce interesting and deeply scholarly engagements with their traditions. *Vyāptipañcakarahasya*, a text of Navyanyāya, gets erudite commentaries in Bengali for instance, well into the twentieth century; and there were scholars of great eminence like Gopinath Kaviraj who continued cultivation of these traditions well into the twentieth century. Still, I think Pollock is fundamentally right: these were scholars of a tradition which had ceased to exist as the primary intellectual force in the life of its own society. They were sustaining that tradition only in the restricted sense of keeping a kind of archive of that knowledge and a form of scholarship which prevented Sanskrit writings from becoming something like hieroglyphs. Even the question 'do these texts continue to exist?' from this point of view, becomes a complicated one. If that question means: do these texts physically exist in libraries, and are they preserved in un-degraded manuscripts which can still in principle be read? Of course, they do. Still it is sobering to think of the amount that we know does not exist any longer. If someone makes a list of works which are referred to in existing texts for which we do not have any extant copy like for instance *Hṛdayadarpaṇa* of Bhaṭṭanāyaka from tenth century Kashmir, it will be a staggering document. But my question is about texts which are physically extant like *Abhinavabhāratī* as to whether the text should be said to have been 'preserved'. If the preservation of a text includes the conditions under which it can be read fluently, the question of its existence/preservation becomes a complicated one. Is a text of an inscription that no one can read, still to be called a text? This shows that preservation, astonishingly, is not a bivalent quality that we can say unproblematically that a text exists or does not: we are forced to think of even existence/preservation in a graded way. Sanskrit texts generally – but I shall soon argue not wholly – suffer from a degraded version of existence.

The interesting thing is that although it is a strongly counter-intuitive thought, modern Indians cannot claim the pre-modern Sanskrit or Persian texts as part of their tradition (Āgama). To understand this paradox we should attend to the two meanings of the term 'tradition', at least the two ways in which it is commonly used in ordinary English. Tradition can mean something like a historical stock, like a warehouse, or a list of plays that a theatre company that existed for a long time has staged over its long history. Alternatively, and I think more accurately, tradition also means the actable part of this stock or repertoire, i.e. only those elements of the historic repertoire which is connected to us by performable practice. In the first sense, *Nāṭyaśāstra* or *Abhinavabhāratī* or *Nyāyamañjarī* are part of my/our tradition: but we can hardly even understand them, so they are not in the second. Colonialism transformed what is near to us, what is at hand. But here colonialism should be taken in a double sense: not just the imposition of some cognitive conditions by the power of the colonial apparatus, but also conditions created by the modern intellectual elites, the custodians of the cognitive traditions of Indian society.

Why are these texts and the ideas they contain part of our tradition in the first, rather lame sense, and not in the second? I shall try to explain that by using an argument from Gadamer's reflection on the nature of historicity. In explaining the nature of historicity Gadamer (1992) introduced an idea of 'effective history'. This meant that although in a tradition of interpretation of past texts some earlier cultures might not be directly used by current interpreters, the effects of their prior interpretations still remain effective. Cultures or interpretations might have been forgotten or become hard to access directly, but remain effective through their consequences. The vital point this adds to our understanding of the past is that the more proximate parts of our pasts have a direct bearing on the current states of historical existence: the previous stages become obscured and remain present in our present not directly, but only through traces of their effects. Under certain conditions, the proximate segment of the past might obscure the more distant ones: temporality, instead of being a connection, becomes an obstacle to our vision. Another way of using this idea would be to say that history can exist in two ways: long and short history. Long history is a form of history in which we recognize that historical states of affairs have long genealogical chains behind them; and by implication, if we really want to understand the past historically, we must painstakingly unravel these long genealogical braids of causality. But it is much more common to live with a short sense of history which must acknowledge that the present state of affairs has a strong explanatory connection with the immediately preceding stage. But this kind of historical commonsense is not really interested in the earlier stages of a long history. Those stages exist nominally, in a way which does not require us to understand their content. In that sense, the previous stage which often has a ruptural continuity with our present, precisely by its cognitive imminence, obscures the stages lying beyond it and causes cultures to forget them. It requires cultures to make a much more decided effort at historical recollection to open up those distanced regions of its past. In effect, the concept of effective history leads to this dismal implication: the lapse of historical time causes a decay of interest and leads to an effect that could be called back-shortening. The further back a time is, the more shrunk it is in our historical consciousness. It is enough to know that those pasts existed, not to seriously know their character.

The Cultural Effects of Colonialism

Added to this in the history of Indian culture is the specific character of the immediately prior stage of our cultural history and the question of the cultural effects of colonialism. The Indian nationalist tradition advanced several powerful lines of reflection about the nature of colonialism and its effects on our society. For understandable reasons, the obvious loss of political sovereignty and the exploration of economic consequences of colonialism dominated these reflections. Inside the complex strands of nationalist thought, thinkers like Gandhi and Rabindranath Tagore thought with deep critical intelligence about the subtler and fundamental damages colonialism caused to culture and intellectual production; but after Independence, the triumph of the Nehruvian version of nationalism put these concerns into relative obscurity. It is only since the 1990s that partly through a revival of interest in Gandhi (much less, incidentally, in Tagore), and partly through the complex discussions around Orientalism and post-colonial knowledge that these questions are being reopened.

Both anti-colonial thinkers like Gandhi and Tagore and post-colonial academics, emphasize the directly political domination of colonialism to explain the decline of Sanskrit knowledge systems. I believe however that the collapse of Sanskrit and Persian cognitive practices were so sudden and so comprehensive that it could not have been caused simply by the political dominance of colonial power. In any case, colonial authorities did not directly restructure educational processes. And as much modern research shows, at least in the initial stages of building a base of knowledge about this society, they had to depend on the factual information traditional intellectuals furnished.[13] I wish

---

[13] There is a tendency associated with this research to suggest that because of this collaboration, colonial knowledge was a benign collaborative project, like modern scientific collaboration. This seriously distorts the historical picture and hides the crucial fact that the new knowledge displaced the traditional intellectuals into becoming intellectual underlabourers. Formerly, they worked within their own knowledge systems; under the colonial dispensation, their own systems were gradually undermined and they were forced to act as suppliers of raw data for a different cognitive system which they did not quite understand and certainly did not control.

to suggest that there was a second process which complicated and hastened the first. Modernity as a social state introduces a new kind of cognitive constitution of society. Modern economic and state practices require knowledge of new kinds, just as much as modern practices of the prosecution of individual lives. Pre-modern knowledge systems crucially did not go through a process of adaptation to these new requirements of the cognitive constitution of society either in terms of their language or in terms of their methodological structures. As our society required these new forms of knowledge, these were accumulated primarily through the linguistic and cognitive instrumentality of English and modern knowledge systems which a new group of Indian intellectuals learnt quickly and began to deploy on their own. But this group had few connections with the older producers of knowledge. Critically significant practices of social life – like the practices of medicine, law, acquisition of social knowledge and their analysis – were primarily transferred to new knowledge systems learnt from the West and delivered almost exclusively in English. The literate intellectual elites who were fluent in cosmopolitan languages of pre-modern India, Persian and Sanskrit, transferred their linguistic and intellectuals skills with relative ease to acquire the new language and cognitive systems, and basically voted with their feet against Sanskrit and Persian.

This argument has a further implication. It is true that pre-modern cognitive systems suffered from a comprehensive collapse of prestige and militant modernists crusaded against any bit of knowledge or information conveyed in these two languages as marks of superstitious backwardness. Actually, however, this shows that knowledge systems were undermined by the associated social practices moving away from them, leaving the intellectual structure hollow and bereft. But this also meant that these systems were rendered obsolete only when the attendant practices moved away from them and went elsewhere.

Our strategy should be to examine if there are segments of Indian culture in which the practice has not moved away from our traditional forms of knowledge.

In numerous parts of Indian culture, systems based on Sanskrit and Persian were not entirely abandoned by practices. The two most evident instances are from religious practice and the fine arts. Clearly, under the impact of Western Enlightenment ideas, the place of religion was transformed but religious life did not suffer a terminal erasure. Even very modern families, if they continued with their conventional religious worship, had to employ priests who knew the relevant language.[14] Modern families in Bengal for instance did not come to offer their prayers to Goddess Durgā in English, nor were Sūfī singers persuaded by modernity to sing their *qawwālīs* in this language. Similarly, in classical music and dance, imaginative artists preserved and returned to their textual traditions associated with their arts. Consider the long pages of the plates depicting dance *mudrās* in the Baroda Gaekwad Oriental series of *Nāṭyaśāstra*.[15] The implication of this argument then is that it is wrong to lament the decline of Sanskrit systems in their entirety; and we should abandon the casual idea of symmetrical obsolescence of the entire Sanskrit corpus. Obsolescence is only an extreme term for increasing inaccessibility. And that gives us the slightly less dismal conclusion that there are degrees of inaccessibility of the corpus. When a young woman learns Bharatanāṭyam she has to use as her normal vocabulary a language which comes down from the tradition of *rasa* theory. A singer training to sing with Oḍissī has to acquire great familiarity with the *Gīta-Govinda*. Inside the practice of music that accompanies much of our classical dances, Sanskrit is not a dead language. The practitioner

---

[14] Though even there the knowledge of Sanskrit of these priests was often unreliable and wholly learnt by rote.

[15] Though even in case of the performing arts, the shift from oral knowledge to texts is a significant one.

has to learn it for the same reason a social scientist has to learn English. But this also leads us to the strange conclusion that Jayadeva, or at least the *Gīta-Govinda*, is better 'preserved' than the much later works of Paṇḍitrāja Jagannātha. He is 'obsolete', but Jayadeva is not.[16]

Let me turn briefly now to a set of other considerations on why and how we should read Sanskrit texts. Three types of interest in Sanskrit texts could be outlined from the earlier analysis. First, the two kinds of historical interest – in short and long history – would direct interest at different bodies of Sanskrit textual material. The insight that modernity cannot be really understood one-sidedly – only through a scholarship which knows the modern in detail – is crucial. Historians of Indian modernity ought to be persuaded to look closely at textual evidence which would reveal what the state of affairs in the immediate pre-modern period was, since the claim of newness associated with modernity is so constitutive. To take an example from Persian, not Sanskrit, anyone interested in the question: 'how did the universe of political power change through colonial modernity?' must attend to the story of India's political life from 1707 (the death of Aurangzeb) to 1781-82 presented in the massive chronicles of the *Seir ul Mutaqherin*.[17] Second, those who are interested in the long history of any subject which constituted part of the Sanskrit knowledge system would naturally have to enter the vast and fascinating world of those texts.

Third, quite apart from these two kinds of interest, there

---

16 I recognize that this skirts around the difficult question of the relation between texts and practices.

17 Ghulam Hussein Khan Tabatabai's *Seir ul Mutaqherin*, is the long, detailed chronicle of the movement of the centre of power from the Mughal court in Delhi to eastern India under the Bengal Nawabs, and eventually to British power in Calcutta. It covers the history of political power in the subcontinent from the death of Aurangzeb to the rule of Warren Hastings.

can be a philosophic interest in Sanskrit texts and the world of their reflections that is not driven by a strictly historical curiosity. I shall take two examples. It could be pointed out that divergent traditions of philosophic thought often encounter similar difficulties, but explore different solutions. It could be suggested that the problems posed by ordinary conceptions of causality were sought to be resolved in Indian philosophy in ways that were interestingly different from the strategies followed in modern Western thought. I find some of the discussions in Kashmiri *rasa* theories of the ninth-tenth centuries full of interesting reflections on questions that are central to an understanding of aesthetic pleasure, but its arguments and intellectual strategies are quite different from the reflective traditions that are more familiar to us from either Aristotle, Edmund Burke, and Immanuel Kant or more modern Western theories of culture. There is an historical aspect to aesthetic enjoyment, but the process of the happening of this pleasure is a general question; and Sanskrit texts from early medieval India can illuminate aspects of this process which remain undeveloped in reflections of Western aesthetic philosophy. *Rasa* theory should be explored not out of a historical interest in how Kashmiri theorists thought about aesthetic pleasure, but of a philosophic interest in ways of grasping how the pleasure of literature is at all possible.

Finally, on a fourth count, in some fields of practice, Sanskrit texts contain a body of knowledge which is of undiminished practical use. In fields like Āyurveda and Yoga, Sanskrit knowledge systems provide cognitive resources about objects which are not subject to significant historical reconstitution. Āyurvedic knowledge was discredited with the initial advent of modernity, as modernist elites embraced a superstitious view that all pre-modern medical practices were uniformly unreliable. More recently, with the exposure of the limitations of modern systems and a widening of the critical appreciation by modern science of the historical traditions of healing, there is an emerging interest in pre-modern medical practice. The same is true of a system like Yoga, which also explains its rising popularity. In a separate category are knowledges of texts which are fundamental to continuing practices in art like classical music or dance. In these fields it is likely that the growth of these artistic practices would augment interest in serious study of the texts associated with these arts, however complex that connection between text and practice might be.

It is possible to argue entirely abstractly that in some fields of philosophical reasoning like logic – where classical Indian thought had been particularly creative – modern scholars might revive serious study of relevant texts. Though here we would come up against some persistent objections. Two arguments are likely to arise in these fields. The first is the idea, often stated by Western philosophers or Indians trained in Western philosophy, that modern Western knowledge in these disciplines – which are not historically sensitive in their subject matter – cover the same questions and have adequate, if not superior, solutions to them. There is thus no clear reason why intellectuals should return to these ideas except in the restrictive form of historical curiosity, through an antiquarian interest in Nyāya. Scholars researching Nyāya doctrines should do their work through an antiquarian interest rather than as a contribution to an understanding of causality.

The second argument is less intellectual, but sociologically compelling. Why should a modern scholar who has been trained in modern Western social science and whose thinking is constituted by its methods and substance, strive to dismantle his intellectual identity? And how should he do it? This raises a very difficult question of intellectual reconstitution of selves. Ultimately, this also links up with the problem of history: paradoxically, for most of modern Indians, the 'tradition' which has constituted us, our immediate past, from which our institutions have evolved, and from which we have got the language we use, is a derivation of the intellectual tradition of Western modernity, entirely dissociated from previous forms of Indian intellectual production. So ironically, if 'tradition' means the actable past from which we have drawn the resources through which we prosecute our lives, it is the modern Western canon. This does not require much proof. Every sentence written or spoken by a modern academic testifies to this prank of our history. The most strident critics of the colonial intervention in history are often also the most unresistingly compliant victims of this rupture. But our social science collective needs to accomplish its own 'discovery of India' – to repeat the reconstitution of the self that is at the heart of that neglected and much maligned work. This raises immediately two questions: of motivation and of means. Where should young Indian scholars gather the motivation for this exploration? And even if they do, what are the means they have for doing this? I do not pretend to have clear answers to this cluster of bafflements: but they obviously need clear collective reflection. My suspicion is that we do not have to dismantle our intellectual selves, as some modernists might fear. Critical perspectives about the modern world are, as most people acknowledge, essential to live thoughtfully inside modernity. Such ideas can and have come from theories which reflect critically on modernity on the basis of modern presuppositions, as illustrated by socialist theories. But pre-modern ideas based on assumptions radically different from modern ones, can often provide powerful impulses for critical thinking. One recent example in Western political theory was the growth in the 1980s and 1990s of the 'communitarian' critique of liberalism which derived some of its central arguments either from Aristotelian philosophy or a re-reading of Christian doctrine. In modern Indian social thought pre-modern ideas were put to similar uses most spectacularly by Gandhi. I feel that if the significant ideas of the Sanskrit–Persian and vernacular textual worlds become more readily accessible to modern intellectuals and they absorb them even episodically and partially, it will eventually shift the line of gravity of their own thinking towards more interesting combinations and experiments.

I began to think about literature through the concepts of standard Western interpretative theory, but soon realized through greater familiarization, that the theory of *rasa* offers us immensely illuminating insights into both the creative and receptive processes bound up with art from angles which are entirely different from the aspects opened up by Western theoretical approaches. Simply because of the intellectual richness and power of these classical traditions, the more we know about them the more these are likely to affect our thinking in the present. This does not mean that we should not explore them for historical interest: it merely supplements that with an entirely unhistorical philosophical argument as well.

There can be a reasonable complaint against some of the specialized scholars who alone hold the key to this rich, but increasingly endangered textual universe. Even in modern times, we suffer from a perversity similar to conventional Brāhmanical privilege. A conventional feature of Brāhmanical culture was the social technique of retaining tight control over its scarce philological skills amongst a small group of scholars. In pre-modern caste societies this made a perverse kind of sense. This constituted a real privilege for them, as this knowledge was both quite scarce and highly valued and those who controlled this knowledge enjoyed the advantages of a precious intellectual monopoly. With the transformations of modernity, this situation has changed significantly. Intellectual skills have to be produced inside institutions which are socially supported and nurtured. With the movement of the elites away from Sanskrit knowledge, those institutions which housed the required skills withered for lack of support. It is the great tragedy of India's cultural modernity that modern institutions like universities did not develop ways of transferring them inside the modern spaces to conserve these knowledges. As these were seen often as false knowledge, they were allowed to decline.

The social world of Sanskrit began to crumble without any effort of the modern economy or culture to secure and conserve its treasures. These skills are becoming even rarer, but the knowledges are no longer highly valued, leading to a deep crisis of classical scholarship in general. Yet scholars who still possess this knowledge – the rare expertise to read such texts with facility and to move intelligently in their mental worlds – value their position in a way which puts this entire knowledge tradition in jeopardy. Sanskrit knowledge can be rescued from the extinction that we fear, if it is partly rescued from their secreting inside Sanskrit. One method of resisting and reversing the decline of Sanskrit knowledge, though surely not the only one, would be to make its contents much more widely available bypassing the linguistic constraint; that is, disconnect the content of the knowledge from the language in which it is stored. After all, if Aristotle had to be read after learning ancient Greek, or G.W.F. Hegel and Karl Marx after learning philosophic German, it is hardly likely that they would have enjoyed the kind of influence they actually have today. Sanskrit knowledge need not be read only in Sanskrit. If Abhinavagupta or Bhoja were available in vernacular translations, or in reasonable English,[18] their ideas may have attracted a much wider group of modern aestheticians. I do not want to be misunderstood: this is not an argument against Sanskrit or a device that makes it less important. Deeper interest in these texts might then inspire scholars to learn the special philology and read them in the original – the usual pathway for closer familiarity. But this procedure too depends on an initial stage in which Sanskrit

---

[18] There are some English translations of fundamental Sanskrit texts which are interpretable only by those who know the original Sanskrit. Much of that translation is in fact pointless.

intellectual production is translated widely and at a high level,[19] which will take us back to the problem of the current crisis.

What thinking about this problem makes apparent is that this requires an interdisciplinary conversation of the most improbable kind; a meeting of people who converse only rarely, if at all. And if they do, they are often separated not merely by their concerns but even by their very languages, both natural and conceptual. Sanskrit scholars need modern social science to understand why the world on which they work became so distanced within their own culture. Social scientists who reflect on the enormity of the colonial rupture in our history must evince some curiosity about the culture which collapsed with colonial modernity, and consider if some parts of it are too valuable to be left to irrecoverable decline. The decline of the world of Sanskrit must be reinterpreted as a question not only for the small number of specialized Sanskritists, but for all those who want to understand modernity as history.

References

Barthes, Ronald, 1974, *S/Z*, Richard Miller (tr.), New York: Hill and Wang.

Femia, Joseph, 1984, "An historical Critique of 'revisionist' methods of studing the history of ideas" in James Tully (ed.) *Meaning and Context*: *Quentin Skinner and His Critics*, pp. 156-75 Cambridge: Polity Press.

---

[19] Those who are familiar with some existing translations of Sanskrit texts would acknowledge that the question of translation itself is a hard technical problem. Modern Bengali translations exist of some high Sanskrit literary texts: for example of *Meghadūta* or *Kumārasambhava*, but many of them do not serve the purpose of serious critical reading that would facilitate entry into the poetic world of the classical literary imagination. Some of them are transcreations into modern Bengali of ancient texts where the ancient world of evocations and associations is excessively faded. In some other, more conventional ones there is often a disastrous conflation of translation and commentary.

Gadamer, H.G., 1992, *Truth and Method*, New York: Crossroad.

Kaviraj, Sudipta, 2010, *The Trajectories of the Indian State*, Ranikhet: Permanent Black.

Müller, Max, 2000, (1883) *India: What Can It Teach Us*? New Delhi: Penguin Books.

Phillips, Stephen, 2008, "Engaging with Philosophical Texts", eds. R. Sharma and A. Sharma *Hermeneutics and Hindu Thought: Towards a Fusion of Horizons*, Springer Science and Business Media.

Pollock, Sheldon, 2011, "Crisis in the Classics", *Social Research*, **78**(1): 22-48.

Skinner, Quentin, 2002, *Visions of Politics: Regarding Method (vol. 1)*, Cambridge: Cambridge University Press.

RESPONSE

Claus Oetke

Presentation of the contribution

Three major issues are (implicitly) indicated in Kaviraj's paper.

The primary issues are:

1. Why should we read ancient texts?

2. How should we read ancient texts?

The third is a secondary issue:

3. Reflections on the persistence of a tradition.

The first 'why' comprises several varieties, which are not explicitly distinguished:

(i) Why should people at present read texts produced in the past, more precisely produced by authors belonging to generations none of whose members is living at present?

(ii) Why should people at present read texts allocated to the Indian tradition, particularly texts originally written in Sanskrit, Middle Indian languages or ancient varieties of south Indian languages produced in the past?

(iii) and (iv) are the same as (i) and (ii) with the exception of 'why should people in India' instead of 'why should people'.

The following considerations constitute possible answers to 1.

(a) A contingent curiosity about history, for example, interest caused by 'biographic accident',

(b) a (better) understanding of the present:

Also

(c) interest in matters of content because items of content exist which are absent in present-day writings, in particular 'philosophic interest' justified by the philosophical significance of pieces of content which are not encountered in modern writings,

(d) embodiment of knowledge which is of practical use or relevance, e.g. Āyurvedic medicine, Yoga, theoretical treatises about arts and literature, and

(e) providing or reinforcing motivations for adopting a critical attitude concerning present states-of-affairs.

Comment: At first glance (a) merely relates to a possible motivation but not to a possible justification of investigating ancient textual sources. If it were, however, granted that the satisfaction of personal curiosity is justified or even a value in itself then (a) could equally indicate an objectively valid reason justifying reading of ancient texts.

With the help of drawing a distinction between 'short history' and 'long history' Kaviraj succeeds in demonstrating that the viewpoint (b) calls for a more sophisticated assessment. Increase of temporal distance tends to diminish the explanatory relevance with respect to a present situation.

As far as one can see, no particular directives are provided in Kaviraj's paper with respect to 2. This is possibly not accidental. Granted that ancient texts can be read on the basis of different justifiable reasons, only a 'formal' answer with respect to 2 appears appropriate: ancient texts should be read in such a manner that the pertinent aims, in so far as they are justified, can be optimally accomplished. More specifically, ancient texts should be read in such a way that some of the objectives indicated in (a) – (e) are optimally realized.

Remarks

The exhaustiveness of the list responding to the 'why' question is crucial particularly against the background of the assumption that answers to the 'how' question depend on answers to the former.

An investigation of exhaustiveness needs:

1. explication of 'text', and
2. explication of 'read'.

The expression 'text' can be understood in various meanings. In particular one could attribute to the word a significance according to which it would stand in opposition to 'document'. The term 'document' might be used to refer to concrete particulars, such as individual manuscripts or printed books. It could equally designate an entity which can be instantiated by various physical objects together, for example, some item stored in the computer of which a multitude of printouts might exist. At any rate, if the term 'text' were taken in a broader sense, then investigation of texts potentially encompasses activities falling beyond the scope of Kaviraj's article: somebody who investigates the historical development of a script or the varieties of orthography might employ and even 'read' in some sense of the term an ancient text with the goal of establishing particular scientific results. A historical linguist could read an ancient text with the aim of ascertaining the historical development of a language, etc.

Since 'read' can refer to activities which do not imply any

understanding or even previous knowledge of the language in which a textual source has been written, it should be presumed that a more specific import of the term is intended in the two main questions. Here we tentatively assume that an import is relevant according to which reading a text encompasses (an attempt at) understanding and interpretation. The crux is that both 'understanding' and 'interpretation' as well as the thematically related notion of 'meaning' are extremely equivocal. This problem particularly affects the initial sections of Kaviraj's article. It appears impossible to attribute to various occurrences of 'meaning' in the first paragraph an import which equals the significance of the word in a statement like:

'Platon war ein großer Philosoph' has the same meaning as 'Plato was a great philosopher'.

As the pertinent use of the expression 'meaning' is not made fully explicit in the article, one can only make conjectures about its relevant sense. A plausible conjecture is the following:

The pertinent import of 'meaning' is intimately connected with that of 'mean' in sentences like: 'The help he offered means (for me) that he is a true friend.'

Given that a meaning of 'meaning' exists which can be explicated by expressions such as:

> Ancient textual sources are read with the aim of ascertaining what they should mean for their readers according to the intentions of their creator (if there is exactly one such creator).

It is easy to recognize that (a)–(e) do not provide a complete justification for this particular type of activity, notwithstanding the fact that the above-presented formulation represents a major objective implicit in traditional textual studies. Nevertheless, any explication of this sort possesses the potential of providing a significant means for assessing the question of justifying studies on textual sources of the past. For by specifying a possible goal of textual investigations a criterion is provided for evaluating the validity of offered justifications. It should be obvious, however, that the above envisaged objective can hardly exhaust all possibilities. On the one hand goals of higher complexity calling for different justifications are conceivable such as:

> Ancient textual sources are read with the aim of ascertaining whether that which they should mean for their readers according to the intentions of their creator is identical with that which they actually meant for their interpreters or commentators.

On the other hand no compelling reason exists to restrict the range of possible objects of meaning ascertainment exclusively to texts. Specifically, ascertainments of meaning with respect to constituents of texts, in particular individual sentences, are equally, and in some regard even primarily, important. On this subordinate level a central goal can consist in the ascertainment of what one might call 'communicative intentions', a term which is applicable to declarative and non-declarative sentences alike and which encompasses several ingredients, such as content, speech and effect of utterance. The circumstance that texts are not the only legitimate objects of ascertainment of meaning possesses relevance with respect to the objectives of the clauses (c)–(e) mentioned above. To read a text of the past with the objective to investigate certain constituent parts, perhaps merely a small number of sentences, because they embody unfamiliar insights or pieces of useful knowledge, should not lose its legitimacy if the remaining sections do not provide relevant information. It deserves to be noted that if apart from (a) and (b) also (c)–(e) are acknowledged as possible objectives of studying ancient texts, reasons for such activities must exist for which the question of whether or not the objects and subjects of interpretation can be assigned to the same culture or tradition is not essential.

Under those aspects, the issue of whether modern Indian

citizens are still representative of the classical heritage is pretty immaterial.

For illustrating the general claim that the list of (a)–(e) does not provide an exhaustive background for ascertaining questions of justification, only three points should be mentioned.

One, there are no clear-cut conditions for the identity or non-identity as well as for the persistence or non-persistence of a tradition. Although this fact is indirectly indicated in the initial paragraphs of Kaviraj's article, the natural conclusion is not explicitly drawn that the circumstance that in some senses parts of the Indian tradition do not exist at present, possesses limited relevance for the issue of why one should read ancient texts. Some allusions made in those sections of the article possess an implication which has perhaps not been recognized, namely that it is not inconsistent to attribute interrupted existence to entities like traditions, entailing possibilities of 'revival' which are – presumably – ruled out for other types of entities, such as human beings.

Two, significance of content is not the only aspect under which matters of content represented in ancient sources can attain relevance. A significant, and still widely unexplored problem, is the identification of factors preventing the attainment of perfection either regarding the treatment of a certain subject matter or regarding the detection of most significant problems, for example in the field of philosophy. This point can be generalized to issues not pertaining to matters of content. A critical attitude towards present events or states-of-affairs is not only promoted by confrontation with aspects of the past whose loss appears deplorable but also by identifications of failures of the past and presumed causes of such failures which can prevail at present. The effects of certain practices of a 'policy of economic austerity' in the past provide a pertinent example. Here the circumstance that the mentioned example concerns events of a fairly near past is not essential because the issue pertains to the general point of 'learning from history'.

Three, it is a natural tendency – not only in certain Scandinavian countries – to consider questions of justification of exploring the past under the aspect of potential utility for the present and the near future. There is no compelling reason to accept this narrow perspective. First it is not evident why consideration of remoter stages in the future deserves to be eliminated. Second, it is not evident that aspects of utility are the only relevant ones in this connection. Could one not argue that explorations of past sources possess an 'ethical' dimension due to the fact that it is our obligation not to ignore persons who have sincerely made efforts of pursuing truths in the past and that in this regard it is absolutely irrelevant whether they have written texts in French like Descartes or texts in Sanskrit like Bhartṛhari? In general the premise that acquisition of knowledge about the past is the only goal of studies on the past deserves a critical reconsideration.

DISCUSSION

P.K. Mukhopadhyaya

The sort of continuity exhibited in modern European culture, including its intellectual culture, is not available in India because of the rupture created by colonialism. In this particular context, how do we go about translating? Most of the things Sudipto Kaviraj talked about are not really about translating but about understanding, interpreting and reacting. Translation only concerns the last one or two points.

I think there is a risk in positing continuity and also discontinuity. The risk of continuity is that in Western culture, particularly in Western philosophy, people think that there is no rupture in their continuous history as is the case in India. So they assume they understand their tradition very well. But to my mind they understand very little of their own history and I think an Indian philosopher could really intervene and excel the Europeans themselves in the field of history, which is lamentably the most neglected area of teaching in India. We teach their logic, their epistemology but we do not pay much attention to their intellectual history, and I am very sure that were it on the agenda, those of another culture would understand Europe's history better than the Europeans. On the other hand, because of this rupture, what is happening to the study of Indian culture is that we think that in order to read our past we must read our texts. But there are two types of scholars who can read them. For real authentic translation we have to depend upon people who are least interested in the particular theory they are translating. As a counter example when Russell wrote the history of Western philosophy, he was the least competent person to write it because he himself was a philosopher. So a type of neutrality is necessary for doing history which is unthinkable for philosophical creativity.

K.D. Tripathi

There is a paradox in your presentation. It appears to me that on the one hand you mention Pollock and appear to be in agreement with him, and you have referred to his understanding of the continuity of Sanskrit poetry. According to him it ends with Paṇḍitrāja Jagannātha. This may be true but at the same time a paradox arises when you consider the continuity of the thought; it continues, does it not, even to Vachasapati and it comes down to Prahlada Char and Mukhopadhyaya. So how can it happen that one portion of Jagannātha is dead, obsolete and another is even now continuing?

Wagish Shukla

There are many questions that can be raised about this paper, but I will concentrate on only one. I fail to see the connection between *Gīta-Govinda* of Jayadeva and *Rasa-Gaṅgādhara* of Paṇḍitrāja Jagannātha. *Rasa-Gaṅgādhara* is a text on poetics while

Gīta-Govinda is an entirely different thing. It is not so much the Oḍissī dance that takes place in the Kamani Auditorium which has helped in preserving it in the sense that I am talking about. The actual technique was practised in the Jagannātha Temple and the two philosophies of performance are entirely different unless they have been replaced by modernity.

There is one *aṣṭapadī – dhīra samīre yamunātīre vasati vanèvanamāli . . .* (*Gīta-Govinda* 5.2), *ratisukhasāre* (*Aṣṭapati Gītam*), which is performed when the Lord is going to sleep. The background for this practice is the following. Apparently there was a girl in the temple garden who was picking flowers to decorate herself rather than preserving them undefiled so to speak, for Lord Jagannātha. This was of course objected to but later on the objectors found that same garland on the Lord (I apologize for the continuous use of the word 'Lord' but it is the only way I can communicate here). And since then this *aṣṭapadī* is performed in the Jagannātha Temple at the time when Bhagvān goes to sleep. Now this aspect is totally absent in any performance we see today and to which we credit the preservation, if you wish, of *Gīta-Govinda*. *Gīta-Govinda* is not preserved by any external, musical or for that matter, thespian activities which are adaptable to any other composition.

S.N. Balagangadhara

I am going to ask for a clarification on a question which I find very troubling. Let me first read how you have formulated the problem from the text: Sanskrit scholars need modern social scientists. What disturbs me in anthropological fieldwork is that Sanskrit literature is made to play the role of native informer to social scientists, with the anthropologists asking themselves as they might with Maori culture: is there something valuable which has been lost?

Claus Oetke also makes the same point. Even if you say that the dialogue between the primitive and the anthropologist is sophisticated, native informers are not merely informants. This idea, this interaction pattern which has existed for the last forty years has a double bias – that of the anthropologist and that of the native informant. They have very powerful dialogues but anthropologists fundamentally take a priori positions, assuming that Sanskritists are the only ones who hold the key: they do not really believe that non-Sanskritists could possibly have anything to contribute.

But it would be absurd to dismiss Indian culture a priori without an investigation into India's intellectual contributions, without entertaining the possibility that Indian culture and tradition might today in a very significant sense be a challenge to the Western traditions which form our intellectual background. Your question shuts it out because it comes from Sanskrit. In your story of the fieldwork model, all Indian parameters answer the sophisticated social scientists model. I am surprised because you have another strand which goes in the opposite direction. But the fundamental framework you are using suggests maximally that we might learn something like Sanskrit aesthetics, *rasa* theory, etc. or even something like curry. This kind of trivialization has resulted from colonialism: it has been and is, very suppressive.

Kapila Vatsyayan

The points that have been raised are very complex and I only want to endorse what Prof. P.K. Mukhopadhyaya and Prof. Tripathi said about continuity. These are issues which will come up later and I will not make any further comments. But since two authors have been mentioned, viz., Bharata and Jayadeva, naturally I enjoyed the discussion, because I have spent more than half a century mulling over what is known as the *Nāṭyaśāstra* and the little great poem the *Gīta-Govinda*.

As far as the *Gīta-Govinda* is concerned, there are innumerable translations and there are also commentaries, nearly forty to forty-five, not to speak of interpretative discussions. So when we talk about this text, I think there is ample scope for further discussions. The more I have perused the multiple commentaries, the more I have questioned myself on what constitutes the text at the level of both word and meaning.

Response by Sudipto Kaviraj

There are a lot of interesting and challenging comments; I hope I will be able respond to all of them.

Very quickly, about the initial comment of Claus Oetke on my paper. Obviously the 'how do we read' question depends, in my view (and that is why I wrote the paper the way I did), on the 'why' question; why we should read the texts. So I think you put your finger on that point. And I agree with most of what you say, but let me put across my point as somebody interested in the Indian state. We need to go back into the Sanskrit texts because when I try to understand, or am curious about the historical–sociological origins of the state, about the nature of the modern Indian state, and when I ask the question: 'is the modern state different from the pre-modern state', I must have a picture of what the pre-modern state' looked like. The question has to be answered scientifically, sociologically, by looking at the features of the modern and the pre-modern states. Are they really different? And in order to do that, I have to look, for instance, at a text that interests me deeply from that angle – the *Vīramitrodaya* of Mitra Misra – a Dharmaśāstra text written in Jahangir's time. Are we really as different from the pre-modern as the modern claims? That is what we have to judge: we cannot presuppose it.

The other comments I agree with but I suppose we have differences on two questions. Let me clarify what I was saying which is different from the way you read it – the point about enrichment, sensitization, etc. I see that as a valid point but it is not the point I was making. When I argued that the *rasa* theory is independently, philosophically interesting what I meant was that it provides a different approach to aesthetics. I thought it was an approach which very deeply affects certain aspects which are not really explored in Aristotle or Aristotle-derived traditions or the modern traditions from Kant and Marx. They have aspects which are very different from the *rasa* tradition. So it is not enrichment in that sense: I meant it in the sense of complementarity. There are some aspects of aesthetics which I can approach by depending on the modern Western tradition but there are some things I can approach much better by looking at the *rasa* theory. So I do not know if we are making the same point. It is true the reason or motivations I was giving are not exhaustive.

I agree with what was said about the identity of a tradition, living or non-living but I would like to come back to it because it gives rise to several questions. The point about rupture is also very important because I think that at some point, for instance in *rasa* theory itself, where a theory went in one direction, one cannot speculate whether it could have gone in another way. I tend to think of it more as thinking interstitially, that you have an argument which is presented in a certain form and there is another argument which is adjacent to it which is presented somewhat differently.

I can give you a modern example. The controversy which I find fascinating in modern times is between Gandhi and Tagore. In many respects they are very close but in others very different. If you look at them closely their actual argumentation is quite different. And what I mean by thinking interstitially is that we can think of developing back the traditional lines of thought or thinking in two senses. I can say that I want to carry on Gandhi's line of reasoning or Tagore's line of reasoning or I can say that these two lines of reasoning have interstitial possibilities which are not developed either by Tagore or Gandhi but which I can develop. Because the questions which Tagore and Gandhi thought about, particularly about modern power, need a kind of critique from which I can develop all that is original in their ideas by thinking interstitially, that is taking the existing ideas in both of them but also producing ones that have been developed on their basis.

I agree with what Prof. Mukhopadhyaya said. It is a deep and very interesting point with which I entirely agree. I think Gandhi says that precisely, that modernity in Europe has cut Europe off not only from other parts of the world but from its own past as well, but it does not understand that. The other matter you raised is true in a complicated sense and I do not have a clear idea of how I should put it, but it contains in itself a very important truth, that our relation to our tradition should not only be mediated by the recovery of texts: there are many other things. We need to have an animated, lively and vivacious exercise searching for things which are known to us in a certain sense, you can use a term like *upekṣit vākyam*: that I have *jñāna* of a thing but it contains a certain kind of *upekṣā* and I have to come back and remind myself that I know about this and then think through it. Then I would have recaptured more vividly what is there. That I think is very interesting. I still believe that we should think very closely about what it means for something to be preserved.

I think that one of the weaknesses of the Sanskritic tradition has been in a certain sense a one-sided textuality and that is the reason why the Sanskrit tradition has not been carried through with vividness, why it is in the state it is. Let us face one question. Either we can say that since some people can compose poems in Sanskrit, there is nothing amiss and we do not need to have seminars like this. But things are obviously not fine, we are worried about Sanskrit; we say we have to revive it, it is not in good health. So I was simply trying to ask myself: is this decline, this decay or inaccessibility if you want to use a less loaded term, uniform or is it varied? I thought it was varied because there are certain practices which surround certain texts, which does not mean that people who dance Oḍissī have a deep, complex understanding of *Gīta-Govinda*. Certainly not, but they have a curiosity which you can develop, on which you can build.

Saying that India is in danger of losing her memory is a rhetorical argument and it depends on how you gloss the term 'memory' to decide exactly what kind of argument you are dealing with. What Pollock said seems to me quite obviously true; this is a very important part of our history about which knowledge in India is becoming thinner, weaker. This is something that we should try to re-grasp.

This question came up in Prof. Oetke's comment on my paper as well, whether the Indian's relation to the Sanskrit corpuses and the Westerners' relation to the same should be treated as different or not. I think it is a very deep, very important question, and I am not entirely sure about how I would answer that. But we all need to think about it.

2

Comparative Studies and the Explanatory Problem

A Methodological Essay

S.N. Balagangadhara

Introduction

THERE are three distinct types or levels of questions that we confront today. At the first level, there is what we can call 'the translation problem': the issue, that is, of translating terms from one language to another. When we settle on 'God' as a translation for *deva* or for 'religion' as a translation for *dharma* and 'letter' for *śabda*, we confront this problem. Even though anthropologists had confronted this problem earlier and the Christian missionaries even before them, its sharpest formulation in philosophy is due to Quine (1960): he speaks of a radical indeterminacy of translation. Many have had an occasion to take issue with Quine, the most notable of whom is Donald Davidson (1984). This is the first level. At a second level, we can talk of 'the interpretation problem', something we confront when we look at the issue of understanding texts. Here, we confront the problem of what it is to understand texts and how to go about doing it. This problem arose in the context of understanding the surface contradictions in the New Testament Bible and in rendering it consistent. Today, the most notable practitioners of this discipline of 'hermeneutics' (Georg Gadamer and Paul Ricoeur, for instance) have gone much beyond the questions that Biblical hermeneutics raised and focus on the process of understanding texts *tout court*.

Both these problems are familiar to students of texts, especially when they look at texts written in different languages. However, there is also a third level, where we can talk of an 'explanatory problem', something which confronts us when we look at the texts as the texts of a culture. Here, the workshop organizers talk in terms of 'Western' concepts and categories the uncritical use of which might repress the native intuitions or thoughts of another culture. Of course, the issue is not one of using 'Western' concepts: most of the concepts we use in the natural sciences have a 'Western' origin and that is not the problem signalled at here. The underlying idea is something like this: there is some kind of a non-trivial relationship between a culture and the texts it produces. Therefore, a simple and straightforward use of theories produced by one culture to understand another culture creates special explanatory problems towards which we must remain sensitive. Of course, I am merely drawing a conceptual distinction. It is a distinction that makes a difference in that the problems these three give birth to and the answers one gives are different from each other.

From this consideration, it does not follow that these problems are unrelated to each other or that one level is independent of the other. In this paper, I want to focus mainly on the third problem from a methodological point of view because I believe, the first two kinds of problems will get reasonably adequate treatment in the course of this workshop.

Thus, I want to focus on the explanatory problem of outlining the relationships between the texts of a culture and the culture that produces them. I shall take Indian and Western culture as examples and presuppose the results of my earlier research: we can use the notion of culture even though some anthropologists throw doubt on the intelligibility of the concept itself; it makes perfect scientific sense to speak of Indian and

Western culture. I further presuppose that comparative research is best suited to tackle the explanatory problem.

However, what is comparative research? What are the methodological problems faced by such research? How can it tackle the explanatory problem? These are the issues I hope to partially answer in the course of this paper. To begin with, let me say that there are and have been many kinds of comparative studies: from comparative anthropology (Holy 1987) through comparative history (Yengoyan 2006), comparative political theory (Jenco 2007: 741-55; Gebhardt 2008: 5-22) and comparative theology (Clooney 2010) to comparative analysis in multiple social sciences (Mahoney and Rueschmeyer 2003). I do not speak about any of those in the present paper; instead, I will add to the existing diversity. Despite this, I hope that the paper is unorthodox enough to provoke far more serious thinking about the methodologies of comparative studies than has been the case so far.

I propose to carry out the task in distinct conceptual steps that constitute the different sections of the paper. In the first section, an argument is built that shows how one can profile the nature of a comparative enterprise by thinking about the problematic relationship between Orientalism and the social sciences. One does not have to endorse the Saidian critique of the Orientalist discourse in order to appreciate the existence of a problem, even though it is convenient to use Said's ideas to introduce it. In the second section, this problem is developed in such a way that it can be formulated independent of whether one endorses Edward Said or not. During this process, I point out a peculiar kind of cultural asymmetry that pervades the intellectual discourse in some domains of the social sciences today. In the third section, three important dimensions of the kind of comparative enterprise that follow from the earlier arguments are isolated. At the same time, I hint at the importance of post-colonial scholarship and its limitations.

In the same section, some methodological generalizations are formulated. The fourth section notices the limitations of these methodological generalizations and seeks interesting ways to find solutions for them. The fifth and the final section relates one aspect of this methodology to a trend in Western philosophy that also establishes why, for this endeavour to succeed, the cognitive condition is that the work of earlier generations of thinkers is adequately appreciated. It also makes clear what that adequacy consists of. If the paper succeeds in its aim, it must provide a new twist to the very notion of comparison itself.

I

Orientalism and the Social Sciences

No matter how critically we do it, if we accept Said's insights into the nature of the Western discourses about non-Western societies, we have to also accept that Orientalism is about how the West experienced the East and gave expression to that experience. In the course of this process, the West built and elaborated conceptual frameworks using resources mostly available from its own culture.

While generating descriptions of other cultures – whether framed in positive or negative evaluative or axiological terms – Orientalism made use of a vast conceptual reservoir. It consisted of ideas and theories about human beings, the nature of languages, the structure of societies, the character of cultures, the importance of religion, the value of history, the problem of politics, etc. In turn, such a constructed discourse had its impact on the evolution of subsequent theorizing about Man and Society. In other words, Orientalist discourse did not evolve in splendid isolation but in continuous interaction with and as a part of the growth of the social sciences. It is not an extraneous and alien growth on the otherwise splendid corpus of social science – it is an inextricable part of the social–scientific discourse.

However, one of the problems with the Saidian terminology is the difficulty in making sense of social science. If '. . . Weber's studies of Protestantism, Judaism, and Buddhism blew him (perhaps unwittingly) into the very territory originally charted and claimed by Orientalism' (Said 1978: 259) what could we say about his theories of the development of capitalism, the relationship between economies and societies and the nature of political authority? If the European writings on 'Hinduism'are Orientalist (Richard King 1999) what about their histories of Christianity? If we assume that Marx's claims in *The Grundrisse* about India are squarely in the Orientalist camp, where do his theses about commodities, money and capital belong? Is Freudian psychoanalysis itself Orientalist because using that theory entails that a non-Western culture, say the Indian culture, is populated by pathological beings afflicted by secondary narcissism and other assorted ills (Carstairs (1957); Moussaief-Masson (1980); Courtright (1985); Kripal (1998))?

To these questions, neither Said nor those inspired by him provide an answer. Inden (1990) criticizes the 'Orientalist constructions of India' by using Collingwood's notion of history. Are we to assume that using Collingwood's concept of history to understand India is non-Orientalist, whereas using Marxist or Weberian notion of history to study India is Orientalist? Or should we assume that Western historiography about the West itself is 'Orientalist' in so far as historians do not make use of Collingwood?

In Said's case it seems as though the existing social sciences are alternatives to Orientalism. This stance has to do with the 'humanistic' orientation that Said entertains. He believes that knowledge about human beings must be both general and specific: 'general' in the sense that it tells us about 'human beings as such' and does not divide them up in arbitrary ways; 'specific' in the sense that it must not lose itself in abstractions or 'collectives' but give us knowledge of 'flesh-and-blood' individuals.

However, there is also his critique of Orientalist discourse. Orientalism as a field of study, stands on its own. It studies the 'Oriental' as a type, an abstraction, a fictitious creature with some 'essential properties' that populates the domain of discourse. This 'Oriental' is a bi-dimensional figure: he is not the 'flesh-and-blood' individual of our world.

Said notices that Orientalist discourse has wittingly or unwittingly borrowed ideas from many social scientific theories:

> Orientalism borrowed and was frequently informed by 'strong' ideas, doctrines, and trends ruling the culture. Thus there was (and is) a linguistic Orient, a Freudian Orient, a Spenglerian Orient, a Darwinian Orient, a racist Orient – and so on. – Said 1978: 22

He is certain too about where the alternatives to Orientalism are likely to come from:

> . . . interesting work is most likely to be produced by scholars whose allegiance is to a discipline defined intellectually and not to a 'field' like Orientalism defined either canonically, imperially and geographically. An excellent recent instance is the anthropology of Clifford Geertz . . .
>
> . . . enough is being done today in the human sciences to provide the contemporary scholar with insights, methods, and ideas that could dispense with racial, ideological, and imperialist stereotypes of the sort provided during the historical ascendancy by Orientalism. – Said 1978: 328

On the one hand, if we follow Said, Orientalism is a massive cultural project which has had a huge impact on Western culture, Western people and their imagination. People produce/reproduce Orientalist discourse without realizing they are doing so and even without wanting to do so. Furthermore, the Orientalist discourse also appears to create and reinforce Western 'self-conception' and 'self-representation'.

Yet on the other hand, if we believe Said, such a discourse has no impact on the growth and development of the social sciences. This enterprise, which is also a cultural project of the West, is completely unaffected by (or even oblivious to) the other cultural project. One cultural enterprise, Orientalism, appears to borrow continuously from the other cultural enterprise, the social scientific discourse. The social sciences, for their part, do not appear to borrow anything from the Orientalist discourse and from the concomitant cultural images about man and society. Not only that. They are also alternatives to the Orientalist discourse. Surely, this suggestion is implausible.

Why is it implausible? The answer is obvious. The existing social sciences which are primarily Western initiatives, make claims about human beings and their societies in both the West and the East. Orientalism does not merely put across claims about the non-Western cultures, it also creates and reinforces certain ideas about Western man and his society. Thus we have two sets of formulations by the social sciences. Because of their subject matter, these claims cannot be irrelevant to each other: either they are compatible or they are not. Because Orientalism borrows from the social sciences, their claims must be compatible. From this it follows that the claims of Orientalism must also be compatible with the claims of social sciences. If this is the case, the existing social sciences cannot provide us with alternatives to Orientalism; instead, they too must continue the legacy of the Orientalist writings. The images of man and society that the existing social sciences either reinforce or take for granted must be continuous with Orientalism.

On Constructing the Orient

When the Europeans came to the East (say, India or Egypt) and wrote down their experiences, they were not hallucinating. They did not write about their dreams nor did they compose stories. Whether of a merchant, a missionary or a bureaucrat, the reports

The first sentence notices the fact that social sciences are 'inherently' ignorant about aspects of non-Western societies and cultures and therefore, they cannot be useful for understanding non-Western cultures and societies. The second notices the fact that they are useful in understanding all aspects of these societies and implies that social sciences do embody knowledge. The first statement is true. The second statement is also true. It is also true that, under the assumption about knowledge and understanding, the implication of the first statement is the negation of the second. Severally taken, both statements merely describe a situation. Jointly, however, they cannot both be true and yet they are. The conditions under which these facts are true require that 'knowledge' and 'ignorance'share the same extension. That is, knowledge is ignorance if, and only if, knowledge is not ignorance. Dipesh Chakrabarty suggests that this claim is not only paradoxical but also true. It is true because the claim is a (partial) description of the situation of Third World intellectuals and that they realize this to be the case as well. In other words, not only are they committed to the truth of this paradox, but they also realize that the situation that forces them to affirm this truth is their own. Thus, these intellectuals live not merely paradoxically but in the awareness of the paradox as well. Their experience, then, involves these two dimensions and both have to do with the social sciences. Similar thoughts have been expressed as challenges elsewhere too. For instance, the Sri Lankan-born anthropologist Valentine Daniel was saying even earlier:

> Enough of Weberizing and Durkheimizing Indian ethnological data. How about Manuizing and Paninizing Western culture, including the science of culture, for a change?
>
> – Daniel 1984: 53. See also Marriott 1976: 195 and 1990

Analogous ideas can also be found in Larson and Deutsch (1988), Loy (1988), Roland (1988), Hall and Ames (1988) and Shweder and Bourne (1984).

Bending the Stick the Other Way

Let me try to capture this sense of unease in more general terms now. To do this, I will formulate the issue in an exaggerated form which will get corrected later on. For now, let us accept that the intuition guiding such thoughts as the above is the realization that whatever their explanatory power or problem-solving capacity, the existing social sciences are not adequate to the task of making the non-Western world intelligible. There is a feeling of dissatisfaction with the conceptual apparatus that obtains today; the disquiet is, that interesting and important issues are not even being formulated as questions for an inquiry. One of the tentative explanations often put across to account for this unsatisfactory state of affairs is that the social sciences of today are 'Western'. That is, the social sciences embody assumptions (whether all of its assumptions or only some of them are 'Western' requires to be made out), which blind them to recognizing issues that are very important to an understanding of non-Western cultures (Claes 1996; van den Bouwhuijsen, Derde and Claes 1995).

However correct it might prove to be later, this intuition is not sufficient for the task of assessing theories from the field of social sciences. To reject the existing conceptual frameworks, simply because we feel that they do not quite manage to do what theories are supposed to, would be a folly. There is no way of assessing theories, except by comparing them with rival theories. We could sensibly begin with theory appraisal if and only if, we have two or more theories which are competitors with respect to the phenomenon they explain (Lakatos 1980; Laudan 1977).

In one sense, it could be said that there are rival theories in the field of social sciences: structural as against cognitive anthropology; the Austrian school of economics against Keynesian economics; Marxian economics against micro and macro economics; Parsonian as against Weberian sociology, etc. Therefore, it might appear that the problems are solved even before their formulation. It becomes merely a question of ascertaining which of these four competiting theories is best suited for the job.

But this is not what these authors have in mind. To explicate that thought better, let us look at the issue this way. Without the least bit of exaggeration, it could be held that the study of societies and cultures is a project that the Western world has initiated. Over the centuries, Western intellectuals have studied both themselves and other cultures and in this process have developed sets of theories and methodologies to understand our social and cultural worlds. What we call 'social sciences' today are the result of gigantic labour performed by brilliant and not-so-brilliant men and women from all over the world over a long period of time.

Let us formulate a hypothetical question in order to express a problem: would the results have been the same, or even approximately similar if, say, the Indians had undertaken such a task instead of the Europeans? That is, suppose that in the imaginary world that we are talking about, it was the effort of the Indian intellectuals reflecting about themselves and European culture as they saw them both, which eventuated in social science. Would the results have looked like the contemporary social sciences? The most natural answer to this question is: 'we do not know'. It is worthwhile reflecting on this answer. The inability to answer the question does not arise from the impossibility of answering questions about hypothetical situations. All our scientific laws describe hypothetical situations and we can say what would happen in such situations. "*Were* I to drop a stone from the top of a building, what would happen? The stone *would* fall downwards. . . ."

The ignorance in our case has to do with the specific kind of hypothetical situation the question picks out, and with the feeling that there is no way to check the veracity of the answers given. That is, because we have no model of such an attempt, we have no way of deciding how to go about answering the question. Worse still, because we have no models where the answers can come out either true or false, we feel that all answers to this question are meaningless and therefore, that the question itself is meaningless. The question has not violated any syntactic or semantic rule, it has not committed any category mistake; yet we do not know how to make sense of this question.

There is a peculiar air about this state of affairs. One is not able to make sense of a question which asks the Indians, literally, how they appear to themselves and how the West appears to them. Yet they have been studying both the West and India for quite some time now. As a result, if you will allow a mild hyperbole, I would assert that neither the problem of 'incommensurability of cultures' nor that of 'indeterminacy of translation' arises. They might become problems when the background assumptions and theories which underlie a study are different. The background assumptions and theories which guide a Western anthropologist studying Asian culture are the same as those of an Asian anthropologist studying his own. Should one of them face problems, so should the other. Both study the same phenomenon (the 'inscrutability of reference' notwithstanding), with the same tools embodying the same assumptions. The nature of some problem and its relative importance are not different for the two and these are so organized by their background assumptions.

With the background assumptions peculiar to it, Western culture problematized phenomena which have taken the status of fact for many of us. One talks endlessly about the problem of 'underdevelopment', the 'question of human rights in India', 'the amorphous nature of Hinduism' and in the same breath, about 'Hindu fundamentalism', 'the problem of modernity and nationhood', 'the women's question in India'; etc. The same is also true for one's perspectives on the West. Surely, there is a problem here. If Indian culture differs from that of the West and if, perforce, its background theories and assumptions are other than those of the West, one could not possibly either formulate questions or assign weights to them, both about India and the West, in exactly the same way the West does. Yet, one does – invariably and as a matter of fact. How could Indians make sense of questions routinely copied from Western social research and go on to answer them by means of empirical studies? Yet they do: they act as though these questions do make sense to them. We, from other cultures, know the West the way the West looks at itself. We study the East the way the West studies the East. We look at the world the way the West looks at it. We do not even know whether the world would look different if we looked at it our way. Today, we are not even in a position to make sense of the previous statement. When Indian anthropologists, psychologists or sociologists do their anthropology, psychology or sociology – the West is really talking to itself.

Thus, it appears as though the problem is not about the presence or absence of rival theories in the domain of social science; instead, it sucks the entire domain of social science into its scope. The challenge that the intellectuals from non-Western cultures face is nothing short of breathtaking: they must attempt to decolonize the social sciences, no less!

On the Novelty of the Task

Whether realistic or not, whether pretentious or not, I do believe that this is the historical task facing intellectuals from non-Western cultures over the coming generations. The emergence of countries and cultures like India and China into world prominence is going to confront their intellectuals with this objective: they too will have to do what Europe and the United States have done so far. And that involves a striving for intellectual hegemony. The increasingly important economic and political role these countries are going to play at a global level is also going to translate into cultural and intellectual realms. About a full 2,000 years ago, the pagan cultures of Greece and Rome met an emerging Christianity which triumphed. Today the circle has come a full turn: two other ancient pagan cultures (non-white and non-Christian in nature) will meet the reigning intellectual and cultural hegemony of a predominantly Christian culture. The challenge of intellectual hegemony is going to express itself as the above-mentioned historical task. Of course, this is inter-generational in nature; no one generation leave alone some individual thinker is capable of bringing such a task to fruition. This qualification, obviously, does not make the task less daunting.

How does this task present itself to intellectuals from non-Western cultures? Does the execution of this job involve postulating the age-old opposition between 'us' and 'them' too? Or do the historical achievements of Western culture change the way the problem is formulated today? Let me first give a short answer, which the rest of this paper will elaborate. I believe that the task is going to present itself as a comparative enterprise. No matter how combative the initial formulations are going to be, one will be compelled to take the hard-won insights and theories of the earlier generations into account, if the task is to be completed. That is to say, the 'decolonization' of the social sciences (or 'provincializing Europe', to make use of Chakrabarty's pregnant if provocative formulation) cannot take the form of a total rejection of the social sciences of today or of the intellectual labour of people from the past centuries. In fact, what makes the coming century exciting is the fact that the task of 'decolonizing' social sciences will either be a collective global effort of intellectuals across the world or it simply will not take place. The intellectual hegemony that the non-Western intellectuals will be forced to seek can only be achieved through negotiation with the intellectuals of the Western world and by means of their cooperation. In this sense, the hegemony of the non-Western intellectuals will not be 'their' hegemony. It cannot and will not take the form of the 'us' and 'them' opposition. This opposition will have to be transcended and that is possible only because of the fact that such an opposition exists today which constitutes our point of departure as well. In the rest of this paper, I shall show how and why that is the case, and why it is a cognitive condition and not a prophetic rant.

II

Let us begin with the following question: how should we look at the Orientalist discourse? One view, let us call this the received view, sees it as a description of the Orient, whether veridical or flawed. In defence of the received view, one could say that such descriptions are flawed in so far as they are wrong or false and they are there only due to insufficient knowledge of the Orient. Here, the wrongness or falsity picks out an almost inevitable phase that all academic disciplines pass through. As more accurate knowledge accumulates, the Orientalist discourse will simply 'improve' and become coterminus with the knowledge of human beings, whether in the West or the Orient. While this received view on Orientalism has its merits, it is not of much use because the notion of 'wrongness' and 'falsity' used here has almost no teeth. In exactly the same sense, one could say that the Greek or Egyptian astrology was flawed or wrong and became the Copernican astronomy as accurate knowledge accumulated.

Our astrophysics will then be seen to supersede Copernican astronomy simply by being 'more accurate'. In other words, such a defence of Orientalism makes discussions about its truth and falsity only marginally interesting from a cognitive point of view. They are only marginally interesting because they do not allow us to come to grips with the growth of scientific theories (Dilworth 2008), the nature of scientific change and the partially incommensurable character of scientific progress (Hoyningen-Huene and Sankey 2010). To understand any of these, one has to discuss the difference between Greek astronomy and Copernican astronomy in terms of their concepts, axioms and theories. To do that, one cannot look back from our vantage point and suggest that one theory is more accurate than the other (Westman 1975). We need to understand them the way they confronted each other historically: as rival and competing theories. As such, they were not trying to propose different solutions to a common and shared problem; in fact, the problems themselves were different. That is to say, one has to differentiate between theories not only in terms of proposed solutions to common problems but also in terms of how each of these theories formulates the problem. For a scientist involved in research, the general claim that all theories (including those from her/his domain) simply become 'more accurate' as 'more knowledge' accumulates is quite useless: s/he needs to know the specific problems that some theory confronts and the range of proposed possible answers. In this sense, the received view on Orientalism merely suggests that a 'more accurate' description of non-Western cultures is an alternative to 'Orientalism', which is just about as useful and illuminating as suggesting that a 'more accurate' description of the natural world will provide us with an alternative to the paradoxes of quantum physics.

The second way of describing the Orientalist discourse, let us call this a comparative view, appreciates this state of affairs and provides a context for situating a possible dialogue between Western and non-Western cultures. That context is the fact that all these cultures are different forms of life and due to globalization, they meet each other as alternatives to each other. In appreciating this historical fact, the comparative view on Orientalism either downplays the alleged Westernization of non-Western cultures or sees it as a process of adaptation by non-Western cultures. Consequently, Orientalism is seen as a description of the Western experience of the Orient. This 'Western way' has to do with the form that such reflections on experience take: they take the form of an apparent discourse about the Orient.

A Cultural Asymmetry

Hopefully, we can now see why these two views on Orientalism need not be at loggerheads with each other, even though they have been so ever since Said published his book. The first is pitched at such a level of abstraction that what it says about Orientalism is applicable to all domains of human knowledge; the second attempts to conceptualize a historical situation, where Western culture (and the discourses emanating from that culture) confronts non-Western cultures *as an alternative*. Rightly or wrongly, Western culture has presented itself as an alternate and desirable form of life to peoples from non-Western cultures, ever since modern colonialism. But there is an *asymmetry* here: while the Western form of life is proposed as an alternative to non-Western forms of life, non-Western cultures are never seen as alternative in the same way that the West is to the other cultures. But this supposition does not fall together with the notion of 'alternation' that we know from logic and linguistics. 'Being an alternative to' is a symmetrical relation: if *X* is an alternative to *Y* then *Y* also is an alternative to *X*.

In this globalized world of ours, it makes perfect sense to suggest that India, Iraq or Pakistan should try to emulate Europe or the US, whereas it appears both obscene and ridiculous to suggest that Europe and the US should try to emulate India or Iraq. This signals that the Western culture is seen as the 'endpoint' for non-Western cultures and only as such does it meet the others in the world arena. However, not many intellectuals want to take such a stance openly. Not only does it smack of the now-rejected developmental ordering of human history it also does not allow for an appreciation of how these cultures are meeting each other today, as alternate forms of life. However, acknowledging this fact implies that there should be symmetry between these alternate forms of life which is implicitly dismissed by the dominant intellectual discourses in the field of social science. We need to keep in mind that the rejection is merely implicit, a hidden premise in the argumentation as it were: no intellectual domain has done the kind of research that shows why Western culture is the only alternative to non-Western cultures. The current understanding of non-Western cultures in the Western world is too thin to allow the generation of this implicit stance as an explicit conclusion. In this sense this is a cultural asymmetry, where Western culture is seen as the only alternative to all other cultures, whereas there are no extant alternatives to this culture.[1] In the first place, comparative research addresses itself to this problem and attempts to restore symmetry (whether crowned with success or not). Taking the rejection of a developmental ordering of human history utterly seriously, the comparative enterprise attempts to make sense of the current state of affairs and restore cognitive consistency to the intellectual parlance of today. The only way of doing that is to try to look at non-Western cultures (or at least the intellectual productions of such cultures) as possible alternatives to the Western form of life. That is to say, comparative studies aim to restore an imbalance that exists between cultures today and allow us to make sense of the fact that different cultures in the world today are different forms of life and confront each other as alternatives to one another.

III

In the process of generating descriptions of non-Western cultures, Western culture built and elaborated many conceptual frameworks. These frameworks also helped in Europe's description and understanding of both the world and itself. That

[1] Note that showing the superiority of Western forms of democracy when compared to, say, the form of governance that Saddam Hussein practised is not an answer to the question. If and only if one can show that these forms of governance are particular products of these two cultures (the Western and the Iraqi cultures), only then will the answer have teeth. I suggest that no intellectual field has come up with this kind of research.

is, in the first place, Europe's description of other cultures is entwined in many untold ways with the way it has experienced and so described the world. If we keep to the post-Saidian distinctions, we could say that Western descriptions of non-Western cultures (Orientalism) are deeply and indissolubly connected to the ways in which Western culture has described the social world (social sciences).

When modern sociology describes the Indian caste system or when modern anthropology studies Hindu practices in some part of India, both presuppose the 'facts' that the earlier generations of Orientalists have dredged up. Facts, as we all know today, are mostly theory-laden and hence they are facts of some theory or another (Feyerabend 2010). Thus for instance, when Mancur Olson Jr. (1984) accounts for the Indian caste system by explaining the facts that Nehru (in his *Discovery of India*) puts across, he is presupposing the truth of those theories and frameworks which Nehru used. Nehru used Orientalist descriptions of the Indian society of his day and made their facts his own. In this sense, Olson is not accounting for the Indian caste system by using the notion of fossilized coalitions in India; he is trying to establish the truth in Nehru's observations (i.e. the truth in the Orientalist descriptions of India) by developing an hypothesis that purports to explain Indian society. This suggests at least one manner of conceiving the relationship between Orientalism and social sciences: where uncontested, there the latter presupposes the truth of the Orientalist descriptions of non-Western cultures. Thus even if we are not enamoured by the field of post-colonial studies, we can appreciate the rationale for its existence and popularity: these studies contest the truth of the colonial descriptions of non-Western cultures. In so doing, they underscore the need for comparative research to exist as a distinct way of studying cultures and societies. This is the first dimension that we should keep in mind.

In order to see why this need arises, we must understand the second dimension by considering the 'what' of the post-colonial contestation. Let us use India as an example of a non-Western culture. India has been independent for more than sixty years. Therefore it is reasonable to expect that there would be no lines of continuity between the way the British described India and the way the post-independent generations look at India (both in India and in the West within the same timeframe). Of course, we are not talking about descriptions of all kinds of facts about the people, the country or its weather, where the absence of continuities would indeed be astonishing. Instead we are talking about the continuities in fundamental and structural descriptions: India is corrupt, caste-ridden, immoral, and so on. As any student of contemporary India knows, such continuities are seen to be present. Surely there is something wrong with this situation.

Many argue that if something is wrong with this situation, it has to do with the Indian society itself. That is, they ask whether there would have been such lines of continuity, if there were no 'truth' to the British portrayal of Indian history, traditions and culture. This stance makes use of the 'fact' of continuity to suggest that the British descriptions are true. The contemporary experience of Indian culture and society appears to lend truth-value to the colonial descriptions of India.

However, the above stance assumes that the contemporary experience is itself unproblematic. What happens if that is not the case? Do the lines of continuity indicate that these experiences themselves are still colonial in nature? (Breckenridge and van der Veer 1993). Such questions would throw doubt upon the 'factual nature' of the British descriptions of India and suggest that these descriptions could be untrue. Consequently, they would also challenge the 'truth' of some of the contemporary descriptions of India. The lines of continuity do not function as evidence for the 'truth' of the colonial descriptions; instead they raise questions about the problematic nature of contemporary experience. In which way is the contemporary experience problematic?

Let me answer this question by focusing on colonialism. To describe the problematic nature of colonial experience, the commonly adopted approach has been to interrogate the intellectuals from India (Gandhi, Tagore, Sri Aurobindo, etc.) about the issues they faced when confronting colonialism as a living system. Whether adequate or not, these interrogations are carried out with the explicit understanding that the current theories of colonialism do not succeed in making the phenomenon intelligible to us today. In this sense, abstractly speaking, the attempt to build an alternative theory can indeed be accommodated within mainstream social science scholarship. However, what makes such an accommodation difficult (if not impossible) is the fact that the existing theories do not question contemporary experiences but presuppose them as true. That is to say, should an alternative theory of colonialism ever come into existence due to this interrogation, there will be rivalry between this theory and the current theories. Their rivalry would reside not merely in the fact that they give different explanations for the phenomenon of colonialism; it would also be constituted by fact that their presuppositions are antithetical in nature. Hence, the very way they formulate problems would be opposed to each other. In this sense, such is the nature of disputes today that there is a need to distinguish between these two kinds of theories by chalking out a domain of comparative research. More generally put, here is the difficulty: while the multiple theories of colonialism that exist today are rival theories because they formulate different solutions to a common problem, their differences from a theory about colonialism which might emerge through comparative research lies in the fact that the latter conceptualizes the problem of colonialism itself differently. If that is the case, the issue becomes: which way of conceptualizing the problem is cognitively more adequate? However, before we settle the issue one way or another, we need to keep the difference between these two endeavours in mind. The existence of a domain of comparative research marks the beginning of such recognition. This, then, is the second dimension.

There is also a third dimension: the kind of 'comparison' involved. Even though the first phase in such a comparison consists of drawing parallels between thinkers from Western and non-Western cultures (say between Gandhi and Rawls), this in itself does not make it 'comparative'. Something more is required.

To elucidate this point adequately, let us return to what was said earlier about the relationship between the social sciences and Orientalism. I suggested that according to the comparative view, the Orientalist discourse is an oblique reflection on Western cultural experience, even though it appears as a description of other cultures. That is, to understand the description of the social world given by the West and the way it has described other cultures is to begin the process of understanding Western culture itself.

In one sense, this stance is congruent with the insight we have about human beings: when a person describes another human being, the resulting description also tells us 'something' about the describer himself. However, like all such insights, it is also ambiguous: what exactly is that 'something'? Does it tell us about the psychology of the describer, or his ideology, or his cognitive assumptions, or his world-view or his prejudices . . . ? In other words, what exactly should we focus on in that description that allows us to say 'something' interesting about the describer? Furthermore, how can we know whether what we identify in such a description is also true or, at least, not false?

Before attempting to answer the last two questions, we need to note their nature. The first question tells us that multiple things could be studied, when we study some description also as a self-description. That means we have to specify very clearly how we approach such self-descriptions in order to study them.

The second question is more generic in nature in the sense that it confronts every hypothesis we make about the world. Therefore, I will ignore the second question in the rest of what follows and focus mainly on the first. What kind of answers would be permitted in the context of comparative studies in this regard?

Consider what a natural scientist does: he provides (or at least attempts to provide) a partial description of the natural world. Assuming such a description to be true, we can study his description of the natural world as saying 'something' about himself. Depending on how we study this description of the world, we can formulate some hypotheses about the psychology of the scientist (which would give us 'psychology of the scientist') or the social forces operating on him (which would give us 'sociology of the scientist') and so on. We could also study the same description as a cognitive product, i.e. as an hypothesis that has specific cognitive properties. We study the hypothesis of a scientist about the world as 'something' that gives us clues about what science is. So when we study many such scientists and study their descriptions of the world as though such a study gives us some clues about the cognitive nature of such descriptions, then we are empirically developing an hypothesis about what science is. To put it even more simply: if we have to understand what 'science' is, then we have to study the cognitive properties of the descriptions that scientists provide about the natural world. In fact, this is how we have been studying sciences for centuries and that is also why we know more about the sciences today than, say, a few hundred years ago. Of course, it is surely the case that 'science' is much more than the cognitive properties of the theories that the natural scientists have produced (Franklin 1986). This claim is not denied here: all that is being said is that the cognitive nature of scientific theories (i.e. the descriptions of the world provided by scientists) can be studied as 'self-descriptions' and such a study gives us at least a partial understanding of what science is. As shown above, these descriptions could yield the psychology of science, the sociology of science and even the epistemology of science. Finally the study of historical presuppositions under which such theories are produced, would give us a history of science.

The same consideration holds good at the level of individual descriptions provided by members of a particular culture. If many members from a particular culture (say, Western culture) have produced descriptions of another culture (say, some specific non-Western culture) in such a way that all such descriptions exhibit some shared pattern or another,[2] then we can also study the cultural conditions under which such patterned descriptions are generated. Studying such cultural conditions as though they constrain creative human thought or as though they produce the pattern in such descriptions is to study the culture of the describer through the medium of his descriptions. Simply put: if all (or even most) individual descriptions of some non-Western cultures exhibit a common structure or a shared pattern, then this structure or pattern allows us to formulate questions for research that reveal the nature of Western culture.

IV

We now need to focus on a single culture in order to explicate the heuristic power of this methodology and once again, I shall choose the Indian culture. Consider the following 'facts' which enjoy a quasi-universal consensus due to centuries of ethnographic work: (a) India has many indigenous religions (Hinduism, Buddhism, Jainism, Sikhism, etc.) and the

---

2 In fact, one of the achievements of Said's Orientalism is to draw our attention to the presence of such patterns in the descriptions provided by members of the Western culture, when such individuals are separated from each other in time and space and are ignorant of each other's work. He called such a pattern 'latent orientalism'.

brāhmaṇas are the priests of Hinduism; (b) native to the Indian society is a hierarchical social structure called 'the caste system', which is religiously sanctioned. To these, let us add another 'fact', accepted till the beginning of the twentieth century, but one which, due to 'political correctness', has disappeared as an explicit claim; (c) Indians are immoral. Leaving aside the theoretical nature of these 'facts' for the moment, let us merely note that these facts constitute the common structure or a shared pattern of works written on India from at least the sixteenth century onwards (Gelders 2009).

As already indicated, there are two ways of looking at this pattern. The received view would take it as veridical: such a pattern is present in the Indian culture.[3] In fact, the disappearance of the third fact as an explicit claim about the morality of the Indians could be used to suggest that because intellectuals took distance from the 'imperialist' and 'racist' attitudes of their earlier generations, such gross generalizations have lost the place they once had. However the received view makes an assumption which is equivalent to saying that whenever natural scientists put across hypotheses, these always describe patterns in the natural world. What creates problems for this assumption is that many such hypotheses have been shown to be wrong or false. That is, before we accept some hypothesis as a true description of the world, we need to submit it to cognitive tests. That many people (or even all of them) repeat and endorse such descriptions is no evidence for the truth of the hypothesis: after all, for centuries, people believed and endorsed the claim that the sun revolved around the earth. In an exactly analogous way, just because centuries of work repeat and endorse the presence of a pattern in Indian culture, that does not tell us that such a pattern is indeed present there.

---

3 One could argue: would all people over centuries repeat and endorse the presence of such a pattern in Indian culture if it was not present there? We shall soon see that this is not the best way to argue.

The second way of looking at the issue, the comparative view, transforms the presence of the pattern into questions for research with a 'how' and a 'what'.

(a) How did the Europeans discover the existence of indigenous religions in India? What enabled them to discover these religions and make them conclude that brāhmaṇas are the priests of Hinduism? What evidence is there for either of the two?

(b) How did the Europeans discover the existence of a hierarchical social structure, when neither its principles nor its mechanism is known to Indians or Europeans? What evidence is there for the claim?

(c) How do we explain the conviction of generations of intellectuals in the West that Indians are immoral, when it is simply impossible to condemn all these thinkers as 'racists' and 'imperialists'? What evidence does our generation possess that they are not?

Notice that these issues cannot be settled by pointing either to the current consensus or to contemporary experience for an additional reason: in the comparative perspective, the line of continuity between the Orientalist discourse and current social sciences is the problem to investigate; what is being interrogated for its truth is precisely the nature of contemporary experience.[4] In exactly the same way that Galileo interrogated our experience of the sun's movement for its truth, comparative research interrogates contemporary experience for its truth.

How shall we go about answering the above questions? How can research begin into any or all of these questions? If we consider the received view on Orientalism, we are not greatly benefitted; it either dismisses the questions or gives an answer like the following: 'through empirical observations, people have

---

4 Nor will it do to say that we accept all cultures are equally 'valuable'; we need good reasons to accept such an axiological claim.

discovered that this is what Indian culture is like'. ('Why do we see the sun revolving round the earth?' 'Because it is the case that the sun revolves round the earth and that is something people have always empirically observed'.) In one sense, the received view takes a commendable stance: the empirical observations or experiences cannot be dismissed. However, in merely assuming such a stance without much ado, it also short circuits the process. While it is true that scientific explanations need to 'save the phenomena' and not deny them, we have to realize that only explanations do so: the theory of Galileo saved the phenomena of the movement of the sun. He denied that our experiences provide us with the truth but explained why we need to experience the movement of the sun on the horizon. In an exactly analogous way, we need to retain the facts that people have reported about India: that it appears to have religions, a hierarchical social order and so on. One cannot claim that entire generations over many centuries have been hallucinating. However these facts do not speak for themselves; we need a theory to explain these facts and experiences. That is what the comparative view does in transforming the presence of patterns into questions for research.

An Example from Religion

Consider the claim that most would give their assent to: Hinduism, Buddhism, Jainism, etc. are the religions of India. Post-colonial intellectuals would probably add two or three qualifications to this claim. They would probably say that it is not possible to speak of one Hinduism, one Buddhism, one Jainism, and, instead, one should speak about many 'Hinduisms', many 'Buddhisms', many 'Jainisms' and so on. Second, they would also raise questions about who could speak for and about these religions. Third, they are likely to add that the British 'created' or 'constructed' these religions in India during the colonial period. Actually, the first two qualifications are cognitively uninteresting because one could simply accept that 'Hinduism',

'Buddhism', 'Jainism', etc. do not name a unitary phenomenon but that they pick out many different sets of practices and beliefs. One could also dispense with the second qualification by suggesting that we are not after 'canonical' descriptions of these phenomena. By far, the most interesting qualification is the third one. Let us look at it closely.

During the colonial period, the British created many things: an education system, a legal system, a bureaucracy, roads and railways. None of these existed in these forms before the British colonized India. Were religions like 'Hinduism', etc. also created in this way? Some post-colonial thinkers are inclined to answer this question in the affirmative: the British created Hinduism as a religion in India, the way they created the Indian Civil Service (ICS). In that case, there is nothing fundamentally wrong with the Orientalist writings on Hinduism. Some of them might have made false claims, but we can correct them as more accurate information accumulates. In that case, contemporary writings on Hinduism, etc. whether from the field of Indology or religious studies, would remain continuous with the Orientalist writings on the subject. This is to say, the 'facts' that the Orientalists provided become the point of departure for the writings in social science. The latter either add to these facts or explain them. This is also the status of the field today: the writings in the humanities and the social sciences maintain an unbroken line of continuity with the Orientalist writings on these 'religions' in India.

If this is the case, one can hardly understand why there is excitement about either 'Orientalism' or 'post-colonial studies'. Of course, if one adds other items to this creation story, one can blame Western culture as the big bad wolf: the British created *satī*, the 'dowry system', 'the caste system' and anything else one feels like. Not only is this exercise in apportioning blame uninteresting, it also transforms the Indians into a bunch of idiots bereft of all reason: the British could do what they wanted with Indian culture, introduce and create whatever took their fancy, while the people stood around without even wanting to move the thumbs they were sucking upon. To put it in the language of the post-colonial thinkers: such a story deprives the colonial subjects of their agency. The post-colonial writers who tell such stories indeed deprive the colonial subjects of their agency in the name of giving it back to them, or they discover in the vigorous sucking of their thumbs an expression of 'resistance' to colonialism. Homi Bhabha, for instance, has made a lucrative business out of telling such stories.

There is however, another way of looking at the claim of creating these religions in India. Despite the limitations, drawing an analogy could make it more perspicuous. Imagine an extraterrestrial coming to earth and noticing the following phenomena: grass is green, milk turns sour, birds fly and some flowers put out a fragrant smell. He is convinced that these phenomena are related to each other and sees *hipkapi* in them. The presence of *hipkapi* not only explains what the above phenomena are but also how they are related to each other. To those who doubt the existence of *hipkapi,* he draws their attention to its visible manifestations: the tigers eating the gazelle, dogs chasing cats and the massive size of the elephants. Each of these is a fact as everyone can see. However neither severally not individually do they tell us anything about *hipkapi*. When more like him come to earth and reiterate the presence of *hipkapi*, other conditions permitting, *hipkapi* not only becomes a synonym for these phenomena but also turns out to be their explanation. Thereafter to ask what *hipkapi* is, or even how it explains, is an expression of one's idiocy: does not everyone see *hipkapi*, this self-explanatory thing? In this analogy, the extraterrestrial visitor has 'constructed' the *hipkapi*. To him, it is an experiential entity. He talks, as his fellow-beings do, about this experiential entity in a systematic way.

This is what the Europeans did. *Pūjā* in the temples, *sandhyāvandana* of the brāhmaṇas, *sahasranāmams*, etc. became organic parts of the Indian religion. Puruṣa-Sūkta was the cosmogony of the caste system and 'untouchability' its outward manifestation. *Dharma* and *adharma* were the Sanskrit words for 'good' and 'evil', and the Indian deities were much like their Greek counterparts. To the missionaries, Indians were idolaters; to the contemporary liberal, they are mere polytheists. In terms of the analogy, the visitors 'construct' a *hipkapi*. To them it becomes an experiential entity. They talk about this experiential entity in a systematic way.

This would entail suggesting that Europeans created 'Hinduism', etc. as their experiential entities. The Orientalists, under this construal, did not describe what exists in Indian culture. Instead, they created a *hipkapi*, constructed a pattern and a structure that lent coherence to their cultural experience of India. In such a case, claims about Hinduism become somewhat akin to claims about having visions of Mother Mary at Lourdes. Only 'somewhat', because the latter could be characterized as an hallucination, whereas one cannot say that the West has been 'hallucinating' about Indian religions. All writings on 'Hinduism', 'Buddhism', 'Jainism', whether their authors are Indian or Western, become suspect because they maintain a line of continuity between Orientalism and their own writings.

Can one tell such a story? It has been told (Balagangadhara 1994, 1998). In this paper, I argue that not only did the West 'imaginatively' create Hinduism, but also explain why it was compelled to do so. Its compulsion is rooted in the nature of religion, and I advance an hypothesis about religion that also explains this compulsion. Consequently it emerges as an alternative, a competitor theory to those in the marketplace, about what religion is. This hypothesis breaks the 'structural unity' that Orientalism has constructed. 'Hinduism', 'Buddhism', etc. become *hipkapis*. Consequently it is possible to investigate which of the 'facts' that went into constructing the *hipkapi* belong together, which do not, and how. One can start probing deeper into one's own culture because one's experience is accessible for reflection. 'What is Hinduism?, what is Buddhism?' translate themselves as tasks which require one to account for the facts that appear to lend credibility to the existence of the *hipkapi* in a non-ad hoc way.

This point is important enough for us to dwell on it longer. It suggests that the West (a) created 'Hinduism' and 'Buddhism', and (b) did so as religions. It is not the case that they created a monolithic religion instead of recognizing the multiplicity of theories and practices that go under the label 'Hinduism'. It is not as though they experienced 'Hinduism' as a monolithic entity. The suggestion is that 'Hinduism' as a concept (and an experiential entity) provided Westerners with a unitary and coherent experience. To the extent it is a concept, it is a construct. It is also a construct because as an experiential entity, it unifies the Western experience. However this concept has no referent in the world, i.e. there is no 'Hinduism' (whether as a religion, or as a multiplicity of religions) in Indian culture. As a result, the double qualification of Said makes sense: 'Hinduism' is both a false description of the Indian reality and is imaginary. It is false not because Westerners gave a false description of the reality ('Hinduism' in this case) but because they falsely assumed that their experiential entity was also a real entity in the world. It is imaginary in the sense that it does not have an existence outside the experience of Western culture. The same considerations apply to what Dirks (2006) does regarding the caste system. The notion of such a system unified the British experience of India; they implemented certain political and economic policies based on their experience. However this experience was not of the caste system. In fact, this experience was of no particular object but the basis of their interactions with Indians. By creating such a 'system' the British lent stability, coherence and unity to their cultural experience. Both the caste system and the Indian religions are constructs in this specific sense.

It is not as though colonialism brought 'Hindiuism' and 'the caste system' into existence. The Europeans spoke about these entities as though they existed. They acted as though these entities were real. However, neither before nor after colonialism do such entities or phenomena exist. They are *hipkapis*. These entities merely lend structure and stability to the European experience, and in the Orientalist discourse they become properties of Indian culture. In other words, language-use does not characterize the Orientalist discourse. Rather, Orientalism characteristically assumes that 'the caste system' and 'Hinduism' exist in Indian culture. The present-day social sciences also assume the same.

In short, the first step consists of recognizing the following: we are studying the descriptions of India in order to understand the cultural conditions under which such descriptions are produced. That is to say, we bracket aside (as a first step) the truth value of the Western descriptions of India[5] and look at them in terms of the cultural experiences of the members of Western culture. As proposed earlier, these experiences are the constraints exercised by Western culture on human observation and thought. Thus we have to reformulate our questions with respect to the Orientalist descriptions of India. Is there something in the nature of Western culture that makes its members believe in (a) the existence of religions; (b) the presence of a hierarchical social order; and (c) an absence of morality in Indian society and culture? In order to answer these questions, we need to undertake research into the history of Western culture with respect to these themes. What are the assumptions guiding the study of religion in Western cultural history? Notice what has happened in this process though: we begin the process of understanding Western culture by studying its description of religions in India (Dirks: 2006). This point can be generalized: to understand Western culture, we need to study how the West has described other cultures.

---

5 Because this is what we have to determine: are they true?

In the second step, we formulate hypotheses that account for why Western culture finds religions in India. When Western intellectuals routinely 'discover' the constitutive presence of indigenous religions (for instance, Hinduism, Buddhism, Jainism, etc.) in India, we can suggest that Western culture considers such a presence important in constituting the identity of a culture.

This suggestion (or hypothesis) can further be tested and strengthened by investigating how religion has been studied in multiple domains in Western culture, ranging from religious studies through sociology to different theologies. This provides us with an hypothesis about the relationship between Western culture on the one hand and religion on the other. This constitutes the third step. The last two steps provide us with a second generalization: to understand Western culture, we also need to study what the West says about the cultural world.

We need to combine the above two generalizations in order to take the fourth step. Western culture is what it says about other cultures and what it says about the cultural world.[6] The (partial) hypothesis about the relation between Western culture and religion can be further tested in two ways: (a) by studying how Western culture has described cultures other than India; (b) what the self-description and self-representation of the West is. If indeed, the predictions made in the third step are confirmed, then one can put across a hypothesis about the relationship between Western culture and religion.

It is only at this stage that we can assess the truth value of the Western claims about Indian culture. This is to say, depending upon what our hypothesis about the relation between Western culture and religion is, we can decide whether the claims about Indian religions are true or false.

---

6 This generalization will turn out later to be surprisingly non-trivial and heuristically productive. See section V.

An Example from Ethics

For a very long period of time, ethics in the Western intellectual tradition has been coextensive with religious beliefs and practices. The contributions of the Greco-Roman world (Aristotelian through Stoic and Sceptical traditions) have been absorbed, reinterpreted and refracted through the lens of a religious tradition. Secular ethics is of relatively recent origin and the relation between religious and secular ethics is a subject of controversy (Stout 1988). The fragmentary nature of our ethical theories has led major philosophers to deny the possibility of a systematic ethics, Macintyre (1984), Williams (1985), others to try and construct one (Arkes 1986), and yet others to champion casuistry (Jonsen and Toulmin 1988).

One of the long-standing ideas regarding ethical differences between cultures has been that the rules of moral behaviour vary from one culture to another. What is considered moral in some culture need not be so seen by others. There is alleged to be a factual diversity of moral rules. For example, 'going to a barber for a haircut and eating chicken after one's father dies' is considered profoundly immoral (!) behaviour by all caste groups in Orissa, India, whereas it is seen as totally non-moral by the Americans (Shweder, Mahapatra and Miller 1987). This factual variety does not damage our normative belief that it is in the nature of moral rules that they ought to hold universally. The requirement of universalizability is an integral part of our very idea of ethics. The norm, for example, that people ought not to be tortured for their religious or political beliefs does not allow for exceptions on grounds of race, time or culture.

My hypothesis is that the fundamental difference will be at the level of the moral domain itself. It is not the case that Indians have a set of moral norms which is different from those of the West; the ethical domain is itself constructed differently in these two cultures.

Different in which way? Consider the following claim: not only is there an absence of the concept of 'morals' in an Asian culture, but also of the very cluster of concepts required to speak about the phenomenon. Thus

> . . . consider as a specific example the classical Chinese language in which the early Confucians wrote. Not merely does that language contain no lexical item for 'moral', it also does not have terms corresponding to 'freedom', 'liberty', 'autonomy', 'individual', 'utility', 'rationality', 'objective', 'subjective', 'choice', 'dilemma', 'duty', 'right' and probably most eerie of all for a moralist, classical Chinese has no lexical item corresponding to 'ought' – prudential or obligatory.
>
> – Rosemont Jr. 1988: 61

This claim is as puzzling as it is startling: it is not possible to speak of 'moral duty' or 'moral dilemmas' or 'moral choices' in classical Chinese. It is not even possible to formulate a rule which uses the notion of 'ought' – either obligatorily ('All ought to do *X*') or prudentially ('If one desires *X* then one ought to do *Y*.'). In the Western intellectual tradition, we believe it to be the 'essence' of a moral principle or norm that it is formulated using the 'ought', either prudential or obligatory. Without it, there would be no difference of kind between factual and evaluative statements and the 'ought' and 'is' statements. Yet it is impossible to do precisely that in Confucianism. The philosophical significance is immense:

> Speakers (writers) of languages that have no term (or concept clusters) corresponding to 'moral' cannot logically have any moral principles. – ibid.: 60

But rightly enough, we take Confucianism at least as an example of a moral system. What is the upshot of the above remark? Rosemont Jr. formulates the issue as follows:

> If one grants that in contemporary Western moral philosophy 'morals' is intimately linked with the concept cluster

> elaborated above, and if none of that concept cluster can be found in the Confucian lexicon, then the Confucians not only cannot be moral philosophers, they cannot be ethical philosophers either. But this contention is absurd; by any account of the Confucians, they were clearly concerned about human conduct . . . and what constituted the good life. If these are not ethical considerations, what are? – ibid.: 64

This problem is not limited to classical Chinese and Confucianism alone. In India exactly the same problem confronts us. The 'ethical' domain itself is constructed differently: ethical language is not a normative language; ethical relations are factual relations; people act ethically without needing norms of ethical behaviour.

The intriguing question, apart from the truth value of these claims, is about their intelligibility. What is identified as the moral domain in Asia? How do they formulate ethical judgements? How do they criticize behaviours ethically? How do they settle ethical disputes? How do they learn to be ethical? Above all, how could we recognize the ethical domain?

Making one culture intelligible using the language of another is merely one face of the coin. The other has implications within the West itself. Unlike the received view (Parfit 1984), I would like to argue that the quandaries faced by Western ethical theories have little to do with their age but with their origin: religion. What virtues and vices are, why they are that; why must norms hold universally and what constitutes a moral life etc. are parts of a theological vocabulary. Should it be possible to demonstrate the truth of this hypothesis, the consequences are immense. Neither the Greek nor the Roman intellectuals can be pressed into the service of a 'secular' ethics. Plato and Aristotle must become radically unintelligible to a culture which calls itself heir to their civilization. The distance between Athens and Jerusalem will then be at least as great as between Mumbai and New York.

An attempt to specify differences along these lines should

help start building a different kind of bridge between cultures. Cognitively speaking, such an attempt might even explain why we have not had a science of ethics so far. Universalizing the provincial experience of a culture does not give us a science of any sort but merely strengthens the illusion of being a universal culture.

The same applies to other domains, whether it is about the presence of hierarchical social structures or the nature of politics. When we study the West this way, we notice that our problems about how to study Western culture are answered in an objective, non-arbitrary and scientific way. Western culture itself is studied in a comparative way. Western culture is what it says about others and what it says about the cultural world. We compare what it says about others with what it says about the world in order to understand what Western culture is. Any hypothesis about Western culture has to account for both the Western descriptions of other cultures and of the world. In condensed form: only an hypothesis that accounts simultaneously for both Orientalism and the social sciences can tell us what Western culture is. From this it follows that before we get 'one grand theory' about Western culture, we need to have multiple partial theories about all those domains that Orientalism and the social sciences straddle. Needless to say, we are far, far from being at that stage today.

It is clear that we see the limitations of current post-colonial studies. Lacking insight into the kind of comparative research that is required, they short circuit the process: they wrongly believe that the self-representation of Western culture is derivable as the antonym of Western descriptions of other cultures. If India is considered 'feminine', 'irrational' and 'superstitious' by the West, then they argue that the West has constructed itself as the opposite: 'masculine', 'rational' and 'scientific'. Not only are these adjectives useless in helping us understand Western culture, they are also empty. In fact, one can argue just the opposite: because of a particular self-understanding, Western culture has described other cultures as its antipode. Surely it matters what one says here: either the self-representation is a derived conclusion or it is the original premise; what choice we make here has its impact on what we say about Western culture or non-Western cultures. In contrast to this, there stands a method of comparative research which claims that understanding the 'self-representation' of Western culture is the end-point of a process; to understand that process one needs an hypothesis about comparative research.

V

At first sight, it looks as though this methodology can be generalized and should also work when we study Indian culture. This culture too is what it says about others and what it says about the cultural world. However if we dig into the Indian intellectual traditions with this expectation in mind, we are bound to come out puzzled: (a) the 'native' Indian traditions have produced very little about 'others' and even less about 'the cultural world'; (b) the modern Indian intelligentsia appears to merely reproduce the Western descriptions of India (when they talk about India) and Western self-descriptions (when they talk about the West). How does one understand or explain these facts and what do they say about a comparative study of Western and Indian culture?

Let us look at these questions separately and do so by beginning with the issue about the absence of 'native' Indian descriptions about the others and the cultural world. What exactly is absent in Indian culture? I will confine myself to the topics already chosen: religion and God; ethics; social structure. The standard textbook trivia which we teach our students routinely assures us not only that there are multiple 'native' religions in India (Hinduism, Buddhism, Jainism, different forms of Śaivism, multiple varieties of Vaiṣṇavism, the Bhakti movements, Sikhism, and many other kinds of 'popular' religions) but also that they arose in conflict with the ruling 'orthodoxies'. For instance, the pure Vedic religion is supposed to have given birth to a degenerate 'Brāhmanism'. The Śramaṇa traditions (exemplified by both Jainism and Buddhism) are alleged to have fought Brāhmanism. The latter itself is said to have mutated into 'Hinduism', partially strengthened by Advaitic religion that later fought Buddhism and so on. In such a case, one would expect a huge volume of literature regarding religion (what religion is, what these individual religions are, etc.) and even more literature in theology. Yet there is hardly any theology in India (if we look at Christianity as an example of what it means to write theological tracts) and there is hardly any explicit reflection on the nature of religion. (All one needs is an acquaintance with the history of Christianity to notice how staggering this absence is.) To this day, neither the scholar nor the layman can answer the question about what makes, say, 'Hinduism' a religion or what is that 'Brāhmanism' against which Buddhism fought. Are we to seriously believe that Buddhism as a religion, fought another religion, Brāhmanism, for centuries on end without even being able to say what made Brāhmanism a religion?

Similar considerations hold good elsewhere. Despite the presence of the voluminous Subhāsita and Dharmaśāstra literatures, India has hardly produced noticeable tracts and sustained reflections on 'ethics' (Van Den Bossche and Mortier 1997). There is no equivalent of an 'Ethica Nichomachea', let alone a 'Summa Theologica' in the Indian intellectual traditions. This does not mean that there is no evidence for intellectual reflections: on the contrary. Yet certain kinds of reflection are noticeable for their absence.

One such is the famous 'Indian caste system'. All and sundry assure us that the Indian social structure is synonymous with 'the caste system' and all we have by way of an explanation (or even justification) of this system are a few verses in the Puruṣa-Sūkta, in the *Gītā* and in some Dharmaśāstras. No Indian could tell you the 'principles' of this system, even though quite a few modern 'theories' about it float around. Indologists (Dumont 1972), sociologists (Bougle 1971), anthropologists (Van den Berghe 1981), political theorists (Olson Jr. 1984) have provided all kinds of descriptions without being sure of what kind of system 'the caste system' is supposed to be.

In this sense, we notice two kinds of facts when we try to study Indian culture. First, there is a noticeable absence of intellectual reflections on these and allied phenomena; second, in the course of the last three hundred years or so, Indian intellectuals have merely reproduced Western descriptions of India's culture and her traditions. When we study India, our question should then be: why is there such a vacuum?

Let me make the above general point in a more concrete way as well. Consider the questions that people in the West routinely ask today: Why do the Hindus wear *bindī*? Why do Indians not eat beef? Is it true that most Indians worship the phallus? What do Indians think about the caste system? Do they still practice *satī* in India? Why do Indian gods have six or eight arms? What is the Hindu religious symbol? Do most Indians worship statues in temples? Do the Buddhists really not believe in God, in which case, why are there temples for the Buddha? Are the Hindus religious? And so on and so forth. Consider now the fact that most Indians do not ask these questions in the process of their socialization. Why are these questions not raised there? I mean to say, why do they not go around asking questions about eating beef, wearing *bindī*, worshipping the Śiva-liṅga, and such like in India? Why have people not found it important to write huge tracts about such practices? Surely, it is not because they know the answers to these questions; if they did, they would have no problems in providing the same answers to Western interlocutors. Here is a simple but a very important answer. It does not occur to most Indians to raise these questions about their traditions. It does not occur to them, not because they are any less curious or intelligent than people in Western cultures but because such questions do not make sense in their cultural milieu. That is, they learn not to ask such questions about their traditions and this learning is a part of learning to become a member of the Indian traditions. Of course, when we say that they do not ask such questions, it does not mean that they have never raised these questions at any point in their lives: for instance, as children they too would have raised many such questions and the answers have satisfied them.

When Indians confront such questions in the West, two things happen: (a) they feel compelled to provide an answer and (b) the answers they give very closely track the answers already provided by Western culture. That is to say, when such questions are asked about the Indian traditions, one should not assume that these questions are intelligible to these Indians: they are not. It is in the nature of Western culture to raise such questions. Furthermore, such questions also outline the kind of admissible answers.

One of the most important consequences of this claim is: when Western culture quizzes Indians about the nature of their traditions, this culture is telling us about itself. To provide answers to the Western interlocutors about Indian traditions one needs to understand the nature of Western culture. Simply put: to understand let alone answer such questions about Indian traditions, one has to understand Western culture.

In other words, we face an asymmetry. To study and understand Western culture, we need to study what it says about the others and the world. However, we need to do exactly the same thing even when we want to study Indian culture. Alternately put, we compare Western descriptions (of others and the world) to understand the West; if we want to understand India, we have to begin by saying what (and in what sense) India is not like the West. Our expectation of wanting to study India by looking at what it says about others and the world is not met.

Why is there such asymmetry? It has to do with colonialism that established frameworks of enquiry into the nature of human beings and societies through the use of power and violence. Once established and generalized, such frameworks continue to draw their legitimacy through sources other than those that are cognitive in nature. Today, this legitimizing process has reached its apotheosis in the guise of an attitude that suggests that a science of culture and sciences of the social are simply impossible because of human and epistemic limitations. Needless to say, a persistent 'anti-scientific' attitude adds fodder to such an attitude.

Why do we have to indulge in this kind of comparison when we study other cultures? Does it mean that Western culture is the 'norm' and that we have to explain other cultures as deviations from this norm? Why can we not, in the process of studying other cultures, study them directly? Why compare? For instance, to study India, could we not simply continue with 'empirical' and/or 'textual' studies produced in India to understand Indian culture?

I would like to answer these questions in two ways. The first is to draw attention to the fact that the only framework that we could possibly use today to study Indian culture will come either from Orientalism or from the social sciences or both. If we use these frameworks, we will merely add to the existing Western descriptions of India and these do not advance our understanding of Indian culture. Of course, one might have no problems with either and merely suggest that in so far as such frameworks allow us to find 'the truth', we should go ahead. This is the received view on Orientalism and the social sciences, whose legitimacy requires endorsements until alternate and rival theories emerge that challenge current understanding. That, in fact, has been my argument so far. However, I am not interested in criticizing this view but in elaborating on the answers given by comparative research.

In elaborating on the comparative view, I would like to return to the Indian case and to the observation made about the Indian intelligentsia: this layer reproduces Western descriptions of both India and the West. This observation is not meant as a criticism; it is just what we say it is: an observation. However, I would now like to nuance this statement in a way that is methodologically helpful.

Even when the Indian intelligentsia reproduces Western descriptions, by virtue of the fact that it is Indians who do this, we can say that they speak both about others and the cultural world. However, in reproducing these Western descriptions about India and the others, something additional intervenes: the Indian intelligentsia too is constrained by Indian culture. This means to say, they do not simply parrot the Western descriptions of India but transform them in the process. Indians reproduce Western descriptions as Indians understand them. This is the nuance that requires addition. This addition opens up a way for us to study India too in a comparative way. There is pattern and systematicity to the Indian transformation of Western descriptions of other cultures, the cultural world and themselves. This pattern provides us with clues about Indian culture. The insight here can be summarized in the following way: to understand India, we need to study how Indians transform Western descriptions of India and the world. This too can be generalized: to understand non-Western cultures, we need to study the way they transform Western descriptions of the world and themselves. Such a study will provide us with insights into the mechanisms of transformation. These mechanisms, in their turn, will provide us with knowledge about the cultural conditions that constrain their thinking.

Underlying comparative research is the realization that both Orientalism and the current social sciences are flawed in some respects. However, this recognition takes a form that is different from simply criticizing them. Their mistakes become problems requiring explanation and therefore, the labour of earlier generations of intellectuals become our point of departure. Instead of rejecting their claims and efforts as wrong, misguided, or whatever else, we need to take their results utterly seriously. Where they are wrong we can improve upon them, provided we understand that we also need to explain their mistakes from within the framework of the theories that we try to build. The dynamic exhibited in such a process is analogous to the dynamic of scientific progress: the earlier theories are both incorporated and transcended by newer theories. In other words, the labour of previous generations of intellectuals (whether from the West or from other cultures) are, as in the natural sciences, constraints on any theory formation that we might undertake.

VI

Beginning with Kant, a new concept made its home in German philosophy: the concept of a 'critique'. Kant claimed that David Hume woke him up from a 'dogmatic slumber' (even though it is very likely that Kant never read Hume) and wrote his *Critique of Pure Reason* as a result. Hegel developed critiques of Kant. However, it was left to Karl Marx to make the notion more widely known than either Kant or Hegel did. He not only wrote critiques of Hegel but also a critique of political economy: his 'economic' theory was seen as a critique of the political economy of his day. Since then, this notion has either meant a 'rejection' of science (as in the case of the Frankfurt School) or conflated with the more mundane and all too familiar word 'criticism'. Of course, in the modern intellectual world, one announces one's radical intention not by saying that one 'criticizes': instead, one always 'critiques'.

One of the reasons why the notion of critique lost its original significance has to do with the lack of clarity about the meaning of the word and the alleged 'troubled' relation between the notions of 'science' and 'critique'. After all, Marx developed a critique of the 'science' of political economy. In the Marxist intellectual traditions, especially in what has been called 'Western Marxism', this gave birth to questions of the following sort: Is *Das Kapital* a 'science' (as Marx claimed) or a 'critique' of a science (as Marx suggests in the subtitle of his work)? How could Marx claim that his work was 'scientific', when he explicitly and emphatically rejects the 'science' of political economy of his day and develops a theory in opposition to those of David Ricardo and Adam Smith? How could the 'science' of political economy be both 'scientific' and a 'critique' of that science at the same time? And so on.

Though fascinating, I do not intend to narrate this century-long discussion here. Suffice it to note that these discussions assume that 'science' and 'critique' refer to the cognitive or epistemic status of the texts (or, in modern parlance, 'discourses') in question: Marx's text (or 'discourse') is either a 'science' or it exemplifies a 'critique' of a science. I would like to suggest that the relationship between a science and a critique should be looked at differently so that it allows us to appreciate their difference properly.

Kant and Marx did two different things: (a) they pointed out mistakes in the work of their predecessors, and (b) developed a theory that explained how and why these mistakes were necessary. Kant for instance, outlined the antinomies of pure reason and explained how these come into being. This explanation is a part of Kant's philosophical theory about knowledge. In the same way, Marx explained why, of necessity, Ricardo committed the mistakes he did and this explanation too is part of Marx's theory. In other words, the notion of a 'critique' picks out a relationship between two succeeding theories: it is a relational predicate that applies to a predecessor theory and to a successor theory. The latter includes within its purview an explanation of the mistakes (including an account of their necessity) of the former. Because it is a relational predicate, one can also speak about it as a property of the succeeding theory: the theories of Kant and Marx are 'critiques'. However, we need to note that this predicate is relative in nature. It is relative to two theories of which one is a predecessor and the other, a successor. In this sense, Marx criticized the earlier science of political economy and also explained its mistakes, by virtue of which, his theory is a 'critique' of the science of political economy. However, to the extent one believes that Marx's theory is also scientific, then to that extent, the relationship between Ricardo and Marx is of the same kind as the relationship between, say, a Copernicus and a Galileo.

A critique is a relational predicate that is applicable to theories, whether they are scientific or philosophical in nature. It tells us that a later theory exhibits and explains the mistakes of the earlier theories as a part of its own explanatory hypotheses about some relevant part of the world. At a generic level, such a cognitive movement expresses the dynamics of the growth of scientific theories: the mistakes and the successes of the earlier theories (for the most part) are explained in the later theories. A comparative science is such a critique: it is a critique of Orientalism and the contemporary social sciences that are influenced by the Orientalist theorizing. On the one hand, without the presence of Orientalism or the contemporary social sciences, such a comparative science would fail to even exist. Thus it presupposes the work of preceding theorists and their theories. On the other hand, such a science also explains the mistakes of earlier works and incorporates their explanatory successes as well.

In this sense, not all scientific theories are critiques, only some are. The appellation signals that some theory or other builds on the work of earlier generations in some domain. It suggests too that the new theory argues that the earlier theories are wrong but that their mistakes were, in some senses, inevitable. Furthermore, it also hints that the new theory is a break of some sort when compared to its predecessor theories. In doing so, it also sketches out an objective starting point for research. Thus it answers the question that had preoccupied centuries of philosophical discussions: with what must a science begin?

Today this question is not considered an important problem in the philosophy of science but that does not mean that it has lost its significance.

Consider a simple way of formulating the problem. How could a comparative science succeed in theorizing about the West and India when generations before us failed to carry out the task adequately? From where should such a process begin? This beginning itself presupposes some implicit theory and there might be good reasons for starting an investigation the way this paper has outlined. Thus it is not research that begins without presuppositions but one which accepts the fact that all research has multiple contexts, linguistic, historical and conceptual. Together these contexts have provided us with a set of problems: why were the earlier generations wrong? How does one explain their mistakes without appealing to ad hoc hypotheses but by incorporating their failures in the process of developing a hypothesis about some part of the world?

To make it more concrete, consider how these questions emerge in some of the sub-domains I have already spoken about. Why did earlier generations think that Indians were immoral? One could come up with many hypotheses as answers: they were racist, imperialist and xenophobes. While many such answers are given, they are both ad hoc and implausible. They are implausible because they transform entire generations into inauthentic bigots in the process of answering the question. A comparative solution to this problem is compelled to answer the same question differently. The answer has to be sought in what ethics is, in the nature of Western ethical thought and Indian ethics. In other words, any such answer emerges as an alternative theory of ethics. At the moment, it is of no consequence how and in what sense it is a competitor to Western ethical thinking. The point is that it accounts for the perception of the Western world about Indian morality by appealing to the nature of ethical thinking. The same considerations hold good in the other two domains I have talked about: religion and the caste system.

In other words, there is a criterion to judge whether or not some theory or another is a critique and as such is part of comparative science. Does the theory explain the failures and mistakes of earlier generations of intellectuals as necessary mistakes, given the nature of the phenomenon under consideration? Does the particular theory explain the earlier mistakes as a part of a theory about the phenomenon that is being investigated? In answering these two questions, the question of where to begin also gets answered. It provides a non-arbitrary and objective point to begin investigating social and cultural phenomena. In doing so, it also suggests why a comparative science could succeed where earlier theorization failed.

References

Arkes, Hardy, 1986, *First Things: An Enquiry into the First Principles of Morals and Justice*, Princeton: Princeton University Press.

Balagangadhara, S.N., 1998, "Comparative Anthropology and Moral Domains", *Cultural Dynamics*, **1**(1): 98-128.

Bougle, Celestin, 1971 (tr. from French by D.F. Pocock), *Essays on the Caste System*, Cambridge: Cambridge University Press.

Breckenridge, Carol A. and Peter van der Veer, eds., 1993, *Orientalism and the Post-colonial Predicament: Perspectives on South Asia*, Philadelphia: University of Pennsylvania Press.

Brill, E.J., 1994, "The Heathen in His Blindness . . ." *Asia, the West and the Dynamics of Religion*, 2nd rev. edn., New Delhi: Manohar.

Carstairs, Morris G., 1957, *Twice Born*, London: Midland Books.

Chakrabarty, Dipesh, 1997, "Post-Coloniality and the Artifice of History:

Who Speaks for 'Indian' Pasts?", in *A Subaltern Studies Reader*, ed. R. Guha, Minneapolis: University of Minnesota Press.

Claes, Tom, 1996, "Theorizing the West: A Second Look at Francis Hsu", *Cultural Dynamics*, **8**(1): 79-99.

Clooney, Francis X, 2010, *Comparative Theology: Deep Learning Across Religious Borders*, Oxford: Wiley-Blackwell.

Courtright, Paul B., 1985, *Ganesa: Lord of Obstacles, Lord of Beginnings*, Oxford: Oxford University Press.

Daniel, Valentine E., 1984, *Fluid Signs: Being a Person the Tamil Way*, Berkeley: University of California Press.

Davidson, Donald, 1984, "On the Very Idea of a Conceptual Scheme", in *Inquiries into Truth and Interpretation*, Oxford: Oxford University Press.

Dilworth, Craig, 2008, *Scientific Progress: A Study Concerning the Nature of the Relation Between Successive Scientific Theories*, Berlin: Springer.

Dirks, Nicholas, 2006, *Castes of Mind: Colonialism and the Making of Modern India*, New Delhi: Permanent Black.

Dumont, Louis, 1972, *Homo Hierarchicus: The Caste System and Its Implications*, London: Paladin Books.

Feyerabend, Paul, 2010, *Against Method*, London: Verso Books.

Franklin, Allan, 1986, *The Neglect of Experiment*, Cambridge: Cambridge University Press.

Gebhardt, Jurgen, 2008, "Political Thought in an Intercivilizational Perspective: A Critical Reflection", *The Review of Politics*, **70**: 5-22.

Gelders, Raf, 2009, "Genealogy of Colonial Discourse: Hindu Traditions and the Limits of European Representation", *Comparative Studies in Society and History*, **51**(3): 563-89.

Holy, Ladislav, ed., 1987, *Comparative Anthropology*, Oxford: Blackwell.

Hoyningen-Huene P. and H. Sankey, eds., 2010, *Incommensurability and Related Matters*, Berlin: Springer.

Inden, Ronald, 1990, "Orientalist Constructions of India", *Modern Asian Studies*, **20**(3).

—, *Imagining India*, Oxford: Basil Blackwell, pp. 401-46.

Jenco, Leigh Kathryn, 2007, "What Does Heaven Ever Say?: A Methodcentered Approach to Cross-cultural Engagement", *American Political Science Review*, **101**(4): 741-55.

Jonsen, Alabert R. and Stephen Toulmin, 1988, *The Abuse of Casuistry: A History of Moral Reasoning*, Berkeley: University of California Press.

King, Richard, 1999, *Indian Philosophy: An Introduction to Hindu and Buddhist Thought*, Edinburgh: Edinburgh University Press.

Kripal, Jeffrey, 1998, *Kali's Child: The Mystical and the Erotic in the Life and Teachings of Ramakrishna*, Chicago: The Univrsity of Chicago Press.

Lakatos, Imre, 1980, *The Methodology of Scientific Research Programmes: Philosophical Papers*, vol. 1, Cambridge: Cambridge University Press.

Larsen, G.J. and E. Deutsch, eds., 1988, *Interpreting Across Boundaries: New Essays in Comparative Philosophy*, Princeton: Princeton University Press.

Laudan, Larry, 1977, *Progress and Its Problems*, Berkeley: The University of California Press.

Loy, David, 1988, *Nonduality: A Study in Comparative Philosophy*, New Haven: Yale University Press.

Macintyre, Alasdair, 1984, *After Virtue*, 2nd edn. Notre Dame: University of Notre Dame Press.

Mahoney, James and Dietrich Rueschmeyer, eds., 2003, *Comparative Historical Analysis in the Social Sciences*, Cambridge: Cambridge University Press.

Marriott, McKim, 1976, "Interpreting Indian Society: A Monistic Alternative to Dumont's Dualism", *Journal of Asian Studies*, **36**(3): 189-95.

—, 1990, "Constructing an Indian Ethno-sociology", in *India through Hindu Categories*, New Delhi: Sage Publication.

Moussaief-Masson, 1980, *The Oceanic Feeling: The Origins of Religious Sentiment in Ancient India*, Dordrecht: D. Reidel.

Olson Jr., Mancur, 1984, *The Rise and Decline of Nations: Economic Growth, Stagflation, and Social Rigidities*, New Haven: Yale University Press.

Parfit, Derek, 1984, *Reasons and Persons*, Oxford: Oxford University Press.

Quine, W.V.O., 1960, *Word and Object*, Massachusetts: The MIT Press.

Roland, Alan, 1988, *In Search of Self in India and Japan*, Princeton: Princeton University Press.

Rosemont Jr., Henry, 1988, "Against Relativism", in *Interpreting Across Boundaries: New Essays in Comparative Philosophy*, ed. G.J. Larson and E. Deutsch, Princeton: Princeton University Press.

Said, Edward, 1978, *Orientalism: Western Conceptions of the Orient*, London: Penguin Books.

Shweder, Richard A. and Edmund J. Bourne, 1984, "Does the Concept of the Person Vary Cross Culturally?", in *Culture Theory: Essays on Mind, Self, and Emotion*, ed. R.A. Shweder and R.A. Levine, Cambridge: Cambridge University Press.

Shweder, Richard A., Manmohan Mahapatra and Joan G. Miller, 1987, "Cultural and Moral Development", in *The Emergence of Morality in Young Children*, ed. Jerome Kagan and Sharon Lamb, Chicago: The University of Chicago Press.

Stout, Jeffrey, 1988, *Ethics after Babel: The Languages of Morals and Their Discontent*, Massachusetts: Beacon Press.

Van den Berghe, Pierre, 1981, *The Ethnic Phenomenon*, New York: Elsevier.

Van Den Bossche, Frank and Freddy Mortier, 1997, "The Vajjalaggam: A Study in Virtue Theory", *Asian Philosophy*, **7**(2): 85-108.

van den Bouwhuijsen Harry, Willem Derde and Claes Tom, 1995, "Recovering Culture", *Cultural Dynamics*, **7**(2): 163-86.

Westman, Robert S., ed., 1975, *The Copernican Achievement*, Berkeley: The University of California Press.

William, Bernard, 1985, *Ethics and the Limit of Philosophy*, Massachusetts: Harvard University Press.

Yengoyan, Arama, ed., 2006, *Modes of Comparison: Theory and Practice*, Ann Arbor: The University of Michigan Press.

DISCUSSION

Manindra Thakur

. . . I have many questions on Balu's observations. I too would like to decolonize the social sciences, because the people of India, not the modern educated ones but those who live in the villages, are still making sense of their lives with traditional philosophy. We undertook a project involving a small amount of fieldwork on Nyāya in the Mithilā area, and we discovered that knowingly or unknowingly this whole idea of Nyāya was in the conscious or unconscious mind. I think that it still makes sense and we are constantly facing conflict between modernity and tradition. In fact if you today visit the Indian countryside as I discovered in the Mithilā area, every village is divided into two groups – the modernizers and the traditionalists, and there is considerable hostility between the two. So I think we need to access our own philosophical tradition, not for reasons of political identity but for making sense of ourselves.

The problem is: in that case how do we do social science? Today we are confronting modern institutions which were never present earlier, not even capitalism – there were markets but not capitalism as we define it. Some social scientists in India are now saying that the idea of social science itself has to be amended. A.K. Saran earlier argued in this vein.

Recently a professor from Jawaharlal Nehru University (JNU) wrote an autobiography which made him very famous. It is titled *Murdaiya*, a word that means *śmasāna* in village parlance. As a young Dalit boy the author spent most of his time in the *śmasāna*, and he has written a story of the *Murdaiya*, looking at the village from the *Murdaiya*'s perspective. It has become an authentic social science text. People who have read it treat it as a good social science text for Indian villages.

So do we have to change the very form of social science? There is a big struggle going on in Indian academia by those who assert that social language terminology is unable to capture our experience. Textual knowledge is one thing but experiential knowledge another. Moreover a large number of persons cannot articulate their ideas well in English, but they have a deep and rich experience of their own reality which cannot be put into the language of social science.

The fact is that social science is itself a colonial project: it was never developed in the non-Western world. Hence the anthropologist McKim Marriott talks about how an Indian social science might be developed from Indian philosophy. Some suggest that since historically we did our 'social science' through narratives, we have here the outline for a brand new project. This is the first point.

Second, if we need to retain the idea of social science then do we need to deal with Hegel, Marx or anybody else, even though it is known we do not understand them? Neither did they, for that matter, understand us. I can argue that Schopenhauer did not understand the Upaniṣads because they were translated by Dara Shikoh into Persian and from Persian into Latin and lastly into German. So there is the possibility of miscommunication. Despite that we need to engage with the other to understand ourselves and the other.

Third, what do we need to prioritize? I am interested in Indian philosophy because I find society is in an unlivable condition. I would like to change this but change demands a major project of human emancipation, without which all projects are useless.

Balagangadhara

I make one response to Thakur. The question requires deeper handling so you will forgive me for the brevity of my response but you will get some idea of where I stand.

Regarding the first question as to whether we reject social science itself, I am aware that many people have made this suggestion. I am not so much hung up on the word 'social science' but I do believe that we need to systematically reflect on our experiences in the world. A systematic reflection on experiences in the form of a theory is what we can conveniently call social science. We need theories about the world to understand the world. Systematic thinking means use of certain criteria to decide which theories are good or not, etc. and which to choose. The best thing would be to appeal to the history of the natural sciences over say four hundred years to see how they have done it, what kind of criteria they used. Thus I belong to the group which advocates systematic reflection on experience, and in that sense I belong to the group which says we need social science.

Your second question was about Indians having different ways of understanding experience: you spoke of narratives and the autobiography of Tulsi Ram. This raises the question of what form these reflections are going to take. To give a crude example: are they going to be mathematized? Will they take the form of scientific laws or of narratives? That is a very interesting question. But all narratives are not social science: in that case every novelist would have a scientific theory. If a text is an autobiography, it is not social science.

3

Translating Philosophical Texts
Challenges and New Avenues

D. Prahlada Char

A SERIOUS and sincere attempt at translating the Indian philosophical classics, as we know, was first made by Europeans at the end of the nineteenth century. Max Müller and others translated the Vedas, Upaniṣads, Bhāṣyas on the *Brahma-Sūtras* and others into English, German and other languages. Later, in the beginning and the middle of the twentieth century, many Indian scholars like Ganganath Jha rendered many philosophical texts pertaining to almost all the philosophical schools of this country, such as Nyāya, Vyākaraṇa, Mīmāṁsā and Vedānta into English. Even in the second half of the twentieth century, particularly in the 1980s and 1990s many translations of philosophical texts were brought out, mainly with the support and encouragement given by the Indian Council of Philosophical Research. Thus, the translation of Indian philosophical classics with its long history of nearly 150 years should have been sufficient for coining technical terms in English that would bring out the exact meaning of the technical terms used in Indian philosophical texts. Technical terms apart, there are some other characteristics of philosophical texts in Sanskrit, which make their rendering into English a challenging task. The long compound words, dialectical style of the philosophical language of Sanskrit, in which the opponent's and proponent's arguments appear to have been intermixed, make the translator who is not traditionally trained and has not gained efficiency in loosening the knots that are abundant in the Sanskrit text, perplexed and liable to commit mistakes. It is time now, I believe, to invite scholars, who have studied the available translations of philosophical texts and found them unsatisfactory, to evolve a methodology of translation, by following which, expert translators can produce qualitatively better translations in future. However, such an effort, howsoever laudable, would not in itself be very useful, because even those translations would remain unintelligible unless the reader is taught, if not the original text the translation of which the reader is trying to understand, some text, the study of which under the guidance of a competent scholar, habituates the reader to the philosophical concepts and also to the terminology used by a particular school. The translation in Gaṅgeśa Upadhyaya's Prāmāṇyavāda of course remains. The translation of Nirvikalpakavāda of Gaṅgeśa by Prof. Mohanty and the translation of Viṣayatāvāda of Gadādhara Bhaṭṭācārya by Sibajiban Bhattacharya can be cited here as examples. I do not think that these can be properly understood by Western philosophers who are well grounded in their own field. These translations are considered very faithful to the original texts and are held in high esteem by scholars, despite their being supported by explanatory notes.

It is needless to say that to produce a readable translation in English, the translator must have a good command over the English language. But, still more important, he should have much more command over Sanskrit and have the competence to notice intricacies of the language by which he can read more appropriate meanings intended by the author of the original text. Still more important is the requirement that the translator have a clear awareness of the exact stand of the philosophical school about issues being discussed in the original text.

With due apologies to the eminent scholar Ganganath Jha, whose translations in English of several philosophical classics have been extensively used by non-Sanskrit students and scholars alike, I would like to show how in certain places his translations/explanatory notes are inadequate or misleading.

The context is the translation of the *Advaitasiddhi* text concerned with the second definition of falsity. The following is the definition in *Advaitasiddhi*:

pratipannopādhou traikālikaniṣedhapratiyogitvam mithyātvam

Ganganath Jha translates it as:

> The unreal is that which is the counter-entity of an absolute negation with regard to the *substratum* in which it is cognized.[1]

The main problem with this translation is the use of the word 'unreal' for *mithyā*. The Advaita school holds that reality is of three kinds namely, *pāramārthika sattva* (noumenal reality), *vyāvahārika sattva* (empirical reality) and *prātibhāsika sattva* (apparent reality). While it treats empirical reals such as worldly objects and apparent reals such as *śuktirajata* and *rajjusarpa,* i.e. shell-silver and rope-snake as *mithyā,* it holds only *cit* (consciousness) as real. Apart from these two, namely, consciousness – the *pāramārthika satya* and *mithyā* (which includes both the empirically real *vyāvahārika satya* and apparently real *prātibhāsika satya*) there is one more category namely *atyantāsat* which is also not real hence unreal. (If the empirical reals and apparent reals are fit to be called 'unreal' because they are different from 'the real' *pāramārthika satya,* the *atyantāsat* such as *śaśaviṣāṇa* (the hare's horn) would also be forcibly included in the scope of the definition; such is not the case for the Advaitins.) According to the Advaita school *śaśaviṣāṇa* (the hare's horn) and *vandhyāsuta* (the son of a barren woman) are *atyantāsat*. The difference between the *atyantāsat* and *mithyā,* according to the school is that while *atyantāsat* is never

---

1 *The Advaitasiddhi* of Madhusūdana Saraswati, 1990, Sri Garib Das Oriental Series No. 102, Sri Satguru Publications, p. 13.

cognized as being existent in a substratum, *mithyā* is cognized as being existent in a locus. Thus the Advaita school carefully avoids calling the *atyantāsat* as *mithyā*. This, being the case the definition of 'the property of being *mithyā*', i.e. *mithyātva* should be applicable only to *vyāvahārika satya* and *prātibhāsika satya* and never to *atyantāsat*. But, the word 'unreal' in the place of the Sanskrit word *mithyā*, gives an impression that the definition is intended to be applicable to all 'unreals' including *atyantāsat*. While *vyāvahārika satya* and *prātibhāsika satya* are unreal since they are different from the real, viz. the noumenally real – consciousness, *atyantāsat* is also unreal as it is different from all the three kinds of reals. In fact, it is inaccurate to call *vyāvahārika satya* and *prātibhāsika satya* 'unreal', as they are also reals in the Advaita school. The translation is misleading, because it gives the impression that the *siddhi* is attempting to define *atyantāsat*.

Another difficulty that we face in this translation is that of the absence of explanatory notes. It is surprising that Ganganath Jha never felt the necessity of adding explanatory notes to his translation of *Advaitasiddhi*, though in some places (indeed very rarely), immediately after translating the sentence, in just one sentence in brackets, he explains what is meant by the original text. The present case itself is an example where he, using brackets, explains the original text, which does not reflect the correct view of the Advaita school. The following is an explanation of the definition of *mithyātva* which he has translated, i.e. by calling the jar unreal, what we mean is that it is capable of being absolutely denied in regard to the point of space and time in connection with which it is perceived.[2]

As per this explanation, the Advaita school considers the jar, etc. worldly objects as *mithyā*, as they are absolutely non-existent in the space and time such as the ground and present time, in connection with which they are perceived. But, the

---

[2] *The Advaitasiddhi* of Madhusūdana Saraswati, op. cit.

Advaita view is not so. It is of the view that just as the cognition of shell-silver is illusory, the cognition of worldly objects also is illusory. However, there is a difference. While shell-silver, etc. things are superimposed on empirically real objects and are considered *prātibhāsika* – apparently real, worldly objects are superimposed on the *pāramārthika,* i.e. the noumenally real object which is *Brahman*, and are regarded as *vyāvahārika* – empirically real. As shown above, had it been the case that worldly objects are superimposed on space and time which are empirically real and are denied there itself, then worldly objects would have been fit to be regarded as apparently real. Thus, the above explanation of *mithyātva* is quite contrary to the concept of *mithyātva* of the world that the Advaita school posits.

These are a few instances where I feel the translation by Jha has some lacuna which should be questioned. In spite of these shortcomings, we will have to ever remain grateful to Jha for his great contribution to Indology through these translations, which, on the whole, gave a very faithful presentation of what the original text contains and kindled an interest in the study of Indian philosophy, in students not familiar with Sanskrit.

As I said earlier, a translator of Sanskrit texts, particularly of philosophical texts, must have a very clear understanding of the subject dealt with in the original text. If the text is highly technical, more than mere familiarity is necessary: he essentially needs to have command over the terminology. If the translator lacks this capacity, the translation would be ridiculous. Examples of such ridiculous translation can be found in the *Encyclopedia of Indian Philosophy* (vol. VI) where the translation of some definitions of *vyāpti* offered by neo-Naiyāyikas appear. I must clarify here that this criticism is limited only to some parts of the volume where translations of highly technical definitions appear. Otherwise, the contribution of these volumes of *Encyclopedia* which beautifully presents a detailed and authentic history of various Indian schools of philosophy, summarizing their views and the philosophical concepts attributed to them, is enormous.

The following is one of the fourteen definitions attributed to a Naiyāyika called Pragalbha and which Raghunātha Śiromaṇi mentions and criticizes in his commentary on the *Tattvacintāmaṇi* of Gaṅgeśa:

sādhyatāvacchedaka viśiṣṭāsādhyasāmānādhikaraṇyāvacchedakasvasamānādhikaraṇa-sādhyābhāvatvakam

The translation of this given in the *Encyclopedia* with an introduction is as follows:

> (Now, say the commentators, Raghunātha discusses three definitions of Pragalbha Miśra.)[3]
>
> Pervasion is *hetu*'s possessing an absence of the *sādhya* which has a common locus with *hetu* and which is the limiter of that generic attribute of *sādhya* by which is limited the limiter of *sādhya*-ness.

Another definition of *vyāpti*, given by a Naiyāyika called Viśārada, and its translation in the *Encyclopedia* are as follows:

sādhyābhāvavati yadvṛttau prakṛtṛnumitivirodhitvam nṛsti tattvam

> Pervasion is that state in which there is no contradiction of an inference proving *hetu* to occur in the locus of the absence of *sādhya* (as *vyādhikaraṇa*).[4]

The translation of the first definition which is too technical, is quite incorrect and meaningless. Pragalbha Miśra cannot say that the absence of the *sādhya* is pervasion, because such an absence is not a property of *hetu* alone; it can exist in other things also which are non-*hetu*. Further, in the definition the *tva* affix is added to *sādhyābhāva*, but the translation totally ignores

---

[3] S. Bhattacharya and K.H. Potter, eds., 1993, *Encyclopedia of Indian Philosophy*, vol. VI, Delhi: Motilal Banarsidass, p. 554.

[4] Ibid.

it. The definition in Sanskrit does not state that the absence of *sādhya* is the limiter of the generic attribute of *sādhya*, but the translation does, and has no sense at all.

The translation of the definition of *vyāpti* by Viśārada also is absolutely meaningless. According to the translation, pervasion is a state. But as per the definition in Sanskrit, pervasion is *tattva*, i.e. possessing the property of being that (*hetu*). The definition in Sanskrit does not refer to any inference proving the *hetu* to occur in the locus of *sādhyābhāva*, while the translation refers to an inference of that kind. The translation is so meaningless that it cannot be applied to any instance of definition.

We find gravely erroneous translations in many places in the *Encyclopedia*. I do not know whether these translations have attracted any criticism by any diligent reader. If they have not, then it suggests that nobody has made serious effort to understand them. In that case, it is needless to say that the very purpose of getting such translations done and publishing them stands defeated.

In places some very absurd translations are made in the *Encyclopedia*. For instance, the two definitions of *vyāpti*, which Raghunātha Śiromaṇi names as *siṁha-vyāghra lakṣaṇa*, are translated as 'Lion and Tiger definitions'.[5] Siṁha and Vyāghra in fact are the names of the two Naiyāyikas whose definitions are mentioned and cited by Raghunātha Śiromaṇi!

Recently some scholars, whose mastery over the Nyāya philosophy is well known, have coined new words and are using them in their translations. The translation of the word *pratiyogin* as 'absentee' by Arindam Chakravarti and the translation of the word *upādhi* as 'the inferential undercutting condition' by Stephen Phillips are examples of this practice. Since the term *pratiyogī* denotes the thing the absence of which is under discussion, the translation 'absentee' which also denotes

---

5 *Encyclopedia of Indian Philosophy*, vol. VI, p. 550.

the same, appears to be very appropriate. However, it does not convey the sense that is etymologically conveyed by the Sanskrit term *pratiyogin*. Till recently and even now, two words in English – 'counter-positive' and 'counter-correlate' – have been used for the Sanskrit word *pratiyogī*. Both the words seem to be quite acceptable, since they convey the meanings of the two constituents of the word *pratiyogī*, viz. *prati* and *yogī*. Even between the two, the translation 'counter-positive' does not seem to be as appropriate as the other word 'counter-correlate', because *yogī* does not mean 'positive'; also because, with regard to an absence of absence, the *pratiyogī* is not a counter-positive.

Stephen Phillips's translation of the term *upādhi* as the inferential undercutting condition, also, I feel, needs some examination. The term *upādhi*, as he himself states in his lengthy introduction to his translation work, has an etymological meaning. The prefix *upa* means 'something that exists nearby'. *Ādhi* is that which superimposes its characteristic on the nearby thing. *Jabākusuma* – a red flower – is an *upādhi* because it superimposes its characteristic red colour on the nearby crystal.[6] On the basis of this etymological sense, some Naiyāyikas made an attempt to define *upādhi*. According to them, an inferential *upādhi* is called *upādhi* because its characteristic, namely invariable concomitance with the *sādhya*, appears in the thing which is not *hetu* but employed as *hetu*. For instance, in the inference, 'the hill has smoke as it has fire', 'conjunction with wet fuel' which is cited as the *upādhi* has actually pervasion with the *sādhya*, but is taken to be present in the so-called *hetu* – fire. Thus *upādhi* must have the pervasion of *sādhya*. However, mere pervasion with the *sādhya* does not make the *upādhi* the vitiator of the inference. Hence, an *upādhi* is also intended to be *sādhya-vyāpaka* – the pervader of the *sādhya*. Thus, an inferential *upādhi* is to be defined as that which is equipollent to the *sādhya* and is

---

6 *Tattvacintāmaṇi*, vol. II, part 1, Tirupati: Kendriya Sanskrit Vidyapeetha Publications, p. 266.

non-pervader of the *sādhana*.

Rejecting this view, Gaṅgeśopādhyāya questions as to why a non-equipollent property is not considered as *upādhi*. Is it on the ground that the etymological sense of the word *upādhi* is not applicable to a non-equipollent property? If that is so, he remarks that there is no such rule that only such a thing which imposes its characteristic property on the object be called *upādhi*. The word *upādhi* is used in our daily dealings in many other senses also where its etymological meaning has no application.[7] Gaṅgeśa further clarifies that the word *upādhi*, used in a śāstric context, is intended just to show that the inference is fallacious – and since a property that pervades the *sādhya* and does not pervade the *hetu* vitiates the inference, the term *upādhi*, in the śāstric context, is only to denote such properties.[8]

Probably these sentences in *Tattvacintāmaṇi* inspired Stephen Phillips to hold that 'the inferential undercutting condition' is the correct translation for the term *upādhi*. But, the question is whether a descriptive phrase should be considered a translation. For the Sanskrit words *gauḥ* and *pācakaḥ* the English words 'cow' and 'cook' are considered the correct translation. But, can we consider 'a specific kind of animal' and 'a person who performs the act of cooking' as the translations of those Sanskrit words? It is true that throughout the chapter of Upādhivāda, Gaṅgeśa, several times, explicitly pronounces that the *upādhi* is cited in the context of discussing the strength or otherwise of an inference, to show that the inference under discussion is fallacious. But this is only one purpose served by the *upādhi*: *upādhi* actually is something else. It is a property that pervades the *sādhya* and does not pervade the *hetu*. It is one of several inferential undercutters such as *vyabhicāra* and *bādha* which are inferential. The difference between *upādhi* and other inferential undercutters is that while *vyabhicāra* etc. as fallacies, directly

7 *Tattvacintāmaṇi*, p. 267.

8 Ibid., p. 268.

undercut the inference which is affected by them, the *upādhi* not being itself a fallacy of inference makes room for a fallacy like *vyabhicāra* or *sat-pratipakṣa* and through them undercuts the inference. Thus when there are many inferential undercutting conditions, it is difficult to understand why the term *upādhi* is so translated giving an impression that it alone is the inferential undercutter.

Phillips's translation of another technical term *bādha* as 'patent falsehood'[9] is also not convincing. According to the Nyāya school, *bādha* is an inferential fallacy. The school defines the fallacy as *sādhyābhāvavatpakṣaḥ,* i.e. the inferential subject devoid of probandum. The inference *hrado vahnimān dhūmāt* – 'The lake has fire because it has smoke' is cited as an instance of this fallacy. Since, a lake having fire is evidently false, it seems, Phillips translated it as patent falsehood. However, the problem is that there are many instances of inference, in which patent falsehood can be found while the fallacy of *bādha* is missing. For instance, the inference – *kāñcanamayaparvato vahnimān dhūmāt* (The golden hill has fire because it has smoke) – does not have the fallacy of *bādha,* but has patent falsehood. It is evident that the inferential subject – the hill does not possess *kāñcanamayatva* – goldenness and thus the inference is patently false. The instances of the fallacy – *svarūpāsiddhi* like – *śabdaḥ guṇaḥ cākṣuśatvāt* – 'sound is a quality as it is an object of visual perception', in which the inferential subject is devoid of the *probans,* patent falsehood is clearly present. However, such inferences are not instances of the fallacy called *bādha*.

Similarly, there are several other words which do not have English words conveying the same sense. The word *adhiṣṭhāna* is yet another such word. 'Substratum', 'locus' are the words being used for *adhiṣṭhāna* in Sanskrit. Though in some contexts the term *adhiṣṭhāna* is found being used in that sense, in some

9 Stephen H. Phillips and N.S. Ramanuja Tatacarya, 2002, *Gaṅgeśa on the Upādhi,* Indian Council of Philosophical Research, p. 147.

other contexts it is used in a different sense. When the conch-shell is said to be the *adhiṣṭhāna* for the super-imposed silver, it is not in the sense of being the substratum of the silver which does not exist in it. In cases such as these, as is already in vogue in some translations, it would be quite helpful to retain the same Sanskrit words with a brief note explaining in which sense the word is being used in the text.

In my view, translation is not very different from a commentary. While the commentary of a text is in the same language elaborating the views of the author of the original text, translation, in addition to reproducing each and every word and sentence in a suitable manner in a different language, also provides information necessary to correctly grasp the stand of the author of the original text. Translations of literary works may not include notes. But it is needless to say that the translation of philosophical texts would be incomplete if necessary notes are not supplied. Translations without notes would only add some more instances to the *Padamañjarīnyāya:*

> *anadhite mahābhāṣye vyarthā sā padamañjarī* ।
> *adhitepi mahābhāṣye vyarthā sā padamañjarī* ॥

> If the *Mahābhāṣya* is not studied then *Padamañjarī* (a commentary on the *Mahābhāṣya* of Patañjali) is useless. Even if *Mahābhāṣya* is studied, *Padamañjarī* is useless.

In the same way, just as a commentator is required to have studied the whole text on which he intends to write a commentary, a translator is also required to make an in-depth study of the whole text which enables him to produce an authentic translation. Kumārila Bhaṭṭa says:

> *anya evaikadeśena śāstrasyārthaḥ pratīyate* ।
> *anyaśca paripūrṇena samastāṅgopasamhr̥tau* ॥

> By a part of the text a different meaning of the śāstric text appears. When all the rules of interpretation are applied then

> with the whole of the text, an altogether different meaning of the text would appear.

However, these words addressed to a person engaged in interpreting a philosophical text are equally applicable to a translator.

At this juncture, scholars of Indian philosophy who are interested in the advancement of the philosophy, have to introspect on the present pitiable condition of Indian philosophy. As we all know, the number of erudite scholars, almost in all the branches of Indian philosophy, is dwindling year by year. In most of the philosophy departments, teaching of Indian philosophy is very superficial. Even in those departments where students are encouraged to take Indian philosophy for their study, the students are not much benefitted because they often have not had an opportunity to learn Sanskrit and thus have not earned sufficient capability to go through the original texts and commentaries and get an authentic knowledge of the philosophical concepts. Even now, there are some *gurukula*s where students are taught Nyāya, Vedānta and other disciplines of Indian philosophy in a rigorous way, but the method they pursue to teach and study is very traditional and the students are absolutely incapable of interacting with the outside philosophical world. Even the number of students pursuing this sort of education is very limited and year by year the number of students opting for this education is going down. If this situation is allowed to continue for some more time, I am afraid, in a few decades, the tradition itself would disappear and the loss, undoubtedly, would be irretrievable. So, I feel that along with our sincere efforts to revive the in-depth study of Indian philosophy in the traditional *gurukula*s, it is important to create a congenial atmosphere in the general universities, in India and abroad to attract intelligent students to opt for the study of Indian philosophy. Needless to say this could only be possible with authentic translations with necessary aids to understand the translations better. Thus we would be in a philosophical world wherein there will be erudite scholars who can efficiently handle original Sanskrit texts and also scholars, preferably with a working knowledge of Sanskrit, or even without any familiarity with Sanskrit, but on a par with traditional philosophers, in explaining the philosophical concepts and even contributing to the advancement of Indian philosophy. We can dream of such a situation only with the help of authentic and at the same time readable, translations.

The pertinent question is whether it is possible to dream of such a world, with the help of just translations. But, it has happened in respect of Greek philosophy. Originally it was in the Greek language but, later only with the help of translations available in English, Greek philosophy was studied, critically analysed and new thoughts emerged. If this could happen with regard to Greek philosophy, I feel it is equally possible in respect of Indian philosophy.

But, again the question is how to make this happen. Before I conclude, I would like to make an appeal to the Indian Council of Philosophical Research to take up or sponsor a project of preparing a translation dictionary of technical terms in various Indian philosophical schools. Under this project ICPR can organize workshops inviting erudite scholars who can authoritatively explain the meanings of the technical terms in different disciplines of Indian philosophy. Such a Sanskrit–English dictionary would be enormously helpful in bringing uniformity in the use of English technical terms. Otherwise, with the ever-changing technical jargon it would be very difficult to understand, especially translations authored by non-Sanskrit scholars.

DISCUSSION

Claus Oetke

One thing that I think that you are right about, and (I) would also like to strengthen your argument, is regarding the *upādhi*.

I think we can nevertheless learn a lesson from that – and I think the lesson is much stronger than the arguments presented suggest. I would say, even if it were not the case that there are other inferential undercutters, the translation which is offered as an undercutter is inadequate as a translation of the term because – and that is the lesson we learn – we should avoid as far as possible to relate a translation to one particular function.

My second remark: this thing with substratum. I think it has a very interesting implication. Here I would like to revitalize a bit of your argument because your criticism is pertinent and convincing, but perhaps it does not give the entire relevant information regarding *adhiṣṭhāna*; hence it is potentially misleading. On the other hand, you can say that if you translate a term you can expect from a reader that he draws certain inferences: in this particular case, that he comes to know the term 'substratum', reading it in a new sense from the contexts from which he gets his information. For instance here substratum means that something of which something is predicable, of which something initiates an attribution of a property wrongly or falsely. Therefore, I think the inadequacy in this case is not so fatal as it is potentially in the other cases.

Bhattacharya

While welcoming the proposal for a dictionary where equivalent terms will be given, I may be allowed to observe a few facts. In Sanskrit from *pramā* we can have *pramāṇa, prameya, pramātṛ*. But when you want to translate into English one word will not always do. You must have a phrase. Previously *pramāṇa* was normally written as 'means of knowledge'. Nowadays I find to be more concise: for *pramā* there is a word 'cognizance' and so *pramāṇa* has become instrument of cognizance – three words. Similarly when some paradigms were found in Aristotelian logic terms such as like *probandam* and *probans* were introduced. However when nothing could be found either in the way of a single word or a compound then the words had to be retained because the idea itself was too complex to be verbalized in another language with one word or even a phrase. This is understandable. Now one problem which strikes me most nowadays is that instead of using 'verbal testimony' for *śabda-pramāṇa*, some people are just writing 'word'; even with small 'w' and that is being encouraged. One translation of a chapter of Jayarāśi's *Tattvopaplavasiṁha* appeared in which 'word' appeared with the lower case 'w'. I asked my friend Arindam Chakravarti why he is using or insisting on this literal translation of terms. These are technical terms used in philosophy only. One *śabda* has several meanings; even contradictory meanings. *Daṇḍa* for example can mean unity, it could mean conflict. So if it is a philosophical text we have to stick to a particular meaning only, however polysemous the word may be. So what I would suggest is that when you translate texts, other than very important notes you have to give, there should be a list stating which English word is being used for a given Sanskrit technical term.

Kaviraj

In my view we can take translation in two ways. Translation as an event; it is not a very precise terminology but what I mean by that is that I take a passage and I do a translation in a different language. But we can also see translation as a larger process of trying to understand something. For instance, take something like *rasa* or the *svagatatva* and the *paragatatva* in the *rasa* discussion. I feel that translation is both unavoidable and impossible as an event that is as a one time thing and that is why we come back to it again and again.

And I think it is also reflected in your own practices because what you say about Ganganath Jha, confirms this character of translation. You are not saying that what he said was wrong, you are saying that what he said was inadequate in a certain sense and you want to come back to it in a recursive manner.

You are also saying something that appealed to me very greatly: that translation must be complex, in the sense that one word might never be captured by another single word. So you have to use several words or phrases surrounding that word in the language in which you are doing the translation. Or let me make another point. The reason for that is that translation is always poised between two audiences and translation is always marked by the tension between correctness and felicity. And for you as the audience, correctness is very important. For some of us who are writing for an audience which is fluent in English language philosophy, felicity is more important.

I will give an example from your own text. You translate *pāramārthika sattva* as noumenal reality. Now if you look at it from the point of view of an audience which in general terms is acquainted with European philosophy, they might actually say that 'noumenon' is a term which has many other connotations. And those connotations make it problematic, so why use 'noumenon' – you should use a term which stays away from the Kantian connotation of this term. I would like to know if you agree with my reading.

You use the term *kāñcanamayatva parvat*. Now *Kāñcanamayatva* has two sides to it. It has the *Kañcana varṇatva*, it also has a *Kāñcanamayatva*, *maya* is not generally the *varṇa*. In English when you say: 'the goldenness of the mountain' what I hear is 'the colour of the mountain'. Colour and content are used differentially in both languages – I think the connotation exists in both languages but in English the content element, I think, is probably more subdued and the colour element is more pronounced. This actually seems to show something which is very central to the activity of translation itself – that it has to be complex and it also has to be recursive – that we come back to it again and again.

And I personally feel that if you see it as a process – I would like to do it this way because this is what I do when I translate things for my students – I would first use a term which is completely familiar to them. Balu said: there is no category of intention in Indian philosophy but I would say that this is an intention because they would understand that. Then I would make it more concise, in the sense that I would problematize that by saying look, it is not intention in the sense that you would take it, its different, so I defamiliarize it, starting from the familiar I would say now you understand it and now let us drop the term 'intention', or let us drop the term 'enjoyment' or something like that for *rasa* – use *rasa* because you have grasped *rasa*. But you cannot grasp *rasa* the first time you say *rasa* – they would not understand, so you say 'enjoyment' – it is wrong but I think that is intrinsic to translation itself.

So translation is an imperfect process and we must understand this peculiar combination of imperfection and the urge to get it right, which is always impossible.

Prahlada

When we teach in a classroom, I think we can use some word which may not be an exact translation of the word in a text, but may add some new meaning to it. But when you are writing and translating a word, then I think, in the translation, you have to try to give some word if not phrase to which you can give a very near meaning of the word. Such words are needed because if you can understand that this particular word is used for this word, you can see more meanings in the text. Either the translation itself uses some words and phrase explanations in a manner that you may not be able to understand the exact meaning of a particular word and you may not be able to see more meanings present in the text. I used the word *noumena* since in some text that word was given for *tattva*. So there are indeed some problems of this kind.

Mullick

I want to draw your attention to the fact that Ganganath Jha was translating, almost a century ago. I think we have to look at the state of the English language at the end of the nineteenth century. This introduces the dimension of the development of the English language all the way down to the present century and to Arindam who is using *word* with a small 'w' for *śabda*. That in itself represents now a very long history of just over 100 years. And of course one could go back even further to nineteenth-century German translations and possibly the English ones as well. There is not only the historicity of the text and the historicity of the translator but (also) the historicity of the language into which the translation is being effected: in this case English. English is a dynamic language, so when we want to approach the original, we have this added complication of what were the tools that were available to translators of the time and which tools are now becoming obsolete. So that *'word'* with a capital 'W' is not perceived as necessary today. The problems we have with Ganganatha Jha's translations today are certainly related to the norms implicit in the Victorian English that he learnt.

Balagangadhara

I want to pick up one aspect of one very important and very good point that Sudipta made which is the following: I think it is very important to use the metaphor 'translation is like building bridges. It must be steady enough to hold you; it must be functional enough to carry you.' So in that sense he is absolutely right in pointing to these two things and talking about the process. There is another point of equal importance he made concerning the aspect of Europeans understanding Sanskrit, and now it goes the other way round: I will go one step further than Sudipta did. In fact you should not translate *pāramārthika satya* as 'noumenal reality' because noumenon is unknowable whereas *pāramārthika* is experienceable and knowable: that at least that is the claim. So noumenal reality can never be used for *pāramārthika satya*. If you want to use the word you must have some philosophical understanding of Kant and not simply say that since other have people used the term I will do so also. It would mean that I am now using methods for which I have criticized the Europeans.

Mukhopadhyaya

I would like to make a few quick points. One important point regarding how to translate has been raised a number of times and is one aspect of the problem, but Prahlada Char's reference to Ganganath Jha has brought in another dimension. Why are we translating? Ganganath Jha was an erudite scholar, a committed traditionalist who had no intention of distorting our tradition. Then why did he make such translations unreadable? Who profited from them? We have to understand his purpose at that time. Ganganath had two significant achievements: he edited and got published innumerable books and texts, as he was very eager to make the *śāstra*s widely available. Had he not used that level of translation, many people would not have studied the Śāstras at all. So the general question is not only who is translating, but why? That is also very important.

And this links up with what you are saying. I know, Sudipta, it is very, very difficult, almost an existential crisis, to make a choice between felicity of reading and accuracy. One has to struggle with it. But there is another important point. Today it is more or less internationally accepted that when we translate a text into another language – whether it is English or French, it does not matter – the crucial expressions are retained in the original. Not only in original French, Greek or German but even in the original script: that has almost become international practice and that is good. But when it comes to Sanskrit, even though the apparatus is available, we do not make use of it.

In addition I want to add to what you have said. I admire the strategy of gradually refining an expression because in one go you will not be able to convey the full meaning. However, you do not give up but gradually refine it. In the case of a book some people feel, keep the original: if they try to explain it in the text itself, it becomes unreadable. So they append a glossary. Retain the meaning and since it cannot be translated in one word, append a glossary. That is also in practice. These two methods taken together can possibly deal with some of the problems.

4

Ways of Rendering Non-Western Thought in Western Languages

Claus Oetke

Thesis: There are no problems of either translation or assessment which are specific to interchanges between Western and non-Western, especially South Asian, communities and cultures.

Comment: The thesis does not call into question the assumption that problems might exist caused by the fact that the item to be translated belongs to the language of the speech community of a different cultural tradition or by the circumstance that the objects of assessment can be relegated to a culture which differs from the cultural tradition assignable to the subject of assessment. It means rather that all the major problems arising with respect to phenomena of non-Western societies and cultures are equally problems arising for translation, interpretation and evaluation in the framework of different varieties of Western culture. The decisive reason is that 'Western culture' can only refer to a non-homogeneous collection of varieties which are often themselves counted as numerically different cultures. A more cautious variety of the thesis could be that in the present state of knowledge no basis exists for the assumption of fundamental differences between interchanges within the framework of Western cultural varieties on the one hand and Western and South Asian cultural traditions on the other hand. This would have as a corollary that problems connected with assessing 'Indian thought in Western terms' tend to be exaggerated.

Two Main Varieties of Rendering Thought: Rephrasing and Assessment

Rephrasing relates to ways of expressing thought by the use of formulations which differ from those originally employed. Translation refers to a special case of rephrasing, where the linguistic varieties employed in the original and the subsequent formulations differ. Assessment encompasses all statements which purport to state some fact about thought as an object. Hence it would follow that 'Vienna is the capital of Germany' is a rephrasing and translation of (the thought expressed by) the German sentence: *Wien ist die Haupstadt Deutschlands*. On the other hand the sentence: 'the thought that Vienna is the capital of Germany is false' or simply 'it is false that Vienna is the capital of Germany' expresses an assessment of the thought which has been expressed by the original sentence. It goes without saying that the class of thought-assessments is far more comprehensive.

Translation

Concerning translation, a number of propositions are relevant in the present context.

(a) Non-existence of linguistically equivalent correlates on the level of linguistic types in some source-language (SL) and some target-language (TL) is a common phenomenon if both SL and TL are modern West European vernaculars.

(b) Varieties of non-equivalence are classifiable for pairs of Western and pairs of Western and non-Western languages alike.

In the realm of general terms the following cases are theoretically possible: (a) A of SL and B of TL are (fully) synonymous, (b) A of SL is more general than B of TL (= B is a hyponym of A), (c) B of TL is more general than A of SL (= A is a hyponym of B), (d) the extensions of A of SL and B of TL partly overlap, and (e) the extensions of A of SL and B of TL are disparate. It can happen that on some particular level, e.g. on the level of lexemes, no unit exists in TL which exhibits the relationship of type (a) to some given expression of SL. TL possesses only expressions exhibiting one or the other of the relations of type (b)–(e) to a word of SL. It can be supposed without argument that this situation arises with respect to Indian and European languages. But exactly the same phenomena occur in the realm of various Western languages. (It is supposed here that further illustration is not needed for substantiating this contention.) Similar relations of higher or lesser specificity or diversity of meaning can be defined for other types of expression, such as declarative sentences.

(c) Devices for rendering expressions of a SL in some TL and of solving problems of non-equivalence are (at least to a considerable extent) identical for pairs of Western and pairs of Western and non-Western languages.

In the framework of theories of translation, in particular in the tradition of the 'Stylistique comparée', categories have been specified representing various possibilities of rendering units of SL in TL. – (Compare Stolze, R.[1]) Examples are (a) direct borrowing (emprunt), e.g. E(nglish) and G(erman) 'know-how', 'jet-set', 'talk show', (b) calque (calque), e.g. E 'growth rate' → G 'Wachstumsrate', (c) literal translation (traduction littérale), e.g. E 'This assertion is false' – G 'Diese Behauptung ist falsch', (d) change of word-category (transposition), e.g. E 'There is no truth in his claim' → G. 'Seine Behauptung is unwahr', (e) adjustment of perspective (modulation), e.g. F(rench) J'ai la chair de poule' or: 'Ça me donne la chair de poule' → G 'Ich bekomme eine Gänsehaut (davon)'. Some of the categories comprise different sub-varieties, such as in category (d) substitution ('Anfangsstadium' → 'initial

1 R. Stolze, *Übersetzungstheorien*, Tübingen: Gunter Narr Verlag, 1994, pp. 59-75.

stage'), dilution ('schutzlos' → sans défense), concentration ('a never ending story' → 'eine endlose Geschichte'), amplification or explication and its reverse, or shift of aspect ('Lebensgefahr' → 'danger de mort') and choice of pragmatic equivalent (équivalence) ('Guten Appetit' → 'Enjoy your meal') in category (e). These devices appear to be equally applicable in translation from, e.g., Sanskrit to English or to German. The supposition that special types of devices are required for rendering linguistic items of South Asian languages in European vernaculars is, as far as one can see, still unproven.

(d) Non-equivalence on the level of 'langue' can be immaterial on the level of 'parole'. If A is a word-type of SL and B is a word-type of TL and if the significance of A and B only partially coincide, certain occurrences of A can nevertheless be adequately rendered by occurrences of B.

Restriction: There are devices of content-compensation on the level of 'parole', such as substituting in TL a noun with a more specific import substituting for a noun with a less specific linguistic import in SL, which are feasible in some cases but not in all.

Example: He has a Greek grandfather ↔ (SE) (Swedish) (a) *Han har en grekisk farfar* / (b) *Han har en grekisk morfar*

One of the alternatives is a possible choice if the token sentence of SL possesses a more specific 'actual import' corresponding to either (a) or (b). This is not always the case. The sentence of SL could be uttered by someone who possesses merely indirect evidence for the truth of his statement, e.g. by having witnessed that some trustworthy person has assertively uttered the sentence which the speaker 'echoes'. In this situation neither belief-state nor communicative intention provide a basis for specifying an actual import in the sense of either (a) or (b). In such cases special translation-devices could be called for. Thus one might use '/' as a device for transferring indeterminacies of SL to TL. A rendering of particular occurrences of Sanskrit *artha-* by e.g. 'meaning/object' can perform this function. But the phenomenon itself is not essentially linked with any difference of cultural tradition.

(e) Need of non-preservation of synonymy in translation is sometimes induced by linguistic properties and does not essentially depend on cultural identity or difference.

Examples: 'They came' ↔ (HI) (Hindi and Urdu) *Ve āye/Ve āyīṁ* 'I think that you saw them' ↔ (HE) (Modern Hebrew) *Ani xośev* (M) *śe atah raitah* (M) *otam* (M) / *Ani xośevet* (F) *śe at rait* (F), *otan* (F) etc. – 'M' = 'Masculine, 'F' = 'Feminine'

Similar phenomena exist regarding the relationship English-Russian, etc.:

'I came' ↔ (RU) Ja prišol / Ja prišla

There are conceivable cases where major cultural disparity *could* generate specific problems of translation. Examples are:

(i) Occurrence of speech-acts in non-Western communities and linguistic devices signalling them which have no parallel in Western linguistic communities.

(ii) Existence of sorts of texts in non-Western cultural traditions which lack counterparts in the West.

In the field of South Asian literatures texts like the Brāhmaṇas or works of 'anonymous literature' (*Mahābhārata*, etc.) could be pertinent instances. But in such cases the task of verifying that theoretically conceivable possibilities are empirically instantiated remains.

Assessment

Many statements pertaining to non-Western cultural objects or their representatives do not entail specific problems caused by employing a Western language. The statement expressed by

'Patañjali's *Mahābhāṣya* has been composed in the second century BCE' might be incorrect for various reasons, such as (a) in fact, no person called 'Patañjali' wrote a (grammatical) treatise with the title *Mahābhāṣya* or (b) somebody called 'Patañjali' wrote a treatise with the title *Mahābhāṣya* but did not compose it in the second century BCE. But under those circumstances the reason for the incorrectness or untruth of the statement certainly does not depend on the employment of a Western language for expressing the statement. To be sure, the employment of the expression 'the second century BCE.' involves a reference to a Western concept and hence it can be definitely ruled out that anyone who might be identifiable as an author of the *Mahābhāṣya* would be disposed to classify himself as a person who wrote some treatise in the second century BCE. But the statement 'Aristotle lived from 384–322 BCE' exhibits the same characteristic but does not concern a representative of South Asian culture – as far as we know.

Thus it can be easily discerned that only a sub-class of statements pertaining to objects or representatives of non-Western cultural traditions can be essentially affected by divergences of language or concepts expressible in language. The idea presents itself that statements whose explicit formulation involves so-called 'intensional contexts' play a special role in this regard. The above consideration conclusively demonstrates that only falsehoods can be stated by sentences which embed the original sentences under 'Patañjali believed that' or 'Aristotle believed that' respectively. But the same consideration also vindicates the view that problems of intentionality are by no means essentially connected with diversities between Western and non-Western tradition. The divergence can at best pertain to matters of detail and degree.

In the field of actions an extensive and important sub-class exists exhibiting the peculiarity of being alternatively describable in terms which in no way reflect anything about the view that the individuals performing the actions possess about them or in terms that reflect in some respect the way in which subjects view their own actions. It is natural to surmise that descriptions of the latter sort are potentially more affected by linguistic and conceptual divergences. The following considerations display that this conjecture is well founded. Suppose that some Dutch anthropologist observes that in some tribal community a number of statues are sprinkled with water, each time at the end of a lunar month. He might express his observation by the statement:

> Always on the last day of a lunar month the statues in the central shrine are sprinkled with water.

Apparently by making this statement the anthropologist does not run a considerable risk of expressing a falsehood due to misrepresentation of the views of other people. However, the researcher could feel dissatisfied with his statement precisely because the lack of reflecting views impairs its relevance. Hence he might pose to some members of the tribe the question of why they perform the ritual at every end of a lunar month and might be confronted with an expression which in his eyes can linguistically mean:

> In order to bring the spirits in the statues to move to another place.

Let us suppose that this experience induces the anthropologist to make a claim which is more ambitious than the preceding one and which reads:

> Always on the last day of a lunar month demons are expelled by sprinkling water on the statues in the central shrine.

Now it is not difficult to imagine a scenario in which the latter statement represents a significant distortion. Possibly the members of the tribe indeed believe that beings inhabit the statues of the shrine which are caused to leave by the sprinkling of water at the end of the month. But contrary to what the expression 'demon' suggests, those beings are not regarded in any way as evil but as human-like creatures which supposedly have concluded a contract with the community for protecting the statues and which are 'remunerated' by the water sprinkled on them and simultaneously 'released' from their obligation so that they can go elsewhere. Against this background the issue is not whether that which the anthropologist has presented is a distorting description but the question of what is responsible for the misrepresentation. For it emerges that the decisive factor can hardly lie in the circumstance that he has formulated his statement in a Western language. English or Dutch or any other European language would have permitted him to make a statement which reveals something about the conception of their own action on the part of the natives without entailing any distortion. This could have been accomplished, for example, by a formulation in which 'demon' is replaced by 'being' and 'expel' by 'cause to leave' or even 'release'. In addition the suspicion that the researcher, who is by hypothesis a Western scholar, has imposed Western prejudice turns out to be unfounded. Presumably the interpretation of the sprinkling of water as expulsion of demons was not caused by experiences in his own environment where such practices do not or very rarely occur but rather by his professional expertise. In this connection knowledge gained from anthropological research concerning other exotic communities and their culture possesses no less potential of generating misunderstanding than knowledge of Western history. The danger of faulty 'over-generalization' is even particularly virulent if correct observations pertaining to communities closely related to the pertinent one are employed as basis of interpretation. In a similar manner linguistic affinities presumably favour faulty over-generalizations in language-acquisition. The crucial fact is that any degree of proximity in localization, time and even history does not guarantee homogeneity in relevant respects. Although the last statement comes close to a truism, it needs to be strongly emphasized because in the present days the tenet has become fashionable that thoughts of foreign cultures have to be interpreted 'in their own terms'. This ill-considered slogan dismisses as irrelevant the possibility that any unit classified as an individual culture or tradition comprises in itself diversities which can exceed divergences with respect to different units. For the same reason the method of interpreting texts 'in the light of their own context' of culture and tradition is potentially pernicious.

One can presume that the results of the preceding paragraphs are transferable to assessments concerning thought or systems of thought, such as philosophical teachings. In the context of descriptions or classifications of philosophical doctrines or theories, the fact that the semantic value of descriptive expressions, including that of technical terms, is usually not rigid, is pertinent. This has on the one hand the effect of diminishing the information-value of classifications using traditional technical terms and on the other, the corollary that the risk of distortion and the danger of incorrectness of information is alleviated, given an awareness of the pertinent semantic indeterminacy.

Example

The term 'logic' is sometimes employed for signifying the study of the principles of deductive reasoning. Yet it is occasionally explicitly acknowledged that this import represents merely a special import of that term. Compare this with Flew's formulation.[2]

However, in its narrower sense, logic is the study of the principles of deductive inference, or of methods of proof or demonstration.

---

[2] A. Flew, *A Dictionary of Philosophy* (2nd rev. edn.), New York: St. Martins Press, 1st edn., 1984, p. 208.

In the Western tradition a distinction between 'deductive logic' and 'inductive logic' is widely acknowledged. The latter variety is supposed to exhibit the characteristic that it 'studies the way in which premises may support a conclusion without entailing it'.[3] On the other hand, we find the following definition of induction:

> A method of reasoning by which a general law or principle is inferred from observed particular instances.[4]

In the light of this definition 'inductive logic' could refer only to inferences in which (a) premises support a conclusion without entailing it, and (b) the premises consist in singular statements or propositions and the conclusion is a general statement or a universal proposition. But precisely the restriction implied by (b) is disputed by I.M. Copi[5] in a statement (attributed to William Whewell) which reads:

> [That] in Deduction we infer particular from general truths; while in Induction we infer general from particular . . . is rejected as inappropriate. The reason is that according to the author of the book the term 'inductive argument' should not only provide room for inferences in which the conclusion is a general proposition based on particular ones, but also for certain arguments in which a universal proposition is supported by other universal propositions or where particular propositions as conclusions rely on a number of other particular propositions. – Here the circumstance that in the view of the present author the quoted sentence also embodies too narrow a conception of deduction need not be taken into consideration.

It should not be difficult to discern the potential relevance of the above depicted diversities for assessments of doctrines

---

3 S. Blackburn, *The Oxford Dictionary of Philosophy*, Oxford, New York: Oxford University Press, 1994, p. 221.

4 Flew, op. cit., p. 172.

5 I.M. Copi, *Introduction to Logic*, New York: Macmillan, 1982.

which are sometimes designated by the term 'Indian Logic' or described as 'theories of inference and proof' or doctrines of *anumāna*. The first question which naturally arises against the present background is: If doctrines of *anumāna* are doctrines of logic are they doctrines concerning deductive or inductive reasoning or of both deductive and inductive reasoning?

From this the following secondary question arises: If doctrines of *anumāna* are doctrines concerning deductive or inductive reasoning can the import of 'deductive' or 'inductive' be taken in some narrower sense, corresponding to the above-quoted sentence, or is it necessary to presuppose a broader import, e.g. that propagated by Copi?

It should be evident, however, that the latter question demands a clarification of the issue of what should count as premise and what as conclusion in arguments which are allegedly the objects of doctrines of *anumāna*. The crux is that if one would content oneself with saying, for example, that theories of *anumāna* pertain to inductive reasoning the information-value is not only impaired by the indeterminacy of the term 'inductive' but also by the doubtfulness of the basis on which this verdict is given.

In the domain of doctrines of *anumāna*-reasoning the issue of the determination of relevant premises and conclusion is in fact crucial. This holds good in the first place because different criteria could be applied for determining the range of premises. A most natural answer would be to identify the elements which are technically called *hetu* with the premises in an *anumāna*-inference. On this basis it would be appropriate to say that, given the broader conceptions of 'deductive' and 'inductive', doctrines of *anumāna* pertain to deductive reasoning precisely if the consequences of pertinent pieces of reasoning are entailed by or follow with necessity from propositions which correlate with a *hetu*. This would imply the remarkable consequence that theories of *anumāna* could be regarded as pertaining both to inductive and deductive reasoning, although this result can safely be vindicated only for particular varieties of doctrine which have been propagated in the course of history. In the first place, it is doctrines advocated in the tradition of Dharmakīrti which exemplify this hybrid character. On the one hand hardly anybody could defend the contention that from the premise that 'sound is produced' follows the conclusion that 'sound at some time perishes' with the sort of necessity characteristic of standard specimens of deductive inference. On the other hand, however, such an assumption is by no means extravagant with respect to arguments to the effect that something is a tree as a conclusion derived from the premise that the pertinent object is an oak. Hence it can be tempting to eliminate the hybrid features of the theory by re-interpreting the specimens in which conclusions are merely supported but not entailed by pertinent premises and to accomplish the desired result by determining the set of relevant premises by a different criterion. It is not difficult to recognize that theories of *anumāna*-inference contain ingredients which could be exploited for this purpose. In this respect the doctrine of the three marks of an acceptable reason, the teaching of *trairūpya*, which existed even before Dharmakīrti, is particularly tempting. The main factor inducing the temptation lies in the idea that one could define as premises all the propositions which have to be true if the postulates of *trairūpya* are satisfied and determine the relevant conclusions as before. It should not be difficult to gather that issues of the interpretation of *trairūpya* potentially affect the outcome of the endeavour to assimilate specimens of reasoning which according to the initial criterion belong to two distinct species. Since in the present article the interpretation of *trairūpya* is not a central concern, only one remark should be made in this regard. Any attempt to assimilate the teachings of *trairūpya* before Dharmakīrti to Dharmakīrti's interpretation on the sole ground that its formulations do not blatantly contradict this interpretation and because such an interpretation could eliminate the hybrid ingredients in doctrines belonging to Dharmakīrti's tradition amounts to an inexcusable methodological flaw. It rests on an unacceptable premise of homogeneity within a broader tradition.

In the present context it is, however, necessary to briefly mention two points:

1. Given that doctrines of *anumāna* could justifiably be classified as doctrines of either deductive or inductive arguments or reasoning it does not follow that this classification reflects everything which is most relevant about them. It might even highlight relatively insignificant properties. Any teaching can in principle comply with various classifications either because it deals with various subject matters as Pāṇini's theory deals with phonological, syntactic and certain semantic issues alike, or because it tackles problems of one field for solving problems in another field, akin to a theory of medicine using chemistry to account for certain medical problems. In the present case the significance of multiple classification represents more than a merely theoretical possibility. It is most natural to combine or even conflate the question of the acceptability or cogency of a piece of reasoning with the question of the existence of epistemic conditions under which a rational being is entitled to assess some propositions as true. Hence even a doctrine which might be justly classified as a variant of deductive or inductive logic could simultaneously qualify for classifications such as methodology of reasoning or epistemology.
2. It is far from certain that teachings of inference classifiable as *anumāna* encompass everything that concerns questions of validity of reasoning or argument. Standard specimens of *anumāna* exhibit a veiled reference to the rule of modus ponendo ponens because they concern conclusions of the form 'Ga' depending on the truth of a proposition 'Fa' whose acceptability relies on the truth of the conditional

'If Fa then Ga'. It is easy to see that the possibilities of supporting a thesis are not exhausted by advocating the combination of some atomic proposition plus a conditional in which the latter proposition occurs as antecedent and the proposition of the thesis as consequent. An alternative possibility lies in demonstrating that from the assumption of the untruth of a proposition a contradiction is derivable which on condition that the contradiction relies on no other premises than the untruth of the proposition, vindicates the truth of the proposition concerned. In this connection it is not absolutely imperative that conditionals supporting the derivation of the contradiction are supported by positive instances. Rather the pertinent conditionals can exhibit a counterfactual nature and the contradiction may partly depend on propositions whose truth cannot be doubted a priori. Given the correctness of a particular interpretation of a debated textual passage it must be regarded as the outstanding merit of the Buddhist philosopher Candrakīrti to have not only detected that this form of valid reasoning exists but also to have realized crucial features on which the soundness of this variety of reasoning depends, in particular the fact that this form of argument is probative only if the contradiction depends on no other debatable assumptions than the untruth of a proposition which needs to be disproven. It might be true that against the background of contemporary logic the decisive features can be exposed with a degree of clarity which could not be depicted with the same amount of precision by the Buddhist founder of the so-called Prāsaṅgika school. But if this is true then it merely follows that the slogan of interpreting non-Western doctrines against the background of their own concepts is conducive to sterility.

The considerations of the preceding paragraphs indeed support the thesis that classifications and assessments of teachings of Indian philosophies using established terms tend to be unfruitful. But the decisive reason of potential unfruitfulness does not lie in the circumstance that the terms or concepts coming into play are of Western origin but either in an inherent deficiency of semantic determinateness or in inappropriate ways of employing them. In the latter respect, lack of clarification of the basis of employing words and employment of preformed terms in contexts where more elaborate analytical tools would be required, are particularly relevant shortcomings. In addition to this the example of the method of *prasaṅga*-reasoning suggests that for an assessment of traditions of thought, comprehensiveness of scope of investigation is more important than the suitability of conventional technical terms.

RESPONSE

S.N. Balagangadhara

In his thought-provoking paper, Claus Oetke states his basic thesis in clear and unequivocal terms:

> There are no problems of either translation or assessment which are specific for interchanges between Western and non-Western, in particular South Asian, communities and cultures.

In the process of commenting on this thesis, he elaborates the idea further:

> . . . all the major problems arising with respect to phenomena of non-Western societies and cultures are equally problems arising for translation, interpretation and evaluation in the framework of different varieties of Western culture.

His paper, thus, is a challenge to those of us who think differently. I intend to respond to this challenge by focusing on his thesis. Of course, I formulate the issues the way one individual sees it. The only purpose of this response is to explain what I mean by 'the translation problem' (and what I think Indians mean when they talk about it).

Even though many of us (myself included) speak of the 'translation problem', there is no one unique problem of translation: there are a plethora of problems, all of which also take the form of 'the' translation problem. Let me begin by mentioning some of these problems.

1. Consider abstractly any two natural languages X and Y. Here, the translation problem takes the form of translating words and sentences from one of them into words and sentences of the other. 'X' could be German and the word 'Dasein'; 'Y' could be English and the translation problem could involve the use of this word by Hegel and Heidegger. We might settle for a hyphenated translation: 'there-being' or 'so-being' for the word 'Dasein'. We might signal the different meanings of the word 'Dasein' in Hegel and Heidegger in glossaries or footnotes. The chosen English words might not accurately translate 'Dasein', as either of the two philosophers use it. But this difficulty does not prevent us from reading and understanding Hegel and Heidegger in English and writing reasonably accurate tracts on their philosophies.

If, instead, one language is Sanskrit and the other English, similar problems confront us: 'God' or 'gods' are not synonyms for *deva* and *devatās* but this problem is no different from translating the Latin 'religio' into the English 'religion'. We can very easily create glossaries and footnotes; we can even introduce new words, say 'pif paf' (for example), as translations ('pif paf' as the translation of *deva*). We can enumerate the different meanings of the word *deva* under the intension of 'pif paf' and leave it to the reader to learn its meaning and use the word properly.

In one sense, we have solved the translation problems involving technical words ('gravitation', 'genes', 'electric current', etc.) in a similar manner by introducing new words into a language. If we can do this in one domain, we can do that in other domains as well: just introduce new words in the English language for 'untranslatable' Sanskrit words; then they can become a part of the English language the way *paṇḍit*, *karma*, 'juggernaut', etc. have become parts of the English vocabulary.

So, here there is no 'special' problem of translation involving two or more cultures. Of course not: there could not be. Just look at the problem formulation: "Consider abstractly any two natural languages X and Y". Here, there is no problem of cultural difference because the problem formulation *abstracts* precisely from all such considerations. However, just because we can describe interactions between members from different cultures in abstract terms also as 'human interaction' pure and simple, it does not follow, therefore, that there are no specific problems of cultural interaction. Such an argument is too general to prove a specific point. The reason is not far to seek: describing human beings as 'children of God' does not make us effectively into children of God just because we can be so described, any more than describing some phenomenon in one way does not entail that other kinds of descriptions are not possible or that they are necessarily false.

2. Consider now two *theories* formulated in two natural languages in conjunction with the use of an artificial language, say Mathematics. (I am calling Mathematics a 'language' in what follows just to illustrate the problem.) Let us say that the theories under question are those of Newton and Einstein. (Let us now abstract from all other considerations.) The issue is this: How does one translate, say the English word 'mass' in Newton's theory into, say, the German language in which Einstein's theory is formulated? Immediately we see that, even though translation between two languages is involved (English and German), the problem is different: in this case, we are dealing with words as they are defined in different theories and see that their meaning in each of these theories is different. Consequently, we are talking about translation of the vocabulary of one theory into another even though the actual job is also one of translating between two different languages. What we need here is not a 'translation science' to help us but knowledge of physics. By the same token, the adequacy of translation depends not on natural language dictionaries but on the consequences of these two theories. Though there is also a translation problem here, there is the additional problem of commensurability of two theories in the same domain.

3. Consider now two theories formulated in a single natural language, say English. Let us say one theory is from the domain of cognitive neuroscience and the other is from the domain of psychology. They are both about the 'same' object, the human brain, and deal with the same topic, say, belief formation. We can be even more specific: let us say that the belief formation involves 'thinking about God'. An MRI brain scan undertaken when some individual Christian prays shows that a specific sub-region of the brain is activated; psychology of religion describes the same activity in terms of a 'total surrendering'. Surely, there is also a translation problem here: translating the vocabulary of the psychology of religion into the vocabulary of cognitive neuroscience.

If we focus on the fact that both theories are formulated in English, we can conceivably say that the translation of one theoretical vocabulary into another is a special case of seeking synonyms. It is a 'special case' because we are not seeking synonyms for some specific word in a natural language but establishing the 'sameness' of meaning between two different vocabularies. If we overlook this aspect, then one could suggest that finding 'synonyms' in one language mirrors the difficulties of translating words across two natural languages and that the problem of translation 'reduces' itself to the problem of finding synonyms. That is, the problem of finding synonyms when we consider only a single language takes the form of a 'translation problem' when more than one natural language is considered. Even were we to make such a statement, we see that the problem of finding 'synonyms' in this particular case also involves a problem of a different kind: the problem of inter-theoretic reduction. What we need in this case is not the **OED**, but multiple theories that would enable us to reduce theories in psychology to cognitive neuroscience.

4. Even though more (and different) examples are possible, these three are sufficient to indicate what I am driving at: just because a 'translation problem' is involved in all the three cases, it does not follow, therefore, that the solutions used in the first case suffice for the other two as well. The 'translation sciences' do not help us in the last two cases, even if they are of some use in the first. Consequently, before one can claim that there are no special problems involved in translating between the languages of India and Western culture, one has to show that issues like the above do not complicate the situation. In fact, one has to do more: show that translating across languages of different cultures cannot create new and further problems for the act of translation. But I believe they do. Let me confine myself to speaking of some four dimensions in this situation, each of which signals the existence of such problems.

5. Consider the English language which has a rich corpus of religious writings. (I am completely abstracting from the problems involved in translating many such writings from Greek, Latin and other European languages into English.) In order to make the problem visible and tractable, let me just speak of 'theology', while ignoring writings like sermons, prayers, liturgical texts and such like. Even here, I speak only of 'Christian theology'. Because there is no 'single' Christian theology but a multitude of them, let me use the convention of speaking about the language of theology in order to signal two things: (a) theologies are kinds of theories; and (b) there is a multitude of them. So, I speak of two kinds of language: natural language and theological language. (Neither, as must be obvious, is meant in the singular.) From now on, when I speak of 'theological language', I refer to theologies in the English language.

5.1. Let me begin with the first dimension and consider the following issue: translation of the theological language into a natural language. Because I am focusing on India and the West, let us assume that this theological language confronts an Indian language, say Hindi. How does translation proceed here? What are the problems we confront? There is, first, the problem of translation between two natural languages, English and Hindi, because the theological language is in English. Second, there is the problem of translating a theory (theology, as I have said, is a set of theories) and, therefore, the problem of translating a theoretical vocabulary: words like 'God', 'grace', 'salvation', 'sin', etc. are theoretical terms in these theologies. Third, there is the problem of identifying the target: into what are we translating these theoretical terms? Into the vocabulary of another theory or merely into another natural language? If we make the claim that the terms from this theological language (considered as terms within theories) are being translated into another theory, what *kind* of a theory are we talking about? That is to say, do we confront a problem similar to translating Newton's theory into the theory of Einstein or a problem similar to reducing psychology to cognitive neuroscience? On the other hand, if we claim that we are translating theoretical terms into a natural language, the task becomes the equivalent of translating Einstein's theory (formulated in English) into Hindi. In that case, one has to introduce new technical terms for all the theoretical terms ('God', 'sin', 'salvation', etc.). How are we going to decide?

Hitherto, this decision process took a very simple form of endorsing as true those assumptions that solved this problem in one particular way. People simply assumed that religion is a cultural universal and that the difference between Indian and Western culture (among other things) lies in the differences between their 'religions'. (While Christianity dominated Western culture, 'Hinduism' (say) has dominated the Indian.) Both religions have notion(s) of 'deity', 'sin', 'salvation' and such like; therefore, both religions have 'theologies'. Consequently, they were convinced that the theological languages are mutually translatable. For centuries, people in the West believed that the Christian theological language was richer (and thus superior) to the Indian theological language, the way Einstein's theory is richer than Newton's theory. This belief at least had the merit of suggesting that, at best, we face the problem of incommensurability of theories when we undertake translations. (Today, even this benefit is lost because one does not, in the academic field at least, speak about the richer language of Christian theology, so we do not know what problems we face or how to solve them.)

However, note that the above assumption is not the result of scientific investigations. The only reason to assume its truth is some sort of 'consensus gentium'. This does not suffice: a similar consensus also existed in the West regarding the sun's movement around the earth. Therefore the conclusions are inevitable: Either (a) one shows (either empirically or theoretically) that Indian culture also has a religion (or many religions), and that words like *deva, mokṣa, pāpa*, etc. are theoretical terms within Indian theologies: then, one can claim that these words can be used to translate 'God', 'salvation', 'sin' and such like. Or (b) one shows that there are no 'native' religions in India, hence there are no 'native' theologies. If it transpires that India does not have native religions (like 'Hinduism', 'Buddhism' and 'Jainism'), then the terms from the theological language (formulated in English) cannot be translated either into Hindi or Sanskrit using words native to these two Indian languages: one has to introduce technical words to translate. *Deva* is not 'God', any more than *mokṣa* is 'salvation' or *pāpa* is 'sin'.

This problem does not arise in the case of translating between the European languages. Nor does it come into existence when the Dutch interact with the Germans. It occurs in an interchange between Western and Indian culture. From this consideration, it follows that Oetke's thesis cannot be true: it is false to claim that "there are no problems of either translation or assessment which are specific for interchanges between Western and non-Western, in particular South Asian, communities and cultures".

5.2. Consider now the second dimension, which introduces one aspect of the relevant cultural difference explicitly: in Western culture, theological language has become a part of the natural language to such an extent that one has lost the awareness that certain words are parts of specialized theories. That is to say, theological language has become a subset of the European natural languages and as theory it defines the meaning of these words and guides their use in natural languages. This, of course, is my hypothesis but there is 'neutral' evidence of sorts: the Biblical phrases and sayings are integral parts of all continental European languages and have seeped into the English language beginning with King James' translation of the Bible. (In Shakespeare, for instance, the Biblical influence is less discernible than in later English.) One does not know today, unless one has done specific research into the theme, which expressions and sayings are Biblical and which not. Together with the Bible, all theological words ('sin', 'God', 'grace', etc.) are parts of the vocabularies of European languages. In fact, such is the penetration of the theological language into English (and other European languages) that even words like 'truth' and 'falsity' carry religious intensions as their core meanings. Nevertheless, people continue to translate 'truth' as *satya* and falsehood as *anṛta*.

The second 'neutral' evidence is the *fact that some natural language sentences in the European languages are seen as category mistakes*, even where they are syntactically well-formed. Recognizing a sentence as a category mistake requires the presence of background theories (minimally, some ontology).

'Cow is God', 'Mother is God' and such like are category mistakes in European languages, whereas 'Jesus is God' is not. (If one is inclined to attribute the category mistake to the use of proper names, substitute names for 'cow' and 'mother' to see that the situation does not change.) Talk of worshipping a rat or a bicycle or a car is a category mistake whereas worshipping God or the Devil is not. (Note that *āyudha pūjā* is not a category mistake in Indian languages, whereas its conventional translation into any of the European languages, is.)

Consequently, when Indians learn the English language the inevitable happens: they map the technical meanings of theological vocabulary on to the meanings of some words from their native languages. They assume as true what they have been taught, namely that these words from a theological language have native natural language equivalents (or semi-equivalents). In the process of learning the English language, they do not learn the underlying theological language that defines the meaning and use of technical terms; instead, they look up Monier Monier-Williams as though this Sanskrit-English dictionary tells us how Sanskrit words are to be translated into English and the other way round.

In other words, a specific unrecognized problem has come to the fore: by not cognizing that some sets of words from English have specific technical meanings, we have ended up distorting English while entertaining the belief that we are translating. When some Indians proudly claim that they *also* think that "Work is Worship" (because they heard or read some or another European relating 'work' to 'salvation' and 'worship'), they are distorting the meaning of both 'work' and 'worship': by identifying 'work' with some or another profession or even just labouring activity; they fail to understand what 'work' means when the Catholics say that 'works are a part of worship'; they distort the meaning of 'worship' when they assume that *pūjā* is worship.

This problem does not arise when a Frenchman learns German or a Belgian learns English. It becomes a problem when Indians learn and use English. From this it follows, again, that Oetke's thesis is false. It is the case that there are "problems of either translation or assessment which are specific for interchanges between Western and non-Western, in particular South Asian, communities and cultures".

5.3. There is also a third dimension that is specific to both India as a country and to its existence as a culture. It has to do with what colonialism is and how it damaged the transmission of Indian culture. By creating a special class of 'intellectuals' in Indian society (for instance, the British created the 'Children of Macaulay' in India), who were more or less completely distanced from native Indian traditions, reflections on and thinking about the Indian culture suffered. These intellectuals thought about India the way Europeans taught them to. Consequently, theory formation using the native reservoir of skill and knowledge about Indian culture and traditions also suffered.

This damage was also inflicted by cultivating and sustaining a very strong belief that native Indian traditions were inadequate and deficient. Colonialism generated, formed and informed an attitude that condemned Indian traditions to obsolescence. A socio-political phenomenon, colonialism, appeared to the Indian mind as a confirmation of the cognitive inferiority of Indian traditions when compared to European achievements. Consequently, the belief grew that there is very little to learn from Indian culture and traditions.

This meant that there was little or no transmission of native theories about the various aspects of human existence unless they were first refracted through the prism of European reflections about man and society. This led to the formation of two distinct groups in India, both of whom are more or less isolated from each other's intellectual influence: a group of *paṇḍit*s and a group of academics. One group, for example, does not know of (say) Rawls while holding forth on *dharma*; the other knows nothing of *dharma* (except as a word) and knows only of Rawls. (Of course, there are people between these two extremes, but they are strictly a minority.)

Why is this important? Indian languages also include terms which have emerged as the result of sustained intellectual reflection. Words such as *sat, asat, manas, citta, buddhi, dharma* and so on are some examples. Unlike in the West, these words have been transmitted only as words in natural languages and not as theoretical terms which they also are, whose meaning and use are guided by theories. Consequently, we face a strange situation: even though Indian languages contain such theoretical terms, there is no clarity about their meaning and use. Unless one has dipped deep into Indian traditions, one cannot answer questions about the meaning and reference of a host of words that one uses 'fluently' in daily discourses: *citta, manas, buddhi* and so on. I am not putting across the suggestion that the native speaker of a language should answer all questions about the meaning and use of words in his language. What I am saying is this: while in the West, there might be disagreement regarding the truth-value of a sentence ('dogs have minds'), in India, by contrast, similar sentences create problems of comprehension ('dogs have *citta*'). This problem arises because of the indeterminacy of reference and meaning of such words and is generated by the lack of 'intuitive' access to those theories that determine both.

Most Indians have no 'natural' access to the Christian baggage, which is understandable. The result of colonialism is that they are also denied a 'natural' access to Indian intellectual traditions. They believe that they understand both Indian and Western culture, while, in reality, they have little knowledge of either. Indians have access to Indian and European languages but not to the implicit 'theories' that are embedded in these languages and transmitted by these cultures. Thus, they reproduce Western descriptions of India when studying India and her culture; they also end up reproducing Western descriptions when attempting to understand Western culture.

Consequently, it is difficult to say what kind of problems we confront when we translate from Sanskrit to English: Is *anṛta* to be translated as 'falsehood' or not? Is *sat*, 'existence' or 'the real' or neither? Is *ātman* the 'soul', the 'Self' or the 'personhood' or none of these? Does the Buddha deny that human beings have 'souls' when, according to some interpretations, he defends the 'doctrine of *anattā*' or does Śaṅkara do the same as well even when he speaks about the *ātman*? How should these translation problems be solved? Should we ask a *paṇḍit* who has studied Sanskrit texts but does not have a clue about what 'soul' or 'falsehood' or 'existence' mean? Should we ask a 'Westernized' Indian academic who knows neither what 'soul' is nor what *ātman* is but thinks he understands Heidegger's 'Dasein'? Or should we consult Monier Monier-Williams who uses a generic Christian theology to translate what he takes to be words from Indian 'theologies'? Or should a German study Sanskrit in the hope that his native language will somehow give him access to Sanskrit without the mediation of many centuries of Christian translations of the Sanskrit language? Or should we train a new generation of Indians to access (through intellectual effort) what they cannot 'naturally' access today?

Whatever the answers to these questions, the point is this: these problems do not arise in Europe, irrespective of whether the 'Western culture' is a collection of individual cultures or names their structural unity. Colonization of some Western country (say, Belgium or the US) by another European nation (say, by the Dutch or the British) has not generated this set of problems for the Flemish or French languages or for translations from these languages into English and the other way round.

From this it follows once again that Oetke's thesis is false. The colonization of India has created problems which also manifest themselves as "problems of translation or assessment" when one talks about the interaction between Indian and Western culture.

5.4. Let us now focus on the fourth dimension which gives birth to a different set of problems. Here, let me begin by assuming that different cultures exist in the world and that these cultures also possess sets of common sense beliefs. Consider now a subset of these common sense beliefs and identify it by the name 'commonplace ideas'. Let me take two randomly chosen commonplace ideas in order to talk further about the issue.

Galileo, the natural scientist from Italy, claimed that 'the book of Nature is written in the language of Mathematics'; Rousseau, the French Romantic thinker, claimed that 'Man is born free but is everywhere in chains'. Even though each of these sentences enclosed in quotes comes from a different European language, both have been accurately translated into all European languages, English included. How do we know that the translation is accurate? Here is the simplest possible answer I can think of: to those concerned, these two translated sentences played the same role and performed the same function as they did for Galileo and Rousseau. Let me explain.

5.4.1. Galileo's claim appealed to a deeply held cluster of ideas in the Christian West that God has revealed His will in two places: in the Bible and in Nature. The Bible was, of course, 'the' book and the medieval Naturalists had paved the way for looking at Nature as a book. They 'read' Nature and natural phenomena to decipher and discern God's will therein. Galileo could assume the stance of 'studying' Nature only because of the labour of a millennium that had already formed such a stance. We need to note that the talk of 'the book of Nature' is not a metaphor; this was not and is not the case either for Galileo or for those who preceded and succeeded him. They did see Nature *as* a Book. Studying this book was one of the fundamental obligations of Man, an obligation that was subordinated only to the duty of studying '*the* book'. In both cases, God imposes these obligations on Man. Because of this stance, this proposition could be readily understood in the Christian West. Galileo's sentence could function as a heuristic in the elaboration of scientific theories only because all those who followed in his footsteps resonated deeply with this thought, irrespective of the language it was expressed in. (For reasons I cannot go into now, it still resonates deeply in the 'secular' West as well.) This would be impossible if the translation did not express the same proposition irrespective of the natural language sentences in which this proposition was expressed.

If we translate Galileo's sentence into any Indian language it does not express the same proposition. In fact, one could even claim that the sentence of Galileo is 'untranslatable' into Indian languages despite the fact that there are 'word equivalents' (using *nisarga* or *prakṛti* for Nature) in these languages. It is an old insight that constructing a syntactically well-formed sentence by translating individual words does not give us the source sentence. That is the case here: we cannot even provide a lexical meaning to Galileo's sentence if we translate it into any of the Indian languages. We cannot understand the sentence-meaning, even where we understand the component word-meanings. The reason is not far to seek: it is in the nature of a commonplace idea that it requires the presence of a cluster of other ideas to make sense.

Even if one does not fully endorse the previous paragraph, the following cannot be denied: what happens when Galileo's sentence is translated into other European languages does not happen when the same sentence is translated into any of the Indian languages. This implies that one or another problem intervenes in one case (translating between Indian languages and the sentence of Galileo), which is absent in the other case (translating between European languages). From this it follows that Oetke's thesis is false. There are some "problems of either translation or assessment which are specific for interchanges between Western and non-Western, in particular South Asian, communities and cultures", even if we cannot, for the moment, formulate *what* those problems are.

5.4.2. Rousseau's sentence has played an immensely powerful role in the development of multiple theories in political philosophy. There are two aspects to this role: (a) it functions as a heuristic in developing theories; (b) the sentence itself is elaborated in different ways into different theories. Let us assume now that we use *svatantra* to translate the word 'free'. Under this assumption, let us try to 'translate' the Rousseauvian sentence into Indian languages. What would the result be? This sentence fails to perform its role in either of its aspects, either (a) because the sentence becomes empirical, or (b) because it fails to make sense as a sentence. The first indicates that it is only an issue of empirical truth or falsity (we cannot speak of logical truth or its negation here because we are considering only an individual sentence), which it definitely is not in Rousseau or in any other coherently conceivable theory. This means that it cannot be a translation of the Rousseauvian sentence. In the second case, it is quite obviously not a translation in any sense of the term. I will be brief in my elaboration here.

If we use *svatantra* as the equivalent of 'free', we need an extremely charitable interpretation of Rousseau's sentence for it to make any sense. *Sva-tantra,* this compound word, refers to *tantra*s and identifies those that are one's own as distinct from other *tantra*s and the *tantra* of others. Being 'born' free makes no sense at all; one cannot use *svatantra* to characterize one's birth. One can only become that: become *sarva tantra svatantra,* for example. So, we need to ignore precisely that element which lends power and poignancy to this sentence: namely, that man is born free, if we have to understand the translated sentence in an Indian language. Of course, one might object to using the word *svatantra* to translate 'free', but doing so compounds the problem: what causes confusion in this choice? The answer is that we have difficulties in identifying the unit of translation: should we look for an equivalent for the words 'born free' (because 'born' free creates the problem if we choose *svatantra*) or for the word 'free'? Introducing technical terms will not solve this problem either: the same issue also confronts us here as well; besides, all those books in political philosophy explicate precisely what it means to speak of being 'born free'. Whatever route we take, note what happens: we have to solve some problems in the case of translating this sentence into an Indian language, problems that do not arise when we translate the French sentence into English. This too shows that Oetke's thesis is false.

Let us look at the other of the two possibilities, namely that Rousseau's sentence is false. Of course, some Christians also consider Rousseau's sentence as false because, they say, man is not born free but under the sway of original sin. Even where they take issue with this religious claim, it does not prevent the very same Christians from developing a political theory on the basis of a restricted interpretation of 'freedom' in Rousseau. That is to say, they also treat Rousseau's sentence as a theoretical claim when they take issue with him. Needless to say, political philosophy looks at this sentence as normative in nature. In short, no thinker in the West treats Rousseau's claim as factual; they cannot, because the 'fact' of being 'in chains everywhere' is being contrasted to how Man is born. Freedom is the ontological status of Man.

If we allow for a very charitable interpretation of a 'translation' of Rousseau's sentence into an Indian language, it requires looking at it as a statement about the world. One has to read the sentence thus: a baby (this is how Man is born) is not born saddled with social, political, economic and family 'bonds' (this is what makes the baby 'free') but acquires them in the course of growing up. This is, indeed, the 'human condition': we are forced to be in chains everywhere. That is why, some Indians might continue, we need to 'liberate' ourselves from *saṁsāra*.

Alternately, one can take another route thus: the baby is not born *svatantra* because, being totally helpless, it is entirely dependent on *paratantra* (its parents and others, for example). It continues to grow the same way and lives all its life enslaved by chains. The usage of 'but' in Rousseau ('born free but in chains') makes his statement empirically false and merely exhibits his ignorance of 'la condition humaine'. That is why, those who follow this route could continue, *mokṣa* is the only possible deliverance because it frees us from *bondage* by liberating us from the cycle of birth and death.

There is no need to emphasize, I suppose, that these sentence-meanings that try to assimilate Rousseau to the Indian *ādhyātmika* traditions have nothing to do with Rousseau's claim. If that is the case, Rousseau's sentence is not translated by the Indian language-sentence under consideration. Of course, one could say that even these interpretations of Rousseau are justifiable because of the presence of 'different' background beliefs in India but that the translation itself is still as accurate as it possibly can be. Whether this claim is correct or not, I am making two different points here: (a) the European interpretation(s) of this sentence are not accessible when reasoning in Indian languages but they are accessible irrespective of in which European language one reads Rousseau; and (b) irrespective of which European language the French sentence is translated into, the aforementioned difficulties in understanding the proposition do not arise there. They do arise when Rousseau's sentence is translated into an Indian language. Thus, from this too, it follows that Oetke's thesis *is false*.

6. One can say more and different things than what I have said so far. But I have said enough, I trust, to explain why I do believe that interesting and important problems arise in the interaction between Indian and Western cultures, some of which manifest themselves in the realm of translations across the relevant languages.

DISCUSSION

Oetke

I had earlier asserted that rendering from a different language can even be rewarding and advantageous. That is the point of my Hebrew example. So if you translate the sentence into German, you can do it automatically. If you want to do the same into Hebrew then you have to make a decision and this necessarily means that you have to get it correct and that means you have to get into matters of translation. It is a very simple example but it shows all the more the advantage of sometimes assessing from a different language because it forces you to raise questions of interpretation which you need to ask if you relate languages which are conceptually alike or are very similar to each other.

But now let us come to the controversy which we have here. When Indians talk about Europe they have a tendency at least, to equate it with modern Europe or with the Christian world. I have a Western background but I attended a school where we had Latin and Greek. So if we think of the European tradition it is most of all the traditions of the Romans and Greeks. And it was unconsciously in the background when I spoke about the Western tradition and the problems that arise in, for example, the Greek texts – Plato, Aristotle, etc. So one needs to be aware of how one wants to conceive the Western tradition when one wishes to contrast it with the Indian.

So I now come to the first really controversial point. If I understand you correctly, all your arguments refute one thesis which can be formulated as follows. Let us just take *E* as an abbreviation of English, *H* as an abbreviation of Hindi and *F* as an abbreviation of French. And there I think you have succeeded in refuting the following thesis which is a little bit technically formulated; nevertheless, I hope it is comprehensible. For all expressions in *E*, if we know that an expression set in *H* exists which translates, let us say *X* then we also know that expression *Y* in *F* exists which translates *X*. So all examples say something of the same kind. Then we have examples where this does not hold. We can translate from English to French: there we have no problems. However, if we start to translate into Hindi then we are confronted with problems. I agree that this thesis is refuted by these examples. But the point is that this is not the thesis of my paper. My thesis also has to do with the background of the Classical European tradition. I first formulate it more technically and then give a more satisfying paraphrase as my thesis could be a bit complicated when expressed in the following manner:

For all expressions of *E*, in all adequacy conditions *C*, the following holds good. If no expression exists in *H* which translates *X* according to *C* then there is also *U* of *E* such that no *V* of *F* translates *U* under this condition. So the intuitive idea is that we now elide this problem which you mentioned. But my claim is that all these problems are of such a type that you can also find some parallel in other languages; not the same expressions but different expressions in, let us say, English and French where you face problems for which one says that the original language cannot be translated, where you cannot adequately translate for precisely the same reasons.

So actually what my thesis amounts to is a rather traditional position, which we had earlier in the West and is now in Sanskrit studies which have fallen into oblivion. So the older generation of us Europeans conceived Sanskrit studies as a parallel to Classical Greek and Latin Studies. And my claim is that all the problems, till now at least, that we have if we translate or interpret works of Indian origin, we have encountered somewhere else. For these types of problems arise if we also interpret Roman and Greek works. This is my thesis and your objections do not meet that because my thesis was different.

The second is also important. You tend to conflate, what I would call the properties of people speaking a language and the speech of a community. So if I look at your Galileo example, what you proved actually is that somebody who is not familiar with the Christian background will, perhaps, not adequately understand or interpret this Galileo statement. But I think this has really nothing to do with linguistic or conceptual matters. It has rather to do with background knowledge. I myself am not familiar with the Christian traditions. But this failure is not due to the fact that I am not Western but just a person to whom Christianity is not so present. It is really the problem of background knowledge. Of course, the background knowledge exists with higher probability and higher degree if you have visited a school in the West but there is no necessary link. So these two issues must be separated.

Then there is the point which is that you presuppose a very reactionary view on the matters of translation because you always bring up the matters of finding an adequate word. This is true but I think nothing new and is also clearly recognized in translation theories. I think we must distinguish between concepts which have attained the status of a philosophical concept and a technical concept. If we ask about the existence of a concept in the non-technical sense, we have to be aware of the fact that having a concept does not necessarily mean having a word. For example, the Indians undoubtedly have a sense of belief; they undoubtedly have a concept of truth although they have not used belief and truth in their philosophical vocabulary. There is a good explanation for that because they did not see any reason to make the concept of belief thematic. The Western tradition also did it at a fairly recent time. Nevertheless the fact that people express their beliefs cannot be doubted and there are different devices for doing that. It is not necessary for there to be a word that is synonymous with belief. In Hindi we have the locution: *mujhe lagtā hai.* That is also a way of expressing belief but with a different syntactical device. So if you ask: is there such and such a concept for encountering foreign cultures, I would say that it is even disastrous casting this question as: 'is there a synonymous word?' and even go further and say 'is there a technical term for it?' So this must be clearly separated and I think in matters of translation it follows that sometimes if you want to convey to a community the desired communicative effect then sometimes you have to revise the entire syntactic structure. It follows that it is not always advisable to present a literal translation and that it is not something new. Of course, what you say is correct but I don't think it really shows that there is something peculiar about India in particular.

My last point is: What do you translate? The naïve point of view is that you translate a sentence or a word, at least a linguistic entity belonging to one language into a linguistic entity of another. But you also speak of different entities which are translated. For example in your paper you speak of translating theories.

Balagangadhara: vocabularies of theories.

Oetke continues: Yes, but I think one may object to the idea that theories are translated. At any rate, there are certain instances where it is suggested that the relata of the translation relations are not linguistic items. I don't want to say that is illegitimate but I think it is important to clearly separate this and also see whether there are other ways of translating different sets of relata and the way we justify what they mean.

One more thing. You might say that for example, different theories, let us say the theories of Chemistry and Physics are equivalent in the sense that they explain the same phenomena but this kind of equivalence is not evident to me at least, that in this case also we have a translation relation between the terms that really make sense. Perhaps this is possible but is not immediately evident.

Kaviraj

I was struck by the fact that the examples that you work with, are primarily from the fields of logic and many from the basic operation of language which are all highly generalized. They are all sciences or fields in which you can refer to a certain kind of common human apparatus. I have no difficulty with the argument that you made right now. Indeed, my argument about *rasa* theory would be very similar to yours in two senses. First of all I find that *rasa* theory looks at questions which modern academic English would call psychologizing, but perceptive observers of *rasa* theory, would immediately say that psychologizing is not a completely correct word, because there is a very strong connection between aesthetic categories and categories which refer to mental states. The technical word that you could use initially would be psychologization. So, I do not have a problem with the idea that there is a kind of psychologizing element in Indian philosophy. And what I said about *rasa* theory is very similar to yours: they have a common problem. Take Aristotle's *Rhetorics* and *Poetics*: I found to my surprise that when I read Ibn Sina on 'literary wonder' I found that the initial questions are very similar, but then they go in different directions which is precisely what makes it interesting and which precisely makes it possible that there are some things which do not figure in Aristotle. I think it would be too strong a phrase to say: 'which Aristotle failed to see'. Because he is not looking for those things so he cannot see those things; those things do not figure in Aristotle's vision and these things actually figure in the *rasa* theory vision and it is because we can have access to both, that we can produce something which is more complete and use them complementarily. A language of course is a vast field in which you have a referential world which is very wide and it has different types of properties. Some part of it – like the human body, the thinking about logic and things like that – those are of one kind and the more cultural you get – for instance when you go into literature or art – there you do not have any reference to something which is independent of language.

So my question would be: would you think that when we talk about a part of the referential world which is more culturally indexed like say language of the emotions or the language of social institutions which do not have an independent existence beyond language – translatability becomes more and more of a problem?

Oetke

I think you are completely right. I say that what follows has equal/even practical relevance. I sometimes suggest that actually making a translation is only a preliminary state, especially if you get to such things like literature in which many expressions occur which are strongly culturally bound then you should actually publish the translation with commentaries. And it is really deplorable that this is so seldom done. This has to do with our economic structures, with our publication industry and so on. There are exceptions to this rule. I recall an Urdu reader which is very old. It is interesting because it explicates the difference between meanings of meaning. It gives a literal translation of the texts then it gives some explanation. And because many of them are Sufi texts, it gives an explication of what they mean against a Sufi background.

So we have three translations – strictly speaking only one is a translation the others are additional information. And I think that is needed if we really want to communicate successfully in both directions. Again here I would emphasize that it is something that we need even with Greek and Latin. So if one translates *deus* with 'god' , then one is inclined to think that it is a monotheistic God. But as we know, it might be Hera or Jupiter or whatever. So there is potential for error; at least information must be added in order to get an adequate grasp of meanings.

Balagangadhara

I want to respond to three of your points Claus. First you are not talking only about the Greeks and the Romans because all the problems arising with respect to the phenomena of non-Western societies and culture are/were equally the problems in the frameworks of different varieties of culture. You not only talk about the Greeks and the Romans, you gave examples about the French and the English as well.

The second point is: you talk about the fact that people face the same problem in Europe of today when they talk about the Greeks and the Romans. You are absolutely right. But that confirms my point, namely, than the Greeks and the Romans had no religion. They were Pagan cultures and this is exactly the problem with India. The Christian culture doesn't understand Greek – the whole of Heidegger's philosophy is an example of that. He says we cannot think Greek. And his whole attempt to speak about what thinking is, what truth is, etc. – is an attempt to rescue the Greek language from what he called the Christianization of Latin. I am aware that contemporary European languages and modern Europe do have problems with the Greeks and Romans. But just because of the fact that Greece and Italy are located in the Western hemisphere does not make them part of Western culture. In an earlier publication, I showed that neither Greece nor Rome were cradles of Western civilization. Western Civilization is Christian Civilization, although you might not agree with that. Greece and Rome do not belong to it. That is why we Indians can understand them. Let me give you a small example – One of the most fundamental notions of Aristotle is *eudaimonia*, which gets translated with great difficulty as 'well-being', 'feeling good', 'happiness' and so on. It is a very difficult word to translate. This is not merely a translation problem because I have had discussions with Greek scholars. Aristotle asks: what is *eudaimonia*? It is very difficult to achieve of course but he says once you have it you cannot lose it. I told a Greek specialist once 'you know nothing about Greek language'. He responded: 'how dare you say that'! So I said: 'here is a simple thing, forget the translation of *eudaimonia*, give me one example of a human property which once you possess, you do not lose.' I said: 'I do not have to understand Greek to understand what *eudaimonia* means.' And of course to this day, no Greek scholar could help me in giving one example of one human property which if once you possess you do not lose – this is a fundamental property of *eudaimonia*. For the Indians here is my answer. *Eudaimonia* is *ānanda*. Once you have *ānanda* you do not lose it. It is equivalent in some conditions to *brahma-jñāna*. And that is happiness indeed, beyond *sukha* and *duḥkha*. So when Aristotle is talking about *eudaimonia* I understand him and I read him carefully. Of course, there is no translation equivalent of *eudaimonia* in any of the European languages but that is because they have no access to that world, that conceptual framework like we have. So indeed, I understand you have a problem with Greece and Rome: we understand them much better.

Two other points – one on Galileo. I am not making a confusion conflating the community of Christians with a community of non-Christians because one of the claims I have substantiated to which in the last fifteen years I have found no counter argument, is the following: My claim is that free thinkers and atheists, even the Communists of Europe, are actually disguised theists. That is to say that Christianity has secularized itself in political theory, in social theory, in rational choice theory; a number of theories. I can show you how assumptions from the Bible have taken secular forms. So by saying for instance, 'look I don't have a religious background', it makes no difference. I know people, who do not have a religious background for generations, are atheists but they continue to have the same excuse for speaking as the Christian does. For example, your ethics will be absolutely no different from

Christian ethics because there is no such thing as non-Christian secular ethics present today. You ought not to kill. Don't tell me that is an example of secular ethics. Even the notion of 'ought not', the normative notion itself, does not come from English: it comes from Christianity, from the Bible.

Aristotle, for example, does not have an 'ought'. Indian languages do not have a 'moral ought' nor do the Chinese in their language in which Confucius wrote. These are not linguistic issues, Claus, these are problems of conceptual apparatuses that are culturally developed. So, it is in that sense that I speak about Galileo and say he made sense to the Europeans. They used his findings to investigate nature because they believed fundamentally that nature has a structure and pattern and a law which has to be discovered by human investigation. They would say that without such a structure the universe should be chaos. The whole of 2,000 years of European culture believes that, and that was Galileo's idea as well. It is a background belief, of course, but it is a background belief of culture and we are talking about difference between cultures. Translation is always a translation between people who use sentences, who use natural languages. So, I am shifting the level of the problem.

Last point, there is something to be said for your claim regarding the notion of belief – that you can have a concept, but do not have a word – that is absolutely true; that is our daily experience. I feel like saying something but I don't know how to say it. So, you can have some sense of a concept but defined psychologically not linguistically or so cognitively. I do not know how to put it in a natural sentence. Right. But you are making out of it logical and philosophical points.

Let me put it very sharply. The notion of having a belief and the belief is always about something; this is a specific conception of man, of human beings – there is philosophical anthropology which attributes some notion of intention to human beings. One of the extraordinary things about the Indian tradition, if you like, is the absence of this notion of intentionality: *ajñāna*. They call it *ajñāna*, they call it *māyā* and many different things. So the nature of human being in the Indian tradition is that we are non-intentional creatures, which is completely incomprehensible within the framework of Christian culture. So, entertaining a belief, having a belief is not a linguistic, psychological, epistemological fact which is applicable to all human beings but is a specific assumption about the nature of human beings that comes from the Bible. So when saying that Indians have belief, you are not making use of any understanding of language – you are making use of a religious concept of man and saying that is what Indians have. Of course, you can say that, people have been saying that for 500 years. That is not the issue. The issue is: is this how Indians understand themselves? In fact, if you look at the languages you find there is greater affinity when you talk of using work words. They do not say 'I got angry' but 'anger came upon me' – this is a very typical old classical Greek way of talking. Why did you say that? I do not know, my tongue moved that way. I am literally translating local Indian languages into English – this is the way we talk. In fact, even the subject notion, is not simply a linguistic subject or verb subject in action, the fundamental ontological notion of subject itself is missing in India as also the notion of agency.

Take the problem about truth: the notion of truth for applying to sentences, to propositions by some other philosophers is a very philosophical disease. If you look at the middle ages take Aquinas for example, he had two notions of truth *adœquatio re* and *adœquatio intellectus*. One is which is adequate to the object; the other which is adequate to thoughts. Hegel used the same notion. Tarski also says there are multiple notions of truth. That notion of truth – *adœquatio intellectus* as it prevailed for 1,900 years in Western culture referred to the fact that objects are adequate to how God conceives them. That is *adœquatio intellectus*; not to human intellects, to God's intellect. *Adœquatio re* had to do with how one related the word to both these notions and emerged not from any understanding of philosophical language, truth, a philosophy or logic, it arose from commenting on theologies and commenting on the Bible.

Mukhopadhyay

I would like to address one or two general issues and then come to some very specific issues that have been raised.

There are very few, very concrete contexts and situations under which translation was undertaken in India. Towards the beginning of colonial rule in India, the colonizers had to depend largely on translations. They needed them for the specific purpose of ruling the Indian people. They had to know their institutions . Quite naturally the first books they translated were the *dharma* – *ācāra* and *vyavahāra* – texts.

The other difficulty is what Indian students particularly feel. In Indian universities in post-colonial India all students, take, for example, philosophy. As a matter of course they have to read Western philosophy. A little Indian philosophy, sometimes as well but Western philosophy they must read. This is not the situation elsewhere. Western students are not obliged to read Indian philosophy. So when we have to read Western philosophy, it is quite natural that we should be able to understand Western philosophy. Now what is our way of understanding Western philosophy? Through the English language. This compulsion the Western students do not feel. Many more people in India know English than those who know Sanskrit. Those who know Sanskrit learnt it for Indological purposes, not for the purpose of philosophy, not for the purpose of science, not even for the purpose of literature.

We do not always see that these Indologists have done the greatest harm to Indian culture in one way. They have marginalized all Indian basic sciences in a sense that if a European writes a history it is described as philosophy but if an Indian writes philosophy it is Indology. Anyway this is the basic situation. And once we are in such a situation what is the problem? The problem is this. Some times we take translation and language in the abstract and we feel that we understand the language so we have understood the culture. Actually language cannot be completely separated from the culture itself. So, our problem is that when we Indians study some subject, whether it is Nyāya or some other philosophy and see some Western people translating it we feel very unhappy, dismayed at times. Why does this happen? The reason is this – they think the knowledge of the literary Sanskrit language is sufficient to translate a text of Indian philosophy like *Tattvacintāmaṇi*, or a text of Gautama. But that is not possible. Similarly if because I know some English, or Greek, can I understand Aristotle? No. Because the language has been segregated from the cultural background itself – the foreigners use language to understand people and we have segregated the language from the people and say that understanding the language is enough. So, we always miss the nuances.

Almost invariably we translate knowledge as *jñāna*. Anyone who knows a little Indian philosophy, knows it is a wrong translation. *Jñāna* is never knowledge, *jñāna* is belief.

That is why I said no Sanskrit philosophical text can be translated into English in the sense that word to word translation and sentences is impossible. You have to translate one paragraph into three pages because we have to communicate the sense in the original language to another language.

In the course of this discussion if we can identify realistically, one or two words or concepts – one or two problems, we can then discuss. Say one logic or epistemological term, for example. It has been held that in India there is no logic or epistemology: there is psychology rather than epistemology. Why do they think like that? The reason is that in contemporary Western philosophy when they discuss epistemology they have removed *śabda*. Today theory of inference and theory of *śabda* are separate branches of philosophy. One is philosophy of logic and the other language. We have to go into it. Why is it that in India we get *śabda* and *anumāna* as part of epistemology as Pramāṇa Śāstra. When I was a student I read texts of logic where among the sources of knowledge *śabda* was included – but now they have removed it. Why? The reason is very simple, they have come to a conclusion that it is not the business of logic to yield truth. It is not the business of language to give truth.

5

Framing the Predicament of Indian Thought
Gandhi, the Gītā and Ethical Action

Vivek Dhareshwar

> I have something far more powerful than argument, namely, experience. –M.K.Gandhi

What appears as a problem of translating Indian thought into English has dimensions that are conceptual and cultural. That is to say, the linguistic problem of translation does not capture the predicament in which Indian thought finds itself. It might be suggested that the problem of translation should be taken in a larger sense, as a metaphor for the problems involved in cross-cultural understanding. I think it is a possible route to take, but my own preference is to see the translation problem that arises in the case of Indian thought as symptomatic of a deeper problem that needs a different kind of framing rather than as a problem of translation/interpretation with which we are familiar, whether we take that problem as formulated in analytical philosophy or in continental thought. In saying this I am of course acknowledging that a proper framing of the predicament is the issue at hand and that will be the focus of this paper. I will not, however, engage with other possible ways of formulating or framing the problem.

Frames and Predicament

Why speak of a predicament? Although I have been speaking

grandly of Indian thought, let's focus for a moment on the by now more than a century-old career of Indian philosophy in global academia. Out of the enormous scholarly output of translation, interpretation, historical reconstruction, it is difficult to name one work that actually uses the resources of Indian intellectual traditions to produce a work of philosophy, a piece of thinking about any aspect of the world or life. So *dharma, satya, avidyā,* or *upādhi* have only been receiving philological attention rather than being employed in thinking: the translation problems they create then seem less urgent conceptually, though important enough from the point of view of accuracy or adequacy. This situation would not have merited the characterization of being a predicament had it not been for the fact that Indian thought is not quite like Aristotle's science. It is not dead yet. It lives on in some fashion (in what condition and vigour and so on are not pertinent at the moment) and there have been attempts, as we shall see with Gandhi, to think with its concepts. There seems to be little connection, however, between the academic enterprise of philosophy and the living stream of Indian thought. Am I contrasting dead academic philosophy with the living stream in the outside world? The contrast is there to be drawn, especially if we take the creative engagement with tradition that Gandhi, a non-philosopher, achieves, and compare it with the dull exegesis and commentary piled up by professional philosophers. But it would be misleading to formulate the contrast this way, as an opposition between these two worlds. We will then fail to notice the more general predicament and the deeper explanatory demand it makes on us. It is partly for this reason that I have been talking about Indian thought, since we are concerned with our life with concepts. Our problem is not simply that we no longer employ terms such as *ātman, avidyā, dharma* to reflect on our experience; the terms that we do indeed use – sovereignty, secularism, rights, civil society and political society, corruption – seem to insulate our experience from our reflection!

Gandhi's *Hind Swaraj* had given us a vivid portrayal of this predicament.[1] That portrayal still captures our attention, even though a hundred years have passed since Gandhi wrote that text. This paper can be seen as an attempt to restate in terms we can (I hope) readily relate to, Gandhi's diagnosis of the predicament so as to better understand his claim that the *Gītā* helped him find a way out. The primary concern however, will be to arrive at a proper framing of the predicament; any productive discussion of the way out can only take place when we begin to diagnose the predicament. My strategy in this paper will be as follows: I will first outline in my language Gandhi's framing of our predicament in *Hind Swaraj*. I will then discuss three very different examples taken from our peculiar life with concepts that will also serve to clarify and illustrate the framework I am outlining. I will then very briefly discuss how Gandhi saw the *Gītā* as showing him a way out of the predicament.

Hind Swaraj is concerned with the particular kind of enslavement that colonialism had brought about and which was wrecking the intricate structures of practical life evolved over a very long period of time. The enslavement of Indians had a peculiar epistemic character: it taught them to ignore the kind of knowledge that organized the domains of practical life.[2] Law, medicine, history, nationalism and the state bring in ways of looking and certain conceptualizations that begin to cleave reflections from the form of practical life in which they are embedded. Thus health, to take an example dear to Gandhi, no longer functions as a matrix of practical action, related integrally and reflectively to ends that inform not only that matrix but other

---

1 M.K. Gandhi, 1997, *Hind Swaraj* (ed. Anthony J. Parel), Cambridge: Cambridge University Press.

2 V. Dhareshwar, 2011, "Politics, Experience, and Cognitive Enslavement: Gandhi's *Hind Swaraj*", in A. Bilgrami (ed.) *Democratic Culture: Historical and Philosophical Essays*, New Delhi: Routledge, pp. 64-86.

adjacent matrices (or possible new ones that can be fashioned). In any case, health is not the state of my bare body. Law is not a resource that helps me resolve my conflictual relationships in my familial matrix or in the domain of business in a reflective way, but an instrument that creates new disputes which I can only deal with in legal terms which extrude reflection. History brings in a perspective that begins to distort my relationship to the Kāvya, Purāṇa and Itihāsa by transforming their function in the practical realm of life. Similar considerations apply not only to nationalism and to the politics centred around the state, but to many more entities and conceptualizations introduced by colonialism. So let me speak of a cognitive/evaluative frame which, as it were, houses these entities, and enslavement to which distorts, devalues and veils the domain of practical life, which I will term 'the actional frame'. Gandhi's concern was to restore the integrity of this frame through learning to reflect on practical life again. So the *āśrama* life he began to construct around action–theoretic concepts modelled on *yama* and *niyama* – such as *aparigraha* and *ahiṁsā* – sought to grasp the function of the form of life that was being attacked by the cognitive/evaluative frame. This point needs to be underlined since this ethical/cognitive activity should not be seen as an attempt to recreate practices from the past.

Although Gandhi did not articulate his philosophy in a systematic way, his thought sought to combine three elements: (i) engagement with Indian traditions, (ii) creation of new concepts, and (iii) social understanding. It is remarkable then, that not a trace of a Gandhian perspective can be found either in the self-understanding of our institutions or in the social scientific discourse on our social world. When he figures, he does so either as a saint or as a charismatic mass-mobilizer with quaint, antimodern and clearly unviable ideas. But *Hind Swaraj* had made clear why his perspective would not find a place in the cognitive/evaluative frame through which India is perceived.

In fashioning his resistance to colonialism and the frame that was enslaving Indians, Gandhi realized that the traditions of experiential knowledge (*adhyātma*) in India have been damaged. He clearly understood that the transmission of ethical learning has been obstructed, driven underground, and distorted. He was expressing this realization when he argued in *Hind Swaraj* that India has become 'irreligious' (by religion he meant the inquiry that for him underlies all traditions and which for him was exemplified in ādhyātmic thought). It was the actional frame of ethical actions that was being muted by the dominance of the cognitive/evaluative frame.[3] Gandhi saw his task as strengthening the actional frame which involved reinvigorating its own reflective dimension. I shall return to consider Gandhi's creative engagement with tradition through the *Gītā* in the last section. Before that I offer some illustrations of our life with concepts, to show how general the predicament happens to be for it is not confined to the practice of Indian philosophy. And unless we diagnose the reason for the generalized predicament, we will neither understand why philosophy shares in that predicament nor whether philosophy can help itself and us to come to grips with it.

Are We Corrupt?

Intellectuals, especially philosophers, usually think of themselves as more susceptible to various kinds of conceptual

---

3 The metaphor of 'frame' appears in very different disciplines and thinkers – in psychology (Amos Tversky and Daniel Kahneman's work on biases and heuristics), in sociology (Erving Goffman's frame analysis), in cognitive science (Daniel Dennett's frame problem) and philosophy (Akeel Bilgrami has used frames in two or three different contexts) – it may be asked where mine comes from. The motivation, function and scope of my frames are different from all these, though there may well be some common features. Nothing at this stage really hangs on clarifying the affinities and differences.

bewitchments or confusions. Gandhi too thought that it is the elite who were enslaved. The discourse of 'corruption', however, demonstrates that it is not the intellectuals alone who share this epistemic condition. Practically everyone seems to think that 'corruption' is rampant in India, or even that we are all 'corrupt'. The puzzle though, is this: whether we take the phenomenon or the moral judgement, there is nothing obvious about corruption. In fact, just a moment's reflection on the standard utterances we hear all round us, which rarely vary from scholars to journalists to politicians to ordinary Indians, will make this clear. It is 'ubiquitous', 'all-pervasive'; 'the rot', so goes the rant by some morally upright figure, 'has set in deep' and so forth. Even if we assume that this can be made sense of, a very hard assumption to make, the conclusion or, at any rate, the implication turns out to be the opposite of what the discourse set out to observe and condemn: that there is indeed a logic, a pattern and systematicity to the actions and the practices they are embedded in. Our first task has to be the cognitive one of spelling out that logic, that frame of action, not the moral one of condemning it without understanding. We want rich, clear and non-ad hoc explanation of patterns of action that by all accounts have such systematicity and ubiquity. Let me admit that it is not an easy point to grasp, but unless we do so we will continue the tirade without even realizing where that moralizing stance comes from. What creates the difficulty is that both the frames we mentioned above are in operation (socially rather than merely cognitively). One of them is actionally effective but otherwise unacknowledged and the other is cognitively/morally/legally operant and officially or publicly legitimate.

What happens when the left or liberal intellectual sits in the cognitive/evaluative framework and writes about nepotistic and other corrupt practices that supposedly pervade Indian culture? It is doubtful if any cognition happens. Certain ways of speaking or writing are adopted, which marks one out as a scholar or an intellectual. One of our most distinguished economists once illustrated the lack of certain values among the poorer and illiterate section of Indians with a report of an interview with a woman, a poor labourer, who, when asked about her well-being, replied that 'we are not well' (and she wasn't using the royal (we) because there was indeed much illness in her family. Assuming that this is a factually correct report, one would have thought that the woman's response reveals an ethical universe, and an understanding which might be richly instructive for social scientists. Instead, her answer is supposed to show that she doesn't understand 'freedom' and 'choice' and such exalted values. As one of Kannada's most sensitive literary scholars Keertinath Kurtkoti[4] once pointed out, when intellectuals use 'feudal' to characterize certain behaviour, attitudes and values, they are using it as a term of condemnation rather than understanding, for the experience is ours, but the understanding is someone else's. He was sceptical that we can arrive at genuine understanding this way. The point is generalizable: when we use the cognitive/evaluative frame for our putative 'observation' (in much of social scientific writing or journalistic reportage) very little cognition or understanding takes place. Instead we 'observe' inefficiency, venality, nepotism, lack of decision-making ability and so on. All actions thus appear as violations of rationality and morality.

We are now in a position to appreciate a remarkable feature of the word 'corruption' that is playing such a crucial role in our lives. That word is not a translation of a native or vernacular word, which should have been the case if the two frames overlapped even significantly if not fully. And whatever word functions as a translation of 'corruption' – in Kannada, and perhaps in many other Indian languages, it is *bhraṣṭācāra* – it simply has to depend on the original to import the right

[4] Keertinath Kurtkoti, 2006, 'Nirupaneya Shakti', in *Uriya Nalige*, Dharwad: Manohar Publishers.

(whatever that is) connotation and evaluative force. (*Bhraṣṭa* is someone who departs from the path of *dharma*, and *ācāra* is practice. I doubt that this term has any currency; I suspect people simply use 'corruption'.) So we do not employ it to understand something, here actions of a certain kind, but deploy it to classify and judge acts. Since there is no understanding, the deployment appears quite arbitrary. Let me clarify this idea of deployment of discourse with another familiar example. Take 'Hinduism'. It is not difficult to show that this term has no referent despite the fact that it has been deployed to refer to any number of things, in an entirely indeterminate way. Though we can understand why it was postulated into existence (roughly because, Europeans could only make sense of the diverse practices they saw by drawing them together into a religion called 'Hinduism'), it is clear that it cannot provide any understanding or experiential salience to Indians. That the discourse of 'Hinduism' is now being deployed by Indians themselves does not reify the entity but creates situations that can range from the harmless, if a little awkward (say Gandhi's use of it) to the positively disastrous, say its use in politics. But either way, it eventually does have the effect of masking the experience of Indians when they wittingly or unwittingly deploy the term. Corruption too was a non-empirical observation/judgement of Indian transactions by Westerners (in fact, most of Asia that they came into contact with was thought to be corrupt). The domain it covered and sought to attack was the whole social ethical world (what I have been calling the actional frame). As in the case of 'Hinduism', when Indians begin to deploy the 'corruption' discourse, the consequences range from the harmlessly ridiculous to the dangerously corrosive. The deployment of this frame and the way of speaking that goes with it has such a grip on us now that it begins to obfuscate whatever implicit understanding we might have had of our own ethical universe and the frame that is operative there. When we Asian philosophers deploy the discourse of 'corruption', we exempt ourselves from understanding the actions that we want to classify or judge as 'corrupt'.

The obfuscation or destruction of the reflective universe of this frame should not be understood sectorially (modern vs. traditional). It is perfectly possible for the items of the so-called tradition to be deployed, that is, to appear in the cognitive evaluative frame in which 'corruption', 'rights' and the language of democracy operate. Let us take seriously the idea that understanding actions in any deep sense itself involves ends; but these are not subjective ends. Although the actional frame is still operative, the reflection on ends of action and experience that was part of that frame has become fractured, indistinct and its transmission sporadic, in part because of the onslaught from the other frame. So when we look at a whole range of actions – the linesman who demands money to fix the phone for which he gets paid, the minister who demands money to grant licences, the professor who uses his connections to get his son a job, the bureaucrat who demands a trip abroad to clear collaboration, the powerful family that expects that its progeny will, as a matter of course, occupy the most powerful elected office of the land – in one frame they all get classified as 'corrupt'. But in the other frame, our evaluations of some of the cases above may be totally different. For example, although most of us would want to make critical remarks about the hold of the Gandhi family on political power, a large number – sometimes the very same people – would also regard Rahul Gandhi as having a privileged claim to the prime ministerial chair. And some instead of regarding the professor's act as nepotism, may consider it as laudable, an act that possibly saved the department. What I am straining to get at is that even when we are deploying 'corruption' to condemn certain actions, there is, at least in some cases, almost simultaneously a different understanding which may get displayed in the action we take but not register in our discourse.

If the cognitive/evaluative frame has fractured, suppressed and rendered silent the actional frame or universe, in another way the force of the latter has appropriated for itself some of the structures, the institutions, the language that belong in the cognitive/evaluative frame. The complication that results from this awaits even an initial description let alone a theorization. Our next example will, however, show why when we take to theorizing, the state of affairs I just described does not even appear as a problem requiring conceptualization.

Our Sovereignty and Our Civil/Political Society?

In this section, I want to highlight the special problem posed by terms that we have come to regard as theoretical or social scientific. The 'forms of experience', as Foucault would put it,[5] that provide the unity and identity of something called the West, cannot be fully understood if we do not regard the so-called human sciences as part of that experience even as they are a reflection (in a sense that we still need to understand) on that experience. To start with let us take a very familiar political concept, namely 'sovereignty'. Emerging some time in the twelfth century,[6] sovereignty encapsulates the problem of arbitrating the jurisdiction or the dominion of the Pope and the Prince, of sacred and temporal secular rule. Although many ideas of the Greek, more specifically Aristotelian political theory found their way into the discourse of sovereignty – body politic, the source of the government in nature and reason – it is important to note how drastically they were transformed by theology. Thus nature becomes the instrument of divine Will, reason the means of providing divine revelation, the body politic

---

5 M. Foucault, 1984. "Preface to the History of Sexuality", in P. Rabinow (ed.) *The Foucault Reader*, New York: Pantheon Books, vol. II, pp. 333-39; see also his 1985, *The Use of Pleasure*, tr. R. Hurley, New York: Vintage Books.

6 H.J. Berman, 1983, *Law and Revolution: The Formation of the Western Legal Tradition*, Cambridge, MA: Harvard University Press.

gets split into the body of the church and the body of the secular polity and gives rise to the problem of which of the two is the true representative of the spiritual body of Christ. The series of questions this theological discourse raises – how God manifests himself in two spheres or communities (the sacred and the temporal) and how a Christian can live in these two communities simultaneously – is completely alien to Greek thought. The discourse of sovereignty thus begins a story that takes in the state, the nation, citizenship, civil society and secularism as it encounters new political and social problems during the course of a history that is still unfolding. Historiography gets forged to narrate and re-narrate this discourse and thus becomes both a part of politics as we now come to understand the term and a continuation of the discourse of sovereignty itself. Let me take advantage of the limitation of space and make a large claim: concepts, such as citizenship and civil society, or entities such as race and nation that are part of the discourse of sovereignty, are not intelligible discretely; indeed, they are constitutive of the forms of experience from which they only seem to stand apart or above. The disciplinization, as it were, of this discourse of sovereignty has a lot to do with why concepts and 'theories' of, say, citizenship or secularism, appear to be separately available as theoretical resources elsewhere.[7]

Now thanks to colonization, this discourse of sovereignty is deployed in non-Western cultures and histories. In India, for example, we are all too familiar with citizenship, civil

[7] The remarks on sovereignty are meant to highlight a problem that Indian historians and political theorists seem to have some trouble noticing. For detailed investigation of the trajectory of secularism, see the work of Balagangadhara and his students: De Roover and Balagangadhara, 2008, "John Locke, Christian Liberty and the Predicament of Liberal Political Theory", in *Political Theory*, p. 36 and De Roover, Claerhout, and Balagangadhara, 2011, "Liberal Political Theory and the Cultural Migration of Ideas: The Case of Secularism in India", in *Political Theory*.

society, secularism and rights. We – that is, the non-Westerners deploying the discourse of sovereignty – should not, however, mistake familiarity for intelligibility. I would like to illustrate and elaborate this point by taking up Partha Chatterjee's attempt to theorize 'civil society/political society' in the Indian context (Chatterjee 2001, 2004).

How should we mourn our dead? In the traditional Indian way or should we adopt Western models of condolence – public meeting, eulogy, etc.? Commenting on this controversy between Rabindranath Tagore and Nabinchandra Sen, Chatterjee asks:

> Does modernity require the universal adoption of Western forms of civil society? If those specific forms have been, in fact, built around a secularized version of Western Christianity, then must they be imitated in a modernized non-Christian world? Are the normative principles on which civil social institutions in the modern West are based so culturally particular that they can be abandoned in a non-Western version of modernity?[8]

Chatterjee's formulation raises the problem of familiarity and intelligibility that I mentioned above. Read in a familiar way, the formulation seems to be raising some valid and even significant issues. Thus when Chatterjee proceeds to designate the 'elite' (in the older terminology) as belonging to 'civil society': 'civil society, then restricted to a small section of culturally equipped citizens, represents – in countries like India – the high ground of modernity',[9] he seems to be saying something significant. But is he? What has mourning got to do with civil society or, for that

---

8 P. Chatterjee, 2000, "Two Poets and Death: On Civil and Political Society in the non-Christian World", in T. Mitchell (ed.) *Questions of Modernity*, Minneapolis, MN: University of Minnesota Press, pp. 35-48.

9 P. Chatterjee, 2001, Democracy and the Violence of the State: A Political Negotiation of Death", *Inter-Asia Cultural Studies*, **2**: 7-21.

matter, with political theory? What does it mean to say, as we so often do, that forms of civil society – the institutions, concepts, practices – are secularized versions of Western Christianity? Is there a theory – Western or non-Western – that tells us what secularization involves? And what do we mean by 'normative' principles? What makes concepts such as citizenship, civil society, secularism, normative? Do we really understand the normativity of these concepts? At the slightest probing the familiar turns out to be unintelligible. Before returning to these questions, let us take a closer look at both 'civil society' and 'political society' as Chatterjee wants to set them up.

Chatterjee explicitly says that he is using 'civil society' in the sense it was used in the Hegelian/Marxian tradition. However, anyone with the most cursory knowledge of Western political theory will see that from Locke through Marx, 'civil society' was not used to designate a section of society. In Locke, everyone who existed in the state of nature belonged to civil society and thereby formed a compact or contract which provided the normative basis for either endorsing or rejecting any political association. In Hegel, this abstract, philosophical concept becomes dialectical – that is, history itself gets permeated by the ideality/normativity of philosophy, so that we (which includes everyone) become reconciled with our social/political world. The early Marx recognized this move for what it is: politics as theology. That explains his trenchant criticism of the duality of citizen and man, political society and civil society, a duality which he thinks cannot be overcome without abolishing the whole framework.[10] In fact, this early essay of Marx is really the first serious attempt to show the normativity of the concepts 'civil society' and 'political society' that otherwise appear purely referential. Whatever one might think of these moves, they

10 K. Marx, 1975, "On the Jewish question", in *Karl Marx: Early Writings* (tr. R. Livingstone & G. Benton), Harmondsworth: Penguin Books, pp. 211-41.

clearly do not involve using 'civil society' and 'political society' to designate a section of society.

Having set up 'civil society' to refer to the cultural elite of India, Chatterjee (2004) uses 'political society' to refer to those sections of society, the 'population', that he says are the target of governmentality. On the one hand then there are the 'culturally equipped' citizens who are the subjects of theory; on the other, the population which leads an illegal or a paralegal existence which is the object of policy. Political society is meant to capture the 'site of negotiation and contestation opened up by the activities of the governmental agencies aimed at population groups' and the latter acts by appealing to the 'ties of moral solidarity'.[11] Our question is: what is Chatterjee doing in using what he calls the terms of classical political theory to designate two sectors or spaces? At one level, he is simply re-describing what the subalterns used to call 'elite politics' and 'subaltern' politics. What does such a re-description achieve? Does it help us understand our present, the character of our institutions and practices and the concepts that inform them? Since neither 'moral ties' nor 'illegality' or 'paralegality' is specific to the sector that Chatterjee calls 'political society', the distinction seems hard to justify theoretically.[12] It would seem then that rather than offering a new political theory for the 'subaltern', Chatterjee's theorization might well be attesting to the subalternity of theory. The concepts of classical political theory seem to appear at best as terms with no theoretical content.

That Chatterjee's uses of 'civil society' and 'political society'

---

11 P. Chatterjee, 2004, *The Politics of the Governed: Reflections on Popular Politics in Most of the World*, New Delhi: Permanent Black.

12 In a recent treatment of the issue, Chatterjee asserts that the illegality of the poor, unlike that of the rich, 'mobilizes moral justification'. This seems more like a laudable sentiment than an empirical observation, see *Lineages of Political Society: Studies in Post-colonial Democracy*, New Delhi: Permanent Black, 2011, p. 16.

have very little to do with the way they were used in Western political theory may be conceded. One might, however, argue that Chatterjee's misuse or misinterpretation testifies to the strange and new career of these Western concepts in non-Western cultures and that what at first appears as a radical misinterpretation or misapplication is indeed an attempt to theorize that career. In the same way as Greek political concepts were transformed beyond recognition by Christian Europe, the concepts of secularized Christianity too undergo radical transformation in a non-Western culture like India. I believe this argument is essentially right; but far from helping Chatterjee's case, it shows both the urgency and the enormity of the task of coming to terms with the fact that the so-called human sciences are part of West's self-understanding rather than being genuinely scientific or theoretical. Let's reflect for a moment on the transformation of the Greek concepts: the forms of experience that took centuries to crystallize – the Christianization of Europe and its secularization – involved a new conception of the self, the shaping of experience in terms of morality (as Nietzsche never tired of pointing out), the emergence of entities such as 'sexuality' (as Foucault began to show us in his later work), political institutions and concepts that cannot be separated from the new conception of the self and the norming of experience. Thanks to the work of Foucault,[13] Balagangadhara,[14] McMullen,[15] et al., we are only beginning to glimpse how we might map this transformation. Consider now the even more daunting task of understanding what happens to Western concepts and institutions when they enter

13 M. Foucault, 1985, *The Use of Pleasure* (tr. R. Hurley), New York: Vintage Books.

14 S.N. Balagangadhara, 1994, *The Heathen in his Blindness . . . Asia, the West and the Dynamic of Religion*, Leiden, New York & Cologne: EJ Brill.

15 R. McMullen, 1997, *Christianity and Paganism in the Fourth to Eighth Centuries*, New Haven: Yale University Press.

a culture whose forms of experience we have not even begun to conceptualize.

The attempt like Chatterjee's then, commits a double error: it first takes as intelligible the concepts that are part of the forms of experience that constitute identity of the West; it then finds it 'useful' to apply those concepts to understand the present of a culture whose forms of experience could not have been constituted by those concepts. Unless one makes the drastic and unjustified assumption that forms of experiences are the same everywhere (or that colonialism has made it so – but this would be unacceptable to the subalterns given their characterization of colonial rule as dominance without hegemony), Chatterjee's kind of attempt cannot avoid committing the double error. It is ironic that Chatterjee uses Foucault's governmentality thesis to characterize his 'political society'. In Foucault, governmentality refers to the process in early modern Europe of norming the state, and his interest in this process of norming is of a piece with his interest in the process of norming that created sexuality. His concern is to study the 'historicity of forms of experience'.[16] Let us note that Foucault explicitly says that

> Rather than embrace the distinction between the State and civil society as an historical and political universal which could guide the questioning of all concrete systems of government, one can attempt to see a form of schematization proper to the particular technology of government.[17]

Such a study can help us in avoiding the double error, since it contributes to the alternative account we must give of the role of the 'human sciences' (including that of the discourse of

---

16 M. Foucault, 1984, "Preface to the History of Sexuality", in P. Rabinow (ed.) *The Foucault Reader*, vol. II, New York: Pantheon Books, pp. 333-39.

17 M. Foucault, 2008, *The Birth of Politics: Lectures at the College de France, 1978-79*. (tr. G. Burchell), Basingstoke: Palgrave MacMillan.

sovereignty) in the constitution of the European experience.[18] Such an account is the theoretical precondition, as it were, for undertaking a theorization of our present.

Our Moral Dilemmas

My last example happens to be from philosophy proper and conveniently involves the *Gītā*, thus providing a nice contrast to my treatment of Gandhi's engagement with the *Gītā* in the next section. I have in mind Matilal's[19] essay on moral dilemmas. Matilal wants to argue that Arjuna in the *Gītā* is confronted with a moral dilemma. There is, of course, a usage of the word 'dilemma', and especially 'moral dilemma', to refer to any difficult situation in which it is hard to know how to act (morally). It is clear Matilal is not using the word in that loose, everyday sense (for then his essay would have no significance). So what is a moral dilemma? The difficulty is not with providing (or borrowing) a definition from the recently burgeoning literature on moral dilemmas. What we need to note is that we do not have an intuitive understanding of what might be a moral dilemma, in the way that we can intuitively grasp what a logical or semantical paradox is when we see an example even if we are not logicians. Matital's own formulation of moral dilemma as 'a species of action-guide dilemma' is rather vague. Here is what he says:

> What is an action-guide dilemma (religious or moral)? A dilemma can be defined here, perhaps, in terms of obligation and evaluation principles. An action-guide dilemma arises in a situation just in case an agent cannot do everything that is obligatory for him to do in that situation. He feels obliged to

---

18 M. Foucault, 2003, *Society must be Defended: Lectures at the College de France, 1975-76*. (tr. D. Macey), New York: Picador.

19 B. Matilal, 2002, *Moral Dilemmas and Religious Dogmas, Ethics and Epics: The Collected Essays of Bimal Krishna Matilal,* vol 2 (ed. J. Ganeri). Oxford: Oxford University Press.

> do, say, both X and Y; but it is impossible to do both of them. For the situation is such that doing X would be undoing Y, and vice versa. You cannot cook your goose and have it alive at the same time. This is that kind of a situation.[20]

Why do obligations create moral dilemmas? What is morality such that it forces you to experience your obligations as a dilemma? Matilal's remark 'doing X would be undoing [not doing?] Y' suggests that he doesn't quite grasp the assumptions one has to make in order to understand moral dilemma. Meeting one moral requirement or obligation prevents one from meeting another moral obligation. And that failure violates a moral norm, that is, makes one immoral. Let me confess here that while it is not difficult to formally understand what constitutes a moral dilemma, I simply cannot grasp it experientially. Nor can I really understand the issues debated by those who argue that moral theories ought not to give rise to moral dilemmas and those who argue that moral dilemmas are inescapable. Aquinas famously held that Christian moral theory cannot allow moral dilemmas to arise, and if moral dilemmas do arise for an agent it can only be because of some prior moral violation on his part. Another, more explicitly theological response could be that it is only in this defective earthly world that one encounters moral dilemmas; in a deontologically perfect world one will never encounter moral dilemmas. The trouble is that the examples presented in the literature do not make a compelling case: they either offer trivial cases, unconvincing cooked up scenarios, or extreme situations (*Sophie's Choice*, for example) or cases taken from literature (Antigone, Agamemnon and now Arjuna) where it is far from clear that the characters experience the situation as dilemmatic.[21] Certainly, the first chapter in the *Gītā* gives no

---

20 Matilal, 2002, op. cit., p. 6.

21 Matilal suggests that Arjuna is confronted with 'must kill and must not kill' situation. That is a double bind rather than a dilemma. For an interesting review of the literature on moral dilemmas, →

evidence that Arjuna is paralysed by a dilemma and Matilal fails to show (even formally) how Arjuna is confronted with a dilemma. I am not suggesting that formally it cannot be done, but only that doing so would require importing into the universe of the *Gītā* kinds of consideration and language that do not belong there. Why engage in such an enterprise, which advances neither our understanding of why the dilemmatic structure has acquired such salience in the secularized moral theories of the West nor throws light on how we are to read the *Gītā*? In fact, we have here a clue to the sterility of contemporary Indian philosophy and social scientific theorizing: a problematic in this case – moral dilemma – that appears to engage Western intellectuals, is taken over without any effort to understand what the problem is, why it appears as a problem, and then superimpose it on material that is not even superficially treating the same problem.

It may seem that both the second and the third examples have a feature that is distinct from the first example: they do not appear to take concepts or problems that lie in the cognitive–evaluative frame. This is only true to the extent that unlike 'corruption', neither the pair of concepts in the second example – civil and political society – nor the problem in the third were used by the colonizers to characterize their experience of Indian culture. With 'corruption' there is enslavement to the way India was experienced, whereas 'civil/political society' or 'moral dilemma' was not so used, even though they figure in the West's

---

← see MacIntyre, 2006. The obsessive and moralistic fixation on the stage-setting first chapter of the *Gītā* too seems peculiar to Western commentators on the text (many of whom recoil in horror from what they regard as immoral injunctions of the text). As Gandhi points out, many great Indian commentators, like Śaṅkara, simply skip the first chapter. Gandhi dismisses such obsessions as irrelevant, but his discussion of the issue is extremely instructive (Gandhi, 2001, *Collected Works*, 33, pp. 887-88).

self-understanding. That is correct, but what is significant is that they track the frame: with these supposedly new concepts drawn from the West, it is as though the theorists are seeking normative salience vicariously. They are misunderstanding the role of such normative concepts in the secularizing dynamic of Western culture. In the recent movement against 'corruption' the massive deployment of the discourse of corruption indexes the extent to which the actional frame has been deprived of its language of reflection. Anna Hazare, coming as he does from that universe, stands in for that language though he cannot speak it, overwhelmed as he is by the discourse of corruption.[22] What Chatterjee, as theorist standing in the cognitive/evaluative frame notices, is the fractured actional frame (what he prefers to call illegality, is really deep down a stripping down of that realm). But he wants to give it normative significance, hence the resort to civil/political society vocabulary. It is as though theorization involves tracking the normative slots and filling them with 'agency' – the proletariat, the woman, the dalit, the subaltern.[23]

---

[22] He is no Gandhi, so despite the moral authority he derives from his universe, he has no understanding of the movement he has generated. Where would he belong in Chatterjee's scheme, in political society or civil society? Which provides any understanding of our present dilemma about the movement? Is it a political society phenomenon misled and mesmerized by the language and the institutions of civil society? Or is it a hegemonizing attempt by civil society to silence political society? These questions highlight the difficulties in this method.

[23] For a discussion of this normative conception of politics, see Dhareshwar (2011). In his recent treatment of this issue, Chatterjee (2011: 3-12) launches an attack on normative political theory for being a-historical and for ignoring or preceding all the political movements. Surely it is a normative narrative that Chatterjee himself is putting in place. The sequence of alternative modernities that Chatterjee prefers is normatively structured too. Polytheism is after all modelled on monotheism.

So far I have been saying that the concepts of Western theory relate to forms of experience and are part of a single history; the concepts both constitute and norm that experience as it has come to be lived and understood. When they appear in our midst, they must be treated as unconceptualized concepts, and not as concepts that tell us how we live or ought to live. In the end, in the same way as 'corruption' masks our experience, the deployment of 'civil/political society' will in effect block any attempt to conceptualize the unconceptualized concepts in the cognitive/evaluative frame. This is no mere word play; rather, that is how we can understand whether and how the frame inheres in the entities or items that it houses – only by reconceptualizing them or by removing those items that rightfully belong in the actional frame but which have been deployed in the cognitive/evaluative frame:[24] the *Gītā*, for example.

Gandhi and the Gītā

When Gandhi encountered the *Gītā* in England through Edwin Arnold's translation, it was firmly placed in the cognitive/evaluative frame. His realization that that frame enslaves one to a perspective in which our experiential world appears as defective, stagnant and degraded, and that the items that get placed there – stories or temples – appear opaque, was achieved through his understanding of the *Gītā*. He learnt from the *Gītā* how to move out of the cognitive/evaluative frame.

> I have something far more powerful than argument, namely, experience. As far back as 1889, when I had my first contact with the *Gītā*, it gave me a hint of *satyāgraha* and, as I read it

---

24 To understand the significance of this point, think of what Marx did to commodity, money and capital, the entities of bourgeois political economy. He reconceptualized them, thereby giving us a different understanding of the fetishistic character of these entities, rather than letting them impose their understanding on us.

> more and more, the hint developed into a full revelation of *satyāgraha*. That a man of Kṛṣṇa's intelligence should indulge in all this wisdom of the *Gītā* for the benefit of an Arjuna in flesh and blood, would be like killing the buffalo for a leather-strap. To believe he did so is to tarnish his name, if it is true that he was the Supreme God, and to do injustice to Arjuna if he was a warrior of experience and judgement. I know you will not dismiss these ideas off-hand. I would rather you embraced and developed them. You will readily admit, I am sure, that learned commentaries are of much less value than the experience of one's limited intelligence.[25]

He was able to do that to the *Gītā* because the *Gītā* enabled him to remove structures that were occluding experience. So in formulating his idea of *satyāgraha*, Gandhi was rediscovering the central insight of Indian thought, namely how to remove *adhyāsa*. But what is *satyāgraha*? How do you stand in *satya* to make your *āgraha*? This, he says, the *Gītā* teaches when it instructs us not to be attached to the fruits of one's action. How do we understand this? Despite its familiarity, it is far from self-evident how one carries out that instruction. The fact that it has acquired a pious, moral (almost Kantian) tone has not helped. Gandhi realized that the *Gītā* is a sustained meditation on the nature of action. Since it 'records', as Gandhi puts it, somebody's experience, 'it must not be beyond us to be able to test the truth of it by repeating the experience. I am testing the truth almost every day in my life and find it never failing'.[26]

To execute an action in the experiential space is a cognitive act. What the *Gītā* teaches is that action when tied to subjective ends tends to increase both unhappiness and ignorance. It is only when one learns how action is carried out within a matrix that one makes discoveries about ends that implicitly organize

---

25 M.K. Gandhi, 2001, *The Complete Works of Mahatma Gandhi*, CD-ROM. New Delhi: Publications Division, Government of India.

26 M.K. Gandhi, 2001, op. cit., pp. 4494-50.

the matrices. To restore a reflective dimension to the hollowed out actional frame is to learn to elaborate matrices, to perform action without conception. Thus learning to understand the concepts and instructions in the *Gītā* is to participate in an action–theoretic exercise. One can cognitively grasp the form and function of the actional frame even when the actual practices may be in need of critiquing or even jettisoning. Action concepts in a practical life-form function differently than as a gatherer of elements that fall under them.[27] To understand how they function we need to figure out how a matrix functions. Let us take dietetics as one such matrix. One is in this matrix when one pays attention to food or substances that nourish, and to actions that help nourishment, help the end of nourishment, which may be health in the sense of well-being. It can be a simple matrix of diet – *pathya* – or it can be an elaborate matrix comprising diet, exercise, and . . . meditation. The presence of the latter in this matrix does not mean that it cannot be part of another matrix. Indeed, criss-crossing matrices are the rule, but the point is that a matrix is an identifiable, individuable unit. Yoga could be a matrix on its own, or it could be part of the dietetics matrix or, to take a seemingly un-Gandhian example, the erotics matrix. I need to say a lot more about the notion of matrix but for now I hope a clear enough sense has emerged for us to understand Gandhi's experiments in the *āśrama* as cognitive acts that were designed to restore the reflective dimension of the actional frame. The experiential world in this frame needs sites of ethical learning to proliferate.

There is a powerful philosophical picture of how action is

[27] For an insightful discussion of the idea of a practical life-form, see Rödl, *Self Consciousness* (2007); Thompson (2008). In Rödl's words, 'A practical life-form is included in the infinite ends that are its elements as the form of their generality: an action manifests an infinite end only if it manifests the practical life-form of which it is a part', 2007, p. 43.

explained that has attained the status of self-evidence, namely the desire/belief model of explaining action. If this picture has attained the status of common sense or folk theory, as philosophers claim or imply, then we can understand why action in general and ethical action in particular has retreated so far that philosophical understanding does not even sense that there is something deeper to explore. My proposal, inspired by Gandhi's reading of the *Gītā*, that action can only be action in a matrix will therefore appear utterly counter-intuitive especially to that common sense and the philosophical understanding that upholds it. In any case, learning to detach or unbind actions from subjective ends involves carrying out cognitive acts. Both ethical action and self-knowledge involve concepts that can only be understood action-theoretically. To grasp the full significance of this extraordinary interpretation of Indian philosophy, we will need to explicate the action-theoretical view of concepts in terms that we can make sense of. That is to say, we will have to evolve our own action–theoretic concepts, in the same way Gandhi did through his engagement with the *Gītā*. One of Gandhi's constant refrains is that the Indian stories in the Kāvyas, Purāṇas, and Itihāsas are not at all historical but are experiential! Without moralizing, they provide structures for clarifying experience and models for situating action within a matrix.

In recovering or reformulating Indian philosophy's original problematic and in restoring its integrity, he used terminologies and strategies that can often be an obstacle to understanding his insight or his particular practices. I would argue that his particular conceptions, bound as they are to contingent circumstances of history, should not become a hindrance. For example, while we can appreciate why he thought that spinning as a symbol of the actional frame enabled reflection of a certain kind, it would be foolish to insist that spinning should be made that kind of symbol again. Similarly, he often used terms and concepts that clearly belonged to what I have been calling the cognitive/evaluative frame although his own concern was to move such items to the actional frame. Thus, he vehemently argues that we cannot separate 'religion' and 'politics', using the terms of the secularism doctrine to express an insight that properly belongs to the actional frame! The profound intuition to which he was giving expression, namely the inconceivability of removing *dharma* from *rājakaraṇa*, needs further articulation, but the cognitive/evaluative frame cannot accommodate it, saddled as it is with a borrowed normative language. Even more intriguing or challenging is Gandhi's use of the 'caste-system', which, like 'corruption' contains the normative evaluation of Westerners experience of Indian domains. When he says that he wants to defend the 'caste-system', his intuition here too is the same as in the case of religion and politics, except the argument needed to clarify and defend that intuition requires alternative conceptualization of the experiential/actional domains.[28]

[28] Gandhi's most subtle interpreter, Akeel Bilgrami fails to appreciate this point (Bilgrami 2003), *Economic and Political Weekly*, 2003, 1-2: 4159-65 which I admit is a difficult one to get hold of (even more so than the 'corruption' phenomenon, with which it has parallels). The advantage of the two-frames idea is that it provides us with the resources to show how what is postulated or normed into being in the 'actional' frame cannot exist there and yet appear, under certain conditions, in the 'cognitive–evaluative' frame. Although it will require immense amount of work to demonstrate the argument, since the context and the framework are in place, let me briefly assert: there cannot be anything called 'the caste-system' in the domains that the actional frame covers. Gandhi was making that point except that he used the term found in the cognitive/experiential frame (as he so often did) to designate what we can only understand after much reconceptualization of the actional domain. That indeed is the work of theorization we need to undertake to break free of the enslavement. In short, to see what Gandhi saw, and to say what he saw, we need new conceptual resources. But if I am right about the frames, there should be no difficulty in getting hold of the intuition, exactly in the same way that we firmly grasp →

It is necessary, therefore, to clear away terminological and frame confusions in order to develop Gandhian alternatives to the dominant left/liberal understanding. This is necessary because the discourses in the cognitive–evaluative frame are a deployment that has tended to obscure and undermine the actional frame that sustains the ethical universe of Indians.

When Gandhi, using his peculiar terminology, called the state a 'soulless machine' he was in essence expressing the same thought. The question for us is whether his critique of the state and, more generally, of the cognitive–evaluative frame (though it would be more accurate to call it quasi-cognitive–evaluative frame) can be developed in such a way that we can today not only effectively show that the continued deployment of that discourse has damaged our practical passionate relation with one another, but also begin to outline an alternative conception of politics. A question critical to the development of Gandhian philosophy is the relationship between the two frames. While it is clear that Gandhi sought to show the distorting effect of the quasi-cognitive frame, to what extent does that frame inhere in the entities that it brings in, such as the natural sciences, normative moral and political doctrines and social scientific discourses? A lot of careful work needs to be done to specify what goes into each frame – in fact, it can be shown that things can get moved between frames. No language or discourse or any such items necessarily come stamped with the frame. As Gandhi clearly saw (and as we have witnessed in the last few decades) the *Rāmāyaṇa* or the *Gītā* could be placed in the quasi-cognitive/normative frame, thereby completely changing their character. But what we need to understand is, what happens when the items from this frame are placed in the actional frame. A theorization of this would enable us to grasp the complexities of our present, for the

---

← Gandhi's argument about never separating 'religion' and 'politics'. There are also extremely crucial comparative questions to be asked about these frames in the context of Western culture.

actional frame, stripped of its ethical reflection, has 'tamed' in some manner the other frame. While Gandhi could be said to have used reflective action against rationality and thus staked everything on regenerating reflection in the actional frame, we would want to say that genuine cognitive activity with regard to the social and cultural sphere is yet to take place but is still possible, even as we would want to agree with Gandhi that making the actional frame reflective is a matter of survival.

Coda

The central concern of Indian intellectual traditions has been how to set up sites of ethical learning. They thought that we needed as many of them as possible, for what is unethical is whatever occludes experience and experience-occluding structures are everywhere, whether it is the body, the sense of 'I-ness' (*ahaṁkāra*) or social structures. So ethics is the attunement of reflection to experience (*anu-bhava*), by removing any and every form of ignorance (*avidyā*) that distorts experience or occludes it altogether. The unethical person in this culture is the person who cannot learn, that is, one who is not attuned to experience. But colonialism brought in structures that effectively disrupted the transmission of ethical learning and displaced the sites of learning. Part of this process involved bringing norms and normativity that effectively created two frames in the cultural universe of Indians. The peculiar coexistence of two frames has created problems of a kind that have not even been registered, let alone theorized as an ethical, political and cultural problem: the description of daily ethical activities acquires a tone of immorality, when seen through the frame of norms (as we saw in our discussion on 'corruption'), but the frame of norms itself has remained alien, because obviously even colonialism could not replicate conditions and institutions that generated normativity in the West. The peculiar misunderstanding and misapplication of normative concepts that we saw in Chatterjee and Matilal is in that sense quite reassuring!

What insulates reflection from experience? The insulating material is discursivity, that is, discourse employed in a certain way. Norming a site, founding a practice, giving reflexivity to practice are all roughly equivalent descriptions. I have used the term 'deployment' for reflection that develops after the insulation and that uses discourse from different sources (thus deployment of feminism, of nationalism, of Indic or Orientalist thought, and so forth). In more concrete terms, all of them involve making discourse pass through a practice, or making a practice discursive. Language or more accurately discursivity plays a central role in constituting normative institutions/structures. Perhaps one of the major reasons for the first frame to go underground, or become mute and ineffective is that when the discursively structured normative institutions/structures – what might be called the garrulousness of the West – are unleashed in India, it is as though they provide their own understanding; the discursive structure, what gets taken to be 'theories', are what compel a sense of understanding by providing a way of speaking. Normativity or the second frame is anchored when we begin to 'buy' into those 'theories' – theory of the state, discourse on freedom and equality, chunks of European history functioning as cognitive schemes (feudalism, secularism, revolution and so forth). It is easy to overlook that they are what need to be understood – what I termed the unconceptualized concepts. We still have not realized that. To reiterate a point I made right at the beginning, the predicament has to do with our life, with concepts generally and not only with concepts of classical Indian thought. It should also be obvious by now that the predicament cannot be understood as a translational problem or a problem of language.

I have tried to frame the predicament of Indian thought. That framing owed a lot to Gandhi; in the last section I tried to show how Gandhi's attempt to find a way out of the predicament brought about a creative engagement with Indian thought.

Implicit in that attempt is the conviction that resuming Gandhian experiment and inquiry is the route to take. We will begin to understand a lot more about that experiment and that inquiry, including why it seemingly never took root, only when we begin to probe the very many different deployments that are holding us enslaved.

Acknowledgement

This paper was presented at the conference, 'Rendering the Categories of Classical Indian Thought in the English Language: Perspectives and Problems', held at the India International Centre, New Delhi, 13-16 December 2011. it was first published in *Asian Philosophy: An International Journal of the Philosophical Traditions of the East*, vol. 22, no. 3, August 2012, pp. 257-74 (Routledge, UK) I wish to thank the organizer Mohini Mullick for many helpful and lively discussions leading up to the conference and the respondent Sudipta Kaviraj for his characteristically thoughtful comments. I have benefitted greatly from the incisive and engaged response of Lata Mani and Indira Chowdhury.

RESPONSE

Kaviraj

I will make two kinds of remarks. First, I wish to set aside the relatively trivial questions. I do not entirely agree with the criticism of Matilal and Partha Chatterjee. I do not think they are doing the same thing. Matilal was engaged in a process of translation from one point of view, and whether you see it is as valuable or not is a different matter. But he was trying to enter into a discussion on moral dilemmas and he used an example from the *Gītā*. I agree with your reservations about using the term 'moral' or the very technical term 'dilemma' but I don't see why it should not be seen as a dilemma. To say that something is not a dilemma is one kind of criticism and to say that it is not a very serious one is a different kind of criticism.

Partha Chatterjee is doing something which is very, very important. What he is trying to do is simply to say that the introduction of democratic institutions in India has historically bent, altered and changed these institutions and their internal logic and dynamics. Western logical theory is inadequate to capture these changes so we have to bend the language (which is what I think Partha is trying to do) and this is a very important enterprise. I also think that the term 'civil and political society' is a popular 'politically correct' yet difficult term. My initial response to Partha was: 'don't use the term 'political' because 'civil and political society' as used throughout Hegelian and other writings is so filled with condensations of earlier meanings that it is very difficult to completely void them and substitute something completely new. Here again we have a difference between the nature of the enterprise and the technical manner of its execution. Thus I agree with your second criticism but not with the first. I think the enterprise is very valuable and very important for people like Partha, me and you who are primarily students of Indian politics or sociology.

I am not sure why you used the term 'cognitive-evaluative' to characterize the Western frame because these are also qualities and properties of many of the frames. If you want to give a similar sort of nomenclature to the Indian frames, even if a singular Indian frame, what words would you use?

But let me now turn to the very significant and important question you have raised in your paper about a problem in current social science that suggests that the language in which we live our lives and the language in which we try to describe it are at very serious variance. This is a real predicament. But sometimes you seem to suggest that there is a kind of unfractured existent language which is just not accessed by us. Now if there is an existent unfractured language then there is not much of a predicament. All we need to do is to make a strong effort to reconnect with and recover that language if it is housed either in our classical or in our vernacular languages. I think we would have a much more serious predicament, and on that your paper is not entirely clear, if the language itself is actually complex and fractured in some ways.

I now come to the problem which is central to your and Balagangadhara's papers that is absolutely central to modern social science as coming from the West. How do we decolonize the thinking of our social scientists? Earlier I made the point that we are not equally decolonized. A part of our lives, the academic and intellectual part is in serious need of decolonization.

In this regard I make three points. First, the nature of the problem. My sense, to put it very crudely, is that the central problem of modern social science from the 1950s onwards is that though practitioners have accumulated vast amounts of empirical knowledge about non-Western societies, the theoretical language of analysis is essentially derived from a distillation of Western history, Western theory and with the experience of Western modernity. This very important problem has two levels: the theory itself and the very valid point that both of you have very persuasively and forcibly made, that even the descriptive level is shot through with theory. As a result it becomes problematic to say that we have empirical knowledge about these societies.

The next point is: what to do about it? And I have no simple way of putting this question to you but it would be a beginning if we start this way: how do we decolonize the conceptual knowledge of the social sciences? There are two ways of doing it. One way would be – and I did not get a very clear answer from your paper Vivek – the argument that you get in Gandhi. But before Gandhi I will give you an example of a Bengali thinker of the nineteenth century, Bhudev Mukhopadhaya, who thought deeply on these lines and adopted and adapted a very distinctive position. He wrote a book *Samajik Prabandho* where he had an argument that was very similar to Gandhi's. It is also expressed more theoretically than Gandhi's in the sense that he argues that we have internal conceptual languages and we should amend our use of them to understand our present reality. That does not seem to me to be very promising. To give an example: I have to think about Indian politics and when I look at the resources of at least the Sanskrit tradition on politics, the *Manu-Smṛti* and *Śukranīti* and so on, in order to bring the texts much closer to our time, I find they cannot provide the intellectual resources by which we can understand the present-day operations of Indian political institutions, but I might be wrong.

The second option which is implicit in what Partha tried to do and I also do in some way is about bending the language that we get from social science. We might start with that language and very often find that the concepts start functioning badly. If we are sensitive enough to try to change that, then we can begin by trying to produce a language which moves gradually away from the received language of modern social science from the West through our engagement with our reality. That is another way of changing the language but it is a very different way. So I would like to know what your sense is of how we move forward. It might be that neither of these seem to be the right way, maybe we need a different combination altogether, but I think we need to answer this clearly and give our own individual answers.

Finally I have a point about Gandhi. You say at various points in your paper; and I think there is resonance in what you get in Balagangadhara where he says that Indian frames of thought do not try to describe the world but to posit it, in a sense it is a logic of action. You also refer to this idea that Gandhi has a kind of an actional frame but I would like to see further explication of this term.

I think we all recognize that Gandhi does something very important and I will give two other examples of people who think very similarly, so that we have a small corpus of people who are trying to do the same thing. What Gandhi aims to do in *Hind Swaraj*, Tagore does through an essay called 'Swadeshi Samaja' in which at times the similarity of phrases and even locution between Tagore and Gandhi is very striking. And the third person who raises this question is K.C. Bhattacharya in his paper 'Swaraj in Ideas'.

But the problem that faces all of us who admire Gandhi for doing something that is very important and powerful is not that it is obscure, but that it has to be taken out of the form in which Gandhi has put it and replaced by a different one, because Gandhi's practice is primarily political and ours is predominantly intellectual. I think what you need to do with Gandhi is what Akeel Bilgrami tries to do, i.e. to think with Gandhi but set out the thoughts in a far more systematic form – go into the assumptions, explicate the structure of the argument and follow it through to the more proximate and more distant conclusions because from this then we have the possibility of the emergence of an alternative form of social science. So what exactly do you mean by the decolonization of modern social sciences and second, what exactly should we do in reading, let us say, texts like *Hind Swaraj* to take them forward?

Discussion

V. Dhareshwar

Sudipta Kaviraj has raised many very pointed questions but I will confine myself to just a couple of them. About Partha Chatterjee you said that the enterprise is itself important but I will try to answer your last question, whether there is an inner conceptual vocabulary. The way I have been trying to set up the problem does not or should not allow me to bend the terminology. It is not a matter of using Western concepts: you can use any concept. This is not a problem of purity. The problem is that we are not able to get hold of what we are trying to grasp. The actional world is stripped of its language. In fact in some way I would like to think that that is what Partha would like to do but his effort gets obscured by the terminological baggage he carries.

S. Kaviraj

Let me ask you a question about that. When you just said the actional world is stripped of its language, what do you mean? There must be a language in which the action is interpreted.

V. Dhareshwar

There are two senses to the word here. For one let us take the phenomenon of Anna Hazare: what happened to him? Nowhere does he measure up to Gandhi, but none today commands authority like he did. When he began his fast for the first time, I was struck by the fact that this old man had paralyzed the whole government, and he was left to recycle the whole language of corruption. But as a crusader against corruption he is demanding relief from the modern state while bringing additions from the same state. Partha is also doing that when he talks of political society and imagines that he wants to look at what he calls 'legality'; but legality is not the problem. The fact is: something is happening to the way the actional world functions, and I like to think that this is what Gandhi was trying to think about in *Hind Swaraj*, with the idea of *swaraj*. His is an attempt to revitalize reflection on experience with the help of some insights from the *Gītā*. I don't know if the anti-corruption movement had some real access to the actional world in the way *Hind Swaraj* did. Had this been so the movement would have gone in another direction, the frustrations would have been articulated differently. That is the sense in which I mean that our access to our experience becomes problematic and why I said that Ambedkar tried to express his frustration by converting to Buddhism, a fact which we write off with unease. I know some Buddhists who are themselves puzzled by this action: it is a phenomenon they cannot recognize.

On Matilal: It may be that this is one of the bad examples in his work but what troubles me is not so much that he makes it but that he then goes to examples like Antigone and others which do not illuminate anything. Matilal even recognizes the fact that Antigone is not faced with a moral dilemma. It follows that if one formulates Antigone's situation as a moral dilemma, one will be using language that is alien to the Greek world. Similiarly, the idea of a moral dilemma in terms of norms is totally absent in the *Gītā*. The question 'what are the norms that Arjuna is confronted with?' itself raises difficulties.

So bending terms is also a problem for people like me (at least for those of us who come from the left) as when for example we think that politics is something desirable, that to be political is a good thing. And then we go to the Western tradition to see what being political means. When I came across Balagangadhara's Heathen [*The Heathen in His Blindness*] I had just written this article on 'Sovereignty and History'. I knew there was a problem here with this idea of sovereignty and history but could see no way out. Balu's work allowed me to make a paradigm shift which basically was to look at these concepts as constitutive of what we might call Western experience, and they appear distinctive because social science is part of their experience. So we start looking upon this as a rupture, if you like, and then when you look at the whole debate on sovereignty you realize that it is not something that can just be taken over. With it one cannot make sense of something like the Gandhian project or our articulation of the Gandhian project as something in *Hind Swaraj* which is also present in Tagore. One cannot make sense of nationalism. If one makes sense of the notion of sovereignty and so on, it remains intuitive. It does not get articulated in a form that we now need. That is what I mean by saying that the task ahead is not so much the bending; when I look at what Partha says from the derivative discourse onwards, I see glimpses of this and the drawing back from it.

At the same time the call for a social theory is implicit in Gandhi even though he did not recognize it. This is the point I want to make when you say that I am not clear whether there is a language or just a structure. My reading of Gandhi is that *satyāgraha* is the setting up of a science of ethical learning. His intuition (and I think it is a profound one) about the Indian tradition is that it tries to set up as many sites of political learning as possible. I see *satyāgraha* as the setting up of a site of ethical learning. Gandhi said it can be practised anywhere against any one – against father, wife, the state. But the meaning is simply this: that being ethical obviously does not mean unreflectingly following any norms that are injunctions from outside.

Mohini Mullick

I find myself quite uncomfortable with the notion of decolonizing social science. What does it mean to even begin to think of decolonizing a science? You have to look at the whole set of presuppositions in the very setting up of a science. In fact I think much of what you say subsequently, and this is perhaps in both the papers, negates the attitude that is implicit and inherent in setting up a science. Vivek says quite explicitly: 'social science' is part of their experience. So it seems to me that it is almost a contradiction in terms to talk about decolonizing science. Modern science was born and evolved in a certain culture: it gave rise to a certain consciousness which resulted in the valorization of (scientific) rationality and a certain conception of method. It is that very culture that also gave rise to imperialism and the colonization of many countries of the world. An interesting question (which I cannot pursue here) is whether there is in fact an *internal* connection between the two, but you can, in any case, see the contradiction I am indicating. The contradiction here becomes more explicit because there is explicit talk about Gandhi's rejection of an attempted description of the world and setting up instead of an actional frame. That is he saw Indian tradition as one in which we learn how to *be* in the world – how to act in the world. I am suggesting that this goes contrary to the descriptive, explanatory and predictive framework that is essential to *science*.

Claus Oetke

I would like to suggest the following: Why not do something which I would call explicatory hardening so that we explicitly define certain terms for a certain area? For example we may define 'corruption' in this area to mean such and such, and then go on to prove that this concept is interesting. And this can be done by explicating definitions of, so to say soft and hard ingredients. We can partly quantify certain variables and also make certain more or less specific terms for a specific science. I tried that myself for example when explicating regional concepts for 'self' to be applicable in any philosophical context, and trying to show that this was a useful term. Thus we get some more hardening and the problem of being misunderstood is decreased because it is backed by an explicit definition. What are the necessary conditions of explication?

Aloka Parasher Sen

To answer both Sudipta Kaviraj and Vivek Dhareswar, I know we can't transplant ideas from the distant past to modern times, but then we were in search of an internal conceptual language and Sudipto thought it was very inconvenient if not useless to draw upon Manu or Kauṭilya or the *Arthasāstra*. So I was just wondering: what about the political language of dhamma? I am using this term 'political language' for *dhamma* but actually the *dhamma* of Aśoka breaks down the barriers between the political and the ethical, and also between what you call the political and civil society and so forth. This is a kind of political experiment within the intellectual or political intellectual tradition which we had in this country at that point of time. And I think the issues of corruption and what is moral are also addressed in that language. And again there is the untranslatability of this word *dhamma* which is not *dharma*. So I think there is some value in looking at this conceptual language which goes a little away from all these examples we have had from the nineteenth and twentieth centuries.

P.K. Mukhopadhyaya

What I find really troubling is the suggestion of the very frequent necessity of breaking or bending the existing language every time we have to search for the meaning of a new thought or concept that we encounter. How far can this breaking or bending of a language go? Is a third language not possible at all? There have been references made to the debate and the commonality between Gandhi and Rabindranath but I want to say that there were extreme differences in their work. Importantly, Rabindranath was a firmly committed internationalist and this must be contrasted with Gandhi's very conscious rejection of internationalism. This has to be taken very seriously, particularly by the social scientists. Vivek Dhareswar, when you think about moral dilemmas, you do not find any in the *Gītā*, not even in Arjuna's case. But a conflict of duties is precisely a case of moral dilemma and there are a number of such cases throughout the *Mahābhārata*. Arjuna again and again is troubled by conflicting duties and Śrī Kṛṣṇa again and again has to rescue him.

S.N. Balagangadhara

There have been many questions and my answers will straddle them together. But first allow me just one sentence which I address to Prof. Mukhopadhyaya. Let us take the word 'duty' for the moment. Conflict in duties does not give you a moral dilemma. For a moral dilemma to occur two necessary conditions must exist: the prescribed sets of duties must be completely logically consistent by virtue of which one is obliged to perform them all. A dilemma pertains to a situation where when one has an obligation to do *A* as well as an obligation to do *B*, but can in fact do only one. It is the perfect consistency of the system of duty that gives rise to the dilemma. A simple conflict will not create a dilemma: a choice between *A* and *B*, between a banana and an orange is not a dilemma. It becomes a dilemma when you want both and can have only one. So a moral dilemma cannot possibly describe a conflict of duties, if one uses the word 'duty' here. A conflict of *dharma*s is not a dilemma at all.

What I mean by decolonizing social sciences is a very simple thing. There are many domains today, sociology, political science, psychology, and anthropology that call themselves social sciences as distinct from the humanities. So I am not talking about decolonizing science in the specific sense given by Mohini Mullick. I do not consider the theories in these domains which call themselves social sciences to be science at all. Today, I see all of them without exception as ideologies. I call my project the 'Comparative Science of Culture', because existing theories are not social sciences.

For instance: political corruption refers to the act of an individual public servant who is part of a state or government and who acts against the public interest of the people or the interest of the state. Because the state has an interest which coincides with the interest of the society, then any action that supports an individual's interest is morally wrong. This is the meaning of political corruption.

I am very conservative. I want a scientific hypothesis in the sense that it solves a problem, has an explanatory potential and there is some way to test it. In this sense political theory is completely bankrupt. I proffer two hypotheses which at least minimally do what you expect an hypothesis to do.

The first is purely historical in nature. You raised a question about the moral evaluatory nature which comes from a completely Western ethic and is not Indian at all. We in India had our own forms of social organization. We had certain indigenous ways of governing, of organizing production. But with colonization came industrialization, bringing with it management institutions from the West; structures were imposed on native Indian industries, on native structures, which today are taught in MBA courses all over India. The result is institutional distortion, so that you come across extraordinary things that baffle management theorists.

More concretely: how were questions asked about tradition? Can we use the resources of our ancient Indian literature to tackle and explain this problem? I find the Indian tradition powerful because it can help generate scientific hypotheses beyond the reach of Western social scientists. That's why I am against the latter, not because they are Western. I am not against everything Western. Physics, Chemistry, Mathematics come from the Western tradition.

Part II

6

On the Availability of Ethics in India

P.K. Mukhopadhyay

THIS paper has two major parts. In the first part we discuss the following more general issues: (i) reasons for why we cannot hope to be able to render categories of classical Indian thought in English, whether literary or philosophical; (ii) reasons why one can still retain one's hope in the matter – some hope of intercultural and inter-lingual communication; and (iii) different dimensions of the problem of translation. The second part deals with the more specific problem of translating central concepts of moral thinking and literature of classical India into the English language in general and in the language of the contemporary Western philosophy in particular.

Many who think it is difficult if not impossible, to effect the sort of rendering in question, have in the back of their minds a belief that disciplines of knowledge like philosophy or even science are culture specific. They also rightly think that the difficulty in question is not unrelated to the further question of who are the persons expected to do the job of rendering categories of classical Indian thinking into English. Third, when we talk of the sort of rendering in question, the history of colonial rule in India and what is known as the Orientalist construction of India are bound to figure as a special context and background of the problem of translation of categories of thought of a subject country in the language of the rulers, whether by scholars of the ruling race or of the subject race.

One aspect of the problem that concerns us most is that many modern Indian scholars including philosophy professionals lack authentic and adequate, let alone deep understanding, of the thoughts and language of classical India and the categories that were used to express these thoughts. Partly to hide (consciously or not) this from others or even from themselves these scholars forcefully deny the alleged culture specific nature of the systems of thought like philosophy or ethics and the categories used there to describe, analyse or critique relevant issues, beliefs and practices. They behave as if there is no great problem of translation of the sort we are discussing here. The views of these optimistic, even complacent, scholars are based on a selective study of classical Indian literature. These are the people who translate the expression *mūrta*, when they meet this word or category in the literature of Nyāya-Vaiśeṣika philosophy, as concrete (as distinct from 'abstract' which they think is the right translation of *amūrta*). These people do not note that the same word occurring in ordinary language has an entirely different meaning from the meaning it has when it occurs in the technical if not formal language of a theory or Śāstra. These are the scholars who have thrown into great confusion the very idea of classical Indian thought. We will return to this situation and show how selective study, of the literature involving use of certain key categories like *dharma, anumāna,* etc. have led men consciously or unconsciously, to essentialise a single or preferred sense of a category leading to partial or even wrong rendering of the categories concerned.

I

Some General Observations and Examples of Mistranslation

There are not one but many problems of translation. Some of them are merely linguistic while others are primarily conceptual. Philosophers are more concerned with the latter, which is also deeper and a more difficult one that figures prominently in intercultural understanding and communication. Except in extreme cases these two sorts of problems of translation are not easy to distinguish. However, to cite one quick example of the problem of the first kind, there are languages that allow bilingual editions of texts in them and languages that don't. There are many bilingual editions of Greek, Roman, or German on the one hand and English on the other. Such editions are hardly possible, when the languages concerned are Sanskrit (particularly Sanskrit of philosophical texts) and English. The problem of translation here relates more to the nature and structure of the languages. We will be concerned here almost exclusively with the other kind of problem of translation where conceptual differences figure prominently.

Rendering in a different language the general thought categories or categories of particular disciplines of knowledge of a certain language and culture is so difficult and vexing, and there are so many examples of failed attempts that people may tend to give up all hope. Let us quickly take some examples. General thought categories used to divide the vast field of knowledge like *parā-vidyā* and *aparā-vidyā* (particularly the latter) seem to admit of no translation in English. Our practice of translating them respectively as disciplines of liberating knowledge and disciplines of useful knowledge may be deemed only as a nearest approximation. Similarly it may be thought unproblematic if one exercises adequate care and translates the word *jñāna,* a term of Indian theory of *pramāṇa,* as 'belief' (instead of translating it carelessly as knowledge) which is a term of standard epistemology of contemporary English language philosophy. For the translation satisfies the standard test of correct translation. Sentences like "a belief can be false as well as true" do not lose their basic meaning or truth value when the word *jñāna* replaces the word 'belief' in them (or vice versa). But still there remains the problem of conceptual difference. According to the conception of it in contemporary Euro-

American epistemology belief is as a rule propositional; but this may not be said about *jñāna* in classical Indian philosophy or *doxa* in early Greek philosophy.[1] Again though we continue to use the same word, 'belief' or 'knowledge' yet the conception of knowledge has undergone many changes – at one time it used to mean idea, later it came to mean as different a thing as sentential knowledge.[2] To cite another example, a number of professional philosophers of modern India tried for many years to formalize *anumāna* or theory of inference (as we find it particularly in the literature of Nyāya philosophy) in the language of modern formal logic of the West. It has been shown that each one of such attempts failed and this has been more or less admitted by those who made the attempts. Later on such attempts were silently given up and the project was shelved without any serious examination of the reasons why the attempts failed. If the scholars considered the possible reasons the results might have been illuminating. It is a common experience that sometimes failures are highly instructive. Another misconception is still alive. Having failed to find much resemblance between Nyāya *anumāna* and the notion of inference/argument in logic, many came to believe that Nyāya logic (theory of inference!) is epistemic logic. Nothing, however, can be farther from the truth. The situation in ethics, we will soon see, is hardly brighter. It is too well known that a number of European philosophers failed to find any philosophy in Indian culture and they said so explicitly. Their utterance can hardly be dismissed as simply idiosyncratic. It is equally widely known that there are authors of deep knowledge of Indian culture and literature who also clearly said that there was not much by way of ethical thought in the Vaidika literature. This remark did not spring from malice

---

1. P.K. Mukhopadhyaya, 2011, "Must Jñāna Be Propositional?", *Journal of Death of Philosophy BHU Anviksiki*, vol. 7.
2. I. Hacking, 1975, *Why Language Matters to Philosophy?*, Cambridge University Press.

or from ignorance of the language of the thoughts of classical India. They originated from cultural and conceptual differences.

Why One Should Still Be Sanguine

Against this general background deliberations envisaged in workshops such as the present one seem to be a non-starter unless we can show some good reason why and how rendering of texts and ideas into the language of another culture may be and should be made possible. We therefore begin by briefly indicating (1) the reasons which still incline us to believe that translation or better intercultural communication is and should be possible, (2) the value it has, and (3) different dimensions of problems of translation.

1. There is one basically wrong reason which makes people hopeful about the possibility of translation in question. It is the belief which many scholars consciously advocate, that academic disciplines or disciplines of knowledge like philosophy and science are not culture specific. This belief is not only wrong, it is resorted to often in order to defend one's inability or unwillingness to train oneself in the language and literature of the culture in question. However, there is one major and good reason why one should believe that rendering categories of Indian thought in English is possible. It is that (a) though there is no necessity that whatever we find in a culture by way of active or operative beliefs and practices of its people must have their (more or less perfect) analogue in another culture, it is unlikely that two (more or less equally) developed cultures would fail to have the same or similar major and broad concerns in the fields of life and knowledge. So it is not unreasonable to think that there is bound to be close parallelism in thoughts, doctrines and theories relating to the major areas of concern and knowledge in two different cultures; and

this largely compensates for the differences in the respective languages and linguistic or even conceptual apparatus.

2. The difficulty of intercultural translation and communication is not to be construed as a very good or compelling reason for cultural insularity. Even the sort of difficulties in question can indirectly awaken us to some hitherto unnoticed dimension of certain issues as well as truths and thus enrich our understanding and appreciation of our own as well as alien culture.
3. The problem of translation has many dimensions. Translation is an important issue in contemporary philosophy of language but the problem is more one of sociology, anthropology and cultural studies than mainstream philosophy. This is all the more so if the source culture is currently or was previously a subject culture and the target culture is the corresponding ruling (or once ruling) culture (or vice versa). The people of the ruling culture need (primarily for extra-academic purposes) to study and understand the beliefs and practices of the subject people and also record those in their own language. This is done by rendering them in the language of the ruling culture which involves rendering the categories of thought of the subject culture by using the allegedly corresponding categories of thought of the ruling culture. This in fact happened in the case of India when during the colonial period the people appointed by the British rulers (as well as foreign Indologists) translated works of classical Sanskrit texts, etc. of law (legal treatises including treatises or provisions of *dharma*) and literature into English. They took the help of local scholars but these scholars, even when the breadth and depth of their scholarship in the respective indigenous branches of knowledge was indisputable, had the same difficulty in

understanding the language and culture of the British people as the latter had in respect of those of India.

The study and understanding of the people of an alien culture and hence the translation they produced of Indian texts could not but be coloured by their background knowledge of respective subjects of their own culture as well as by their knowledge of their own language. This resulted not infrequently in the distortion of Indian culture and thought. While this could hardly be avoided, absolute cultural insularity is neither (strictly speaking) possible nor desirable. So we need to risk translating the thought of one culture in the language of another culture. But after some time the thought of possible risk tends to disappear from our explicit awareness; not only the foreigners but the native people also tend increasingly to overlook the distortions of the culture and thought of the concerned culture or become indifferent to them. This happened in the case of India during and after the colonial period. What idea many modern or contemporary Indians have about India is primarily the construction of the orientalists. Against this background scholars like Mariott wrote about the need for understanding India through Hindu categories.[3] The book bearing this title was dedicated to Radhakamal Mukherjee who in his writings displayed acute awareness of the distortions Indian culture had suffered in the writings about India in English.

It may be thought that it makes perfect sense to say that there is need to exercise caution while trying to understand an alien culture or rendering in one's own language the thoughts or categories of thought of some alien culture. In the present case it should be a problem for the English people of how to translate in their language, the thought categories of Indian culture. How can it be a problem for Indian scholars? Why are Indian scholars so concerned about it? The fact is, it is doubly

---

3 McKim Mariott, 1990, *India Through Hindu Categories*, University of Michigan and Sage Publication.

problematic for these scholars. Many Indian scholars do not have direct access to the language in which thoughts of Indian culture were originally written. In the scholarly world and the world of professional philosophers of India today, English is the language in which classical Indian thoughts are discussed and written. Though English is recognized in the Indian Constitution as one of India's languages yet it is not the original language used in disciplines of knowledge which flourished in classical India. Besides English is not even derived from Sanskrit, which was primarily the language in which thoughts were expressed and recorded in classical India. While modern Indian scholars use the English language for the purpose of describing or discussing Indian disciplines of knowledge of classical India, they cannot prevent smuggling in the associations which the expressions of English have in the culture of Europe or European thought. A randomly chosen example is the rendering of *varṇa* as caste: we unconsciously make a shift from a predominantly moral to a predominantly social context as these are distinguished in the European culture. And great distortion is created when *varṇaśreṣṭha* is translated in English as 'dominant caste'.

Many modern and contemporary Indians are so habituated to looking at Indian culture through the eyes of Europe that they hardly notice it. And many Europeans do not pay much attention to the fact that before they can render Indian thought in their language they need first to learn the nuances of the categories which are used in understanding, describing or rendering Indian thoughts – beliefs and practices of the people of India authentically. Thus the risk of distortion increases greatly. One hastily imposes European categories on Indian thinking.

In short we need to carefully understand first the people and the culture and then the fundamental categories we seek to translate in a different language. We further suggest that understanding cultural differences is a more secure way of authentic rendering than emphasizing too much the slightest similarity and parallelism. We need also to remember, as said before, that it is more likely than not, that more or less equally developed cultures will agree in their major concerns. If we keep all this in mind and do not seek, demand or construe rendering as exact translation, serious and sincere efforts are possible to reconcile the point made by sociologists like Mariott and the project of translating thought categories of a culture in a different language. Such translation, in the case of Indian categories, should follow, and not precede the understanding of Indian culture in terms of, what Mariott describes, as Hindu categories.

II

The Problem and Prospects of Rendering Categories of Indian Moral Thinking in English

We distinguish between translating into English the thought categories of classical India and the English translation of theoretical categories of science, philosophy or ethics of India. Categories of a certain theory of a culture can be translated in terms of the categories of the corresponding theories of a different culture. To put it differently, a theory can be translated into, or formalized within, the language of the corresponding theory of another culture. Failure to notice or emphasize this important distinction led many Indian authors of philosophical texts to translate thought categories and technical expressions of Western philosophy into, say, literary Sanskrit or Bengali and the like. They often translate the word 'idealism' as Bhavavāda and realism as Vastuvāda or *Vāstavavāda* and so on. Such practices are causing great harm to our academic enterprise. Translating thought categories of Indian philosophical literature of the classical period into philosophical English in general is what we are concerned with at present. One needs to bring it and keep it in one's explicit awareness that the expressions of the language of a certain culture have standard meanings and established associations (including historical associations) in that culture. These can create problems even when they are otherwise appropriate to translate thought categories of an alien culture. In such cases sometimes, accuracy of translation (of sense at least) is best served by making a departure from literal meaning. Many professional philosophers of modern India know the English language and philosophy sufficiently well but do not know classical Indian philosophy as well or the language in which it was originally written. But there are many who know both. Similarly there are many foreign Indologists who know the Sanskrit language and philosophical literature written in it quite well. And they fail to find in India anything comparable to the developed moral thinking of Europe. This is really what deserves serious attention and discussion. To give just one example Prof. Keith wrote that he did not find too much ethical thought in Vaidika literature; the little that he found there was "negligible and valueless". But Deussen was overwhelmed by the grandeur and nobility of thought in that very literature which, according to him, surpasses all that is available in other cultures.

Another important source of difficulty, as already discussed, is that in European culture it often happens that the expression remains unchanged but the corresponding ideas undergo several important changes in the course of history. (In this matter Sanskrit language and its expression are more stable in respect of meaning than the expression of English language.) This point can be best illustrated if one compares the two expressions *darśana* and philosophy. In the present context of translatability of classical Indian thought categories, etc. we need to emphasize the well-known fact that the word ethics, as also *dharma*, *vidhi*, duty, etc. mean so many disparate things. So we begin with the difficulty of deciding what if anything in classical Indian thought and literature can be legitimately translated as ethics. We can similarly ask the question if philosophy of language is available in India. Now ethics in the sense of a certain identifiable broad concern or natural disposition, to borrow a term from Kant, is certainly available in every developed culture. Thus quite independent of moral institutions or ethical theory man carries a sort of sensitivity which is the sign of his being a moral man or having morality. There is a well-known saying in Indian culture (there are similar sayings in other cultures too):

> *idam puṇyam idam pāpam etyetasmin padadvaye asamudra manuṣyanām alpam śāstra prayojanam*

This means, in short, man does not need ethics to be moral. What then is ethics and what need does it serve? Ethics is best understood as moral theory and like other theories its task is to provide the criterion needed to decide borderline cases and bridge the gap between beliefs on the one hand and the evidence we have for them. That such cases exist and the need for theory exists is well attested by the *Bhagavad-Gītā "kimakarmakimkarmet kavayopymohitai"*. That is even God finds it difficult to decide what one should or should not do. Throughout the *Mahābhārata* Arjuna is repeatedly found to suffer from indecision of a sort that can rightly be said to be moral indecision which one suffers in the context of conflict of duties.

Once we go beyond or outside the sphere of broad concerns and gut feelings it becomes difficult to decide what, if anything in Indian culture corresponds, strictly speaking, to ethics as theory of morals or to the distinction between ethics and meta-ethics, normative ethics, theoretical ethics and so on. Rough correspondences and near parallels are always found. What is however difficult to meet but should be met is the demand that cultural insights find their adequate representation in the translation in an alien language. What are the important cultural differences between ethical thinking and whatever is supposed to correspond to it in classical Indian culture?

Not only normative ethics (or code of conduct and/or scheme of values) but also the philosophy of morals of a country are informed by its conception of man – his nature and destiny – as well as of the meaning and purpose of his life in the world. Among the pervasive thoughts of India are: (i) man is (born) a suffering being, (ii) men are born unequal, (iii) though life's highest fulfilment and goal are the same for all, and (iiia) all are destined to attain it through they may do so through largely different ways and means – by performing different sets of actions which are therefore appropriately enjoined on them. There are other differences also which we will soon describe but rooted in the Indian views just listed, is a feature of Indian ethical thinking which inclines European scholars to deny that there has ever been such a thing as ethics in India. The feature in question is the lack of universalism. Many have argued that Indian society is too discriminative to allow ethics to develop. For universalism is at the very heart of ethics or better morality, so far as European culture is concerned. For example those who advocate "the good-reasons approach", and do not accept exclusively either emotivism or cognitivism in ethical theory maintain that no matter how emotive or performative moral utterances may be, when we make a moral judgement, it must – logically must – satisfy certain requirements to count as a moral judgement. In making a moral judgement, we must be willing to universalize the judgement in question and it must be possible to give factual reasons in support of the oral claim. European sociologists also think along the same line. Max Weber's work in the field is the best example. He and other scholars like him tend to emphasize the caste system and the beliefs and practice of *svadharma*.[4] Weber even believed that in India there was no universal ethic, "but only a status and professionally differentiated *dharma* according to caste". It is a different matter however that Weber grossly misunderstood the idea of *svadharma* or extended it to an absurd limit. It is

---

4 Max Weber, 1935, *The Religion of India*, The Free Press Macmillan, NY, Hans Gerth and Don Matrindate.

interesting to note that the presence of that which determined men like Weber to miss ethics in Indian culture led some otherwise highly knowledgeable scholars of India to emphasize *sādhāraṇa dharma*. This emphasis may be due to the influence of a modern European mentality on aspects of Hindu ethics which display universalism at the cost of those other aspects in which Europeans find evidence of the lack of universality in the so-called moral beliefs and practices of Hindu society as well as in its theory of morals. These Indian scholars emphasize *sādhāraṇa dharma* more than *varaṇāśrama dharma*. Kane's work is a case in point.[5]

Before we proceed to further details of the difficulty of rendition in question, we would like to mention some other broad features of Indian culture and perspective which determined what in India corresponds to ethical thinking in Europe and America. Multiple life ideology as against single life ideology on the one hand and soteriological orientation on the other, have profoundly affected the moral thinking and practices of the Indians. Again in the European view morality is by and large social morality. But in Indian culture it is society that is conceived of as moral. This has profound implications for the question of the source and justification of moral ideas and practices. And this was an issue that was hotly debated during the national movement of India – and men who were involved in the debate include such noted personalities from outside mainstream philosophy as Mahatma Gandhi and Rabindranath Tagore.

Now what are the central categories of moral thinking? What are the categories used to distinguish philosophical writings on morals from philosophical writings on epistemology for example? India's classical literature, philosophical writings and thinking cannot be exactly fitted into Western philosophical

[5] P.V. Kane, 1936, *History of the Dharmaśāstra*, 5 vols., Poona: Bhandarkar Oriental Research Institute.

categories such as metaphysics, epistemology, logic, ethics and so on. Broad divisions used to be drawn between Prameyaśāstra or Padārtha-śāstra as theory of object – regardless of whether the object is ethical, metaphysical or whatever – and Pramāṇaśāstra or theory of knowledge. Regarding matters moral we have in classical Indian thought and literature categories like *karma* (human action), *vihita karma* (positive duty), *niṣiddha karma* (negative duty), *codana* (moral injunction), *dharmapravṛtti,* etc. Some other important categories are *pravṛtti-lakṣaṇa dharma, nivṛtti-lakṣaṇa dharma, niṣkāma karma,* etc. And there are also discussions about how we can know of these things and how we know that our beliefs in these matters are true or false as the case may be.

Theories and/or literature about *dharma* are mainly of two kinds, hortatory texts and parts of philosophical works. The former deal primarily with normative ethics or codes of conduct and injunctions which enjoin them. The philosophy of morals deals with the analysis of moral concepts, tests of the truth of moral judgements and justification of moral principles. Hortatory literature is basically of three kinds: Śruti, Sūtra and Saṁhitā; in addition there are *nibandha*s.

Let us now turn to some specific categories of Indian moral theory and thinking. *Dharma* and *vidhi* are among the broad and central terms in this sphere. It is now an old cliché that *dharma* is not and cannot be translated as religion. It is widely translated as duty. We may note in passing that religion which some distinguish sharply from *dharma* actually comes under the purview of *dharma* injunctions. Second, the word *dharma* is ambiguous and in some of its uses and senses it cannot be translated as duty. However, there is a sense in which *dharma* stands for a certain kind of action. But this does not warrant us to think that it is unproblematic to translate *dharma* as duty since duty means morally right action. The majority of *dharma karma*s are not only enjoined by moral authority (*vihita*) but also deliver good results (*artha*). Again *vihita* cannot be understood to mean primarily or solely what is socially approved. Scripture is the primary source of our knowledge of *dharma*. This is believed so literally and absolutely that when certain actions are found to be performed by all men of a certain description we are permitted to infer appropriate scriptural injunctions in case no such injunction is available in the extant scripture. Again moral injunctions are sentences which are prescriptive in form and nature but these are also believed to be at the same time descriptive. One more point to note is that in classical Indian moral theory the idea of the "prescriptive" is not radical. In European philosophy the division of sentences into descriptive and prescriptive is too radical to allow the same sentence to be both. And this has its analogue in the division of fact and value. In Indian moral thinking no injunctive sentence in the field of *dharma* can fail to be descriptive also.

In Indian thinking the scope of *dharma* is very wide and the actions it covers admit of division in European eyes into rites (religious or magical) such as sacrifices and enabling performances (*saṁskāra karma*), duties (such as the study of the Veda) and soteriological practices (*yama* and *niyama*). It even includes *iṣṭapūrta* which can be best described as social service. Sometimes *dharma* is extended to cover *vyavahāra* as distinct from *ācāra* or *dharma* proper. These are actions that come under the purview of legal considerations or jurisprudence.

It is very hard to find any parallel in Western ethical theory to the division of *dharma* into *pravr̥tti-lakṣaṇa* and *nivr̥tti-lakṣaṇa*, or *dharma* for worldly people and *dharma* for ascetics. Similarly the concept of *nitya karma* (unconditional duty) restricted to a particular group (*varṇa* or *āśrama*) is almost impossible to translate into English.

Again *dharma* involves essential reference to the non-natural. It has been said that *dharma* is the non-natural (*alaukika*) means to attain a non-natural good. Ethics being goal oriented, seems to lack autonomy; it is not an end in itself. Further this goal is good and commendable, its affective value is positive or pleasurable. However, it is pleasure of a kind which is attainable at some cost which normally men are not willing to pay. The natural tendency of man is to desire pleasures that are not too distant, that can be achieved in real time and that can be had at a cost which is not too great. *Anāyasa-labhya* and *acira-labhya sukha* and *duḥkha-abhāva* are man's natural objects of desire and his natural goal of life. Men who desire such pleasures or goals naturally have a desire to perform actions that will lead to these goals. It is natural desire (*rāga*) that motivates a man to perform these natural actions. These actions are therefore called *rāgaprāta*. Dharmaśāstra or *vidhi* has no function or authority in respect of these actions. There are, however, other actions which are means to a greater and higher good and pleasure which rationally should be done, but for which men have no natural inclination. Injunctions not only state these actions as worth doing but also compel us to do them. Thus injunctions, in the case of these actions substitute for (natural) desire in other kinds of actions. This is what is meant by *dharma*. This view led to the development of a highly intricate theory of language as the seat of moral force. This also has no parallel in ethics.

It may be thought that this account of *dharma* might suit the paradigmatic cases of *yajña* but not of such other *dharma karmas* (moral actions) as truth telling or non-violence. How does the above account of *dharma* apply to these cases? It may seem that the account of *dharma* as in the Mīmāṁsā is not in agreement with the account of *dharma* found in the *Gītā* and the *Prajñādarśana*, say.

We cannot decide if 'duty' can be the right translation of *dharma*. But this translation is central to what is called Indian ethics. We will miss the very basis of what is called Indian ethics if this translation is not permitted. The Indian conception of *dharma* includes such diverse actions and practices which are very difficult to bring under one head and certainly many of these actions do not resemble duty.

The above account makes it impossible to render the categories of Indian moral thinking in English. But we suggest that this is not so great a loss as some may want us to believe. For the very fact that we can identify and express important differences in otherwise parallel conceptions of diverse cultures, intercultural communication and communication in alien language of culture-specific matters including thought categories are largely possible. The risk of distortion can also be minimized if we take the pain of acquainting ourselves thoroughly and deeply with both the source and culture and their respective languages. In short we should go for intercultural communication rather than direct translation of expressions of one culture in the language of a different culture.

RESPONSE

Purushottam Aggarwal

Regarding this colonial sense of inferiority, that any absence is a sign of deficiency I completely agree with you that absence produces a sense of deficiency. This is itself reflective of a colonized mentality, and quite naturally this colonized mentality has outlived colonialism per se, not only in academic but also in popular discourse. Sometimes when the two levels of the popular and the academic converge, then you get some very interesting, at times hilarious, if not at the same time, problematic results.

I have in mind the last visit of the Pope to India in 1998 or 1997, when the Hindutva forces were organizing demonstrations against his visit. An advertisement was issued in all the national papers by hundreds of *dharmācāryas* led by Sri Sri Ravi Shankar welcoming the Pope and requesting him to remove misgivings prevalent amongst Christians that Hinduism is not a monotheistic religion, and therefore they should cease trying to convert Hindus, who already have a monotheistic tradition. In other words being monotheistic becomes a *lakṣaṇa* of religion or *dharma*, and since we are charged with not being monotheistic Hindus have to prove that they also are monotheistic. Personally, as a Hindu, I believe that it is a great asset of my tradition that we are not monotheistic. I have my reservations about the term 'pagan' used by Wagishji yesterday, but the fact remains that not being monotheistic cannot be a deficiency: it is in fact a positive asset.

Second, Prof. Mukhopadhyay is absolutely right in his paper where he has written about the problem of rendering "the thought categories of a particular culture into another culture – that it is more a problem of sociology, anthropology and cultural studies than mainstream philosophy". I feel that the very discipline of anthropology has a certain inbuilt colonial prejudice. There is sociology for industrial societies, sociology for advanced societies and anthropology for primitive societies. While it is not exactly pertinent here, this observation of yours brings to my mind the tragi-comedy of the translation of *Manu-Smr̥ti* in the eighteenth century. The colonial rulers wanted to understand the Hindu system of law, discipline and punishment and instituted a project of translation. The head or supervisor of this project, Mr Hallhead knew no Sanskrit. So the text was translated first from the Sanskrit into Bangla, from Bangla into Persian and from Persian into English, after which it was published as *The Hindu System of Discipline and Punishment*. Sir William Jones found this translation absolutely ridiculous if not corrupt. But he attributes the corrupt nature of the translation to the corrupt nature of brāhmaṇas in particular and Indians in general, completely overlooking the peculiar and ridiculous process adopted for the translation. So translation in many ways becomes a colonial activity, instead of a dialogical exercise. Instead of a means of understanding the other, it became an exercise in domination through the so-called understanding.

The third point I would like to introduce for discussion is whether the best way to deal with translation problems is to retain the original terms. There is no need to translate *dharma* into religion or Nyāya into logic and so on. But can we adopt this practice beyond a point? It may be feasible in very strict academic discourse but not necessarily at a more general or popular level. For example, should we retain the term 'democracy' in Hindi instead of using *lokatantra* or other equivalent terms in other Indian languages? Do we wait for our own categories to evolve into linguistic constructs in our own language?

Another problem: there has to be some kind of universality or some kind of universally analogous nature for the concerns and imaginations of all human beings that, theoretically speaking, in a positive sense is the *raison d'être* of translation, that even if I cannot speak this particular language I can perhaps understand it. Or a translation is possible because of the presence of universal features or characteristics of consciousness, without which translation, even from Bangla to Hindi will not be possible. I remember when I read the Bengali classics as a young boy (for any north Indian youngster, reading Tagore or Sarat Chandra was part of growing up) I found and was puzzled by the word *puṣkarṇī* in a Sarat Chandra novel. A Bengali gentleman explained that despite its being so high sounding; it just meant a pond behind the house, nothing very pious and lofty as I had presumed. So translation problems need not always result from colonial relationships. Can we evolve some strategies to deal with domination in translation, because in the case of history and various academic disciplines, with their inherent eurocentricity, translation has been a source of domination. The challenge for scholars from the non-West is to change this domination, not only vis-à-vis Europe, but maybe also within and outside South Asia.

Why this exercise is extremely important is my last point.

In his fascinating book, *The Heathen in His Blindness*, Prof. Balgangadhara has given not only a number of examples but has also analysed them in a thought-provoking way, bringing out the violence in the so-called attempt to understand the non-West – which includes not just India but China, Japan – all other traditions. I largely agree with him that there cannot be a society without a religion; even where there is no religion we have to impose one to give meaning to a society. So can we think of ways where translation becomes indeed an exercise in dialogue instead of domination?

DISCUSSION

Wagish Shukla

To start from the last observation of Purushottam Aggarwal, it is not only religion that has to be imposed. There are many serious thinkers in the West who believe that any society which does not have an alphabet is not worth studying, or is not a civilization. I have given specific examples in my paper. By alphabet I mean strictly the alphabet, not any system of writing, i.e. there must be an aleph and bet as in the Hebraic system or *A* and *B* as in the Roman. There are many societies and many serious thinkers, even scientists who believe that the wheel is the basis of science. If a society does not have the wheel, it has no science. This entirely rules out the consideration of the Incas as a civilization, because they did not have any system of writing and no wheel. It is worth remembering that the Inca civilization or empire or state, was larger than the Spanish state which invaded and destroyed it. So what constitutes a civilization or a culture has indeed been an extremely brutal and narrow concept. But this apart, let us not worry about what others have been saying or thinking about us or other non-West civilizations.

Since *dharma* has been mentioned, let me ask as a specific question; let us forget the problem of translation for the time being. In the *Bhaviṣya Purāṇa* there is a situation based on the *Mahābhārata* where the Pāṇḍavas say that they have not fought enough, they have not been given an opportunity to show off their valour, and there are also some appeals that the Kauravas should be given at least one chance to win. In response Kṛṣṇa says 'alright, we will do this and initiate the Kaliyuga' or 'I will do the *dharmasthāpanā* of Kaliyuga'. Now whether Vyās or somebody else wrote the *Bhaviṣya Purāṇa*, the author of this sentence could not have been unaware of the following sentence in the *Bhagavad-Gītā: dharma-saṁsthāpanārthāya sambhavāmi yuge yuge* — in every *yuga* I will be here so as to do the *dharmasthāpanā*. Reading these two together, the question arises, where do we seek the *dharma* of the Kaliyuga? There are two possibilities. It is either to quash or destroy the *garv*, the pride of the Pāṇḍavas or it is simply to establish the *dharma* in the Kaliyuga where evil will triumph. Which of the two possible meanings should I adopt? (Regardless of whether I know any English or any colonial interpretation.)

Now add to this a passage from *Yogavāsiṣṭha* in which Vasiṣṭha, confined in a rock *vyavasthā*, is relating his various incarnations. He says: 'I saw many worlds in which there were no Vedas, no Śāstras, no caste system no *varṇa-vyavasthā*, and I saw many worlds in which Rāma killed Rāvaṇa and many other worlds in which Rāvaṇa killed Rāma'. Now this kind of statement, apart from indicating that there are possible worlds in which the basic systems which are explicitly recognized as Hindu or Brāhmanic – superficially I must add – do not pertain (and *dharma* as we understand it depends on most of these things), claims that there are distinct indicators that such worlds can exist. If there is a possibility of creation in which all these basic physicalities, so to speak, are absent, what is the concept of *dharma* to which no doubt apart from all the *darśana*s. . . . *Yogavāsiṣṭha darśana* also adheres to. . . .

Mukhopadhyay

Yes it is absolutely necessary that translation should not be a weapon of domination. If it is not obvious it has to be investigated. I completely agree with you: what is the point if I cannot communicate with my father or brother or friends if human language necessarily means that it is used as a means, as a vehicle of domination.

So it should be possible. But at the same time, there is always the danger – as I told you – certain problems cannot be resolved. We have only two options: either we live with this language and the difficulties intrinsically associated with it or we give it up. But we cannot give it up because we are human beings and without language we cannot live, and at the same time we cannot free this language from these possibilities. So we have to learn to live with certain problems. But we should not add to these problems, as does the colonial mentality, introducing that which is neither inherent in language, nor inherent in human beings, nor inherent in the Śāstras. These are avoidable problems.

Before I partially respond to Wagish Shukla's observation, I have to clarify a little more about *dharma*.

In the first place I again come back to this modern mentality of first contesting that everyone has misunderstood *dharma*, and then while explaining and translating *dharma* we fall into the trap of (using) their selfsame categories. In the attempt to explain and translate *dharma* and related categories, with awareness of what the West wants us to take within in order that they can accept it, apparently we try to show that the West is wrong in understanding our ideas. But in fact we fall prey to their categories. I take one or two examples, of which one is not that useful. In his recent book – *Being Different* – the author very forcefully argues that Indian categories cannot be translated; he gives a list of such categories and the first is of course *dharma*. *Dharma* cannot be translated into Western languages because

Western and Eastern cultures are so different. And when he tries to show what the differences are he falls prey to the same Orientalist construction, scientific analytic vs. the mystic. He says that talking of cultures – there are various categories – I had pointed out that some Western categories divide cultures into scientific–religious and analytic–mystic, and he employs these very categories – analytic and mystic. He uses analytic for the West – then where to place the other? – into the only other category, mystic. There is no other. This is exactly what the Westerners say.

When the West does not find any ethics in India what are they missing? Weber makes a very clear statement that India cannot have an ethics or a morality or a moral theory because India does not have a moral society. His argument is that India's is a fragmented society made up only of castes. A caste society is fragmented, so there cannot be any *dharma.* Balagangadhara rightly again and again points to the assumption of universalism. The West believes that without universality there can be no morality: Indian society is fragmented so there is no morality. They fail to understand our attitude. Today we also play their game: we have concocted an expression 'unity in diversity'. What does it mean? – nothing. Traditionally, Indians did not view this 'fragmentation' negatively. If the West tried to find out how we managed these diversities and differences they would find that the stability and growth of society is preserved only through diversity. If one uses force to remove these diversities there is bound to be conflict. They do not understand that diversity is a conflict management technique. Prof. Kane observes that because Weber does not find any universality, the only example of *dharma* he has taken is *svadharma* – that is *dharma* according to *varṇa* and *avarṇa* and he has carried it to such an extent that he says, well if this is so then *dharma* is so fragmented that even dacoits have their own *dharma* – which is not the meaning of *svadharma.*

Kane in his most comprehensive book *The History of the Dharmaśāstra* deliberately avoids discussing *varṇāśrama dharma*. He only discusses *sādhāraṇa dharma* and takes his definition of *dharma* not from Mīmāṁsā, or Dharmaśāstra but from *Arthaśāstra*. Why does he ignore the Dharmaśāstra? He notes the usage in Dharmaśāstra but prefers to use *dharma* as in the *Arthaśāstra*. He clearly says that if there is *only universal dharma and the varṇāśrama, then dharma has gone.*

Now I come back to Wagish's observation. What is *dharma,* if one studies the text? I have not studied it as proficiently as Prof. Wagish – there is a very clear statement on *dharma,* as to why there should be *dharma* at all? The story goes that *dharma* was the second creation of God. His first was *jagat*. . . . After the *sṛṣṭi* of *jagat* the question arose, how to preserve it – *rakṣā – dharma rakṣā, jagat rakṣā, sṛṣṭi rakṣā*. For the *rakṣā* of *sṛṣṭi* he had to create *dharma*. *Rakṣā* means preservation; as a mother preserves her *santāna* to ensure stability and growth, *dharma* is used to ensure stability and growth. Now when the Purāṇa asks whether the Pāṇḍavas or Kauravas will survive and which will be the corresponding *dharma*; whether *dharmasthāpanā* will come through the triumph of the Pāṇḍavas or the victory of the Kauravas. In *Bharata Savitri* you know what Pāṇḍava and Kaurava meant. The Pāṇḍavas personify *dharma* and Kauravas *adharma*, so the definition of *dharma* in different ages varies. Of course, we have *deva dharma, manuṣya dharma, dānava dharma* – Rāvaṇa was a great dhārmic. So the question is whether *dharma* or *adharma* survive, because the death of a society occurs only when there is *dharma-viplava*. When there is *adharma* then there *sṛṣṭi* is finished.

Kaviraj

I wanted to make three remarks. I like very much what you said and also what Purushottam said towards the end, about translation, and I would put it with a slight modification – the anxiety of domination. But the two comments are slightly different.

I think in translation we must remember that language is internally complex; it is a heterogeneous entity and different parts of language, like speech and writing work differently. I think what we should try to do as translators is to try to replicate – I do not know how it can be done but we cannot do it if we do not see the need for it – replicate in writing what we spontaneously do in speech. Which is that, you say that this is *dharma*, I say this is religion, you say, do you mean religion and I say no I do not mean religion – I mean this. So there is a dialogical quality in that sense. And dialogical quality also requires a temporal coming back, which is very difficult to do in writing but I think we should try to devise ways in which something that can be done in speech can be imitated in a certain sense in writing.

The second point: I would say that today the notion that English is the ruler's language is both true and false. It is true in some ways, false in others. I will give you an example which troubles me, again because I think our society, our cultures, are to a large extent already de-colonized in some parts though not in all. As a student of politics, I look at how politicians behave, how they behaved during Nehru's time, their political imagination at that time was heavily dominated by the West, they were steeped in Western history, Western categories which acted as constraints: before taking simple actions they asked themselves whether this is something I can see in the British parliamentary proceedings. In a certain sense that kind of imaginative control or domination in our politicians' thinking has receded. Today they do not know about European history, and they are freed of the anxiety of being concerned whether what they are doing conforms with a European precedent. Large parts of our society have been freed from the weight of European history but it has not lifted from the intellectual culture of our society. There again the picture is not uniform: in literature it has lifted. It is in academic life that de-colonization is a very serious problem even now, and my suggestion would be that we should think about it instead of simply saying it is wrong. Obviously it is wrong. But the question is to find out why it has not gone, because now it is not the British who force us to read Hobbes and Locke, we read them ourselves. It would be simplistic to say that we should not blame colonialism, but we must find other ways than only relating these problems to colonialism.

Dhareshwar

My question relates to the remark you made, which I think is very right in the sense that there is no reason to take offence about some remark from the West and take it as devaluation. There are incidents even as late as the early twentieth century of people like Ramakrishna who were completely indifferent to what was said. In fact, he used to converse with the Brahmo reformers just out of curiosity but he had no anxiety. So the question is: is it a fact that in the philosophical community these were taken seriously? The very fact that you began to remould the content of whatever was called Indian thought in the Western philosophical mould itself shows that it was taken seriously. So this remark is valid but you can always find people like Ramakrishna and Ramana Maharshi who were completely free of this. The interesting question, surely for us is: what happened to the tradition? What happened to Indian philosophy for example? With more research, as Mohini said we should be ready to say that there is no Indian philosophy. Maybe, I should say Indian thought. So isn't that the question to ask: what prevented the development of Indian thought?

Ramkrishna Bhattacharya

Mine again is not so much a question but an observation. When we speak of *dharma*, why should we confine ourselves to the Brāhmanic tradition only? After all the Buddhists and the Jainas are no less conscious about the impact of *dharma*. In fact, Aśoka's inscriptions were the first to be translated so far as Indian history is concerned, they were translated into Greek and Aramaic and there the word *dharma* always posed a problem. *Dharma* could not find its proper equivalent either in Greek, Hebrew or Aramaic. So the term *eusebia* . . . or some word in Greek which meant justice was used. And that's how it all started. And *dharma* is a central concept to *ahiṁsā* both in the Buddhist and Jaina traditions. *Ahiṁsā paramo dharmaḥ* is something that is on the lips of everybody amongst the Jainas and the Buddhists as well. So would you say, that all these things have a singular point of reference or do they emanate from different sources.

Claus Oetke

Regarding domination I think we should make a conceptual differentiation because this word can be used in a stronger and weaker sense. The stronger sense is 'ruling' and in the weaker sense it is like 'prevalent'. And regarding the stronger sense, I find it extremely implausible to say that any way of translation or interpreting can be a means of domination because it is counter-intuitive, at least, because the normal view of the Orientalist studies is that they are too irrelevant for them to perform the function of domination. So if it were clear that the enterprises of translation and interpretation could ever be a means of domination in the stronger sense, then it is entirely incomprehensible, why.

But in the weaker sense, in the sense of prevalence, it makes (to me at least) a certain kind of sense with certain demands that hang together with the existence question. So actually it is a matter of fact that the questions which are prevalent are always present in every culture; something like our ethics or what we see as ethics or what we see as philosophy, is to be found everywhere. It is true in the sense that these questions are natural ones because every culture looks for, or every citizen

him took the liberty of understanding its foundational essence in the scientific category of 'race' to build a comprehensive conception of Indian 'caste' society. They also consciously brought with them the baggage of framing their ideas through the prism of Christianity. A couple of years before Wilson compiled his magnum opus, the missionary contact with the subcontinent had already made this assumption. Thus for instance, Rev. Sherring wrote:

> . . . in designating many castes I have frequently employed the word 'tribe', and not the word 'caste', and have preferred the use of ethnological terms to a term which is used only very partially in an ethnological sense, and is associated with other and different questions.[6]

These (other and different questions) were garbed in Sherring's aversion to and utter disdain for 'the Hindoo institutions', which he regarded 'as monstrous engines of pride, dissension, and shame, which could only have been invented in an utterly diseased condition of human society'. He goes on to give us his total perspective when he states that ". . . intense conviction is, that, next to the universal prevalence of the Christian faith, the greatest boon to India would be the absolute and complete renunciation of caste".[7] In a similar vein Wilson too prefaced his remarks on defining 'caste' when he asserted that:

> [i]t is emphatically the curse of India and the parent of India's woes. It is the great enemy of enlightenment and improvement and advancement in India. It is the grand obstacle to the triumphs of the Gospel of peace in India.[8]

Apart from the missionary zeal of these writers, for the British administrators, the late nineteenth century was a difficult period. It was one of tremendous change and therefore of flux

---

6 M.A. Sherring, 1974, *Hindu Tribes and Castes as Represented in Benares*, Delhi, repr., p. xxiii.

7 Ibid., pp. iv-v.

8 Wilson, op. cit., p. 12.

in both ideological and political terms. This often led to a need to deeply understand and continually reformulate their attitude and policy especially in relation to the diverse population of the subcontinent.

The imagining of 'caste' in this way got great impetus from a publication on tribes and castes by Sir Herbert Risely that stabilized the earlier views and articulated the official stand on how Indian 'caste' society was to be understood.[9] In the 1909 edition of the same book Risely added two new chapters to the earlier edition, in which he assessed the role caste might play in the future of India's political development. Here he approvingly quoted Sir Henry Cotton to the effect that "the problem of the future is not to destroy caste, but to modify it, preserve its distinctive conceptions and to gradually place them upon a social instead of a supernatural basis".[10] Risely, of course, was not alone in his formulations. Rather, he can be taken as an example of the most systematic manifestation of the way caste was in the process of being reconstituted in the colonial period. As pointed out by Sekhar Bandhopadhyaya, the prominent concern for the British was to put in place social controls that would ensure the maintenance of the British Empire after 1857 and that could only be done by keeping Indian society neatly compartmentalized into castes.[11] Likewise, Dirks aptly argues that "the constitution of caste as a necessary complement to social order and governmental authority, a new kind of civil society for the colonial state" was essential for governance and a means to control as diverse a society as India's.[12]

The theoretical and methodological parameters embedded

---

[9] Sir H.H. Risely, 1891, *The Tribes and Castes of Bengal*, Calcutta.

[10] Ibid., p. 282.

[11] Sekhar Bandhopadhyaya, 1990, *Caste, Politics, and the Raj: Bengal 1872-1937*, Calcutta: K.P. Bagchi & Co., pp. 10-30.

[12] Nicholas Dirks, 1992, "Castes of Mind", *Representations*, Winter, **37**: 71.

in categorizing, naming and understanding 'caste' within the broader colonial context were thus implicit in their task of administering the conquered peoples. The vagaries of administrative tasks on hand especially when ethnographic data from India began to pile up, ensured that certain predilections came to the forefront that made even census officials admit:

> At each census the question arises which of them should be classed as Hindus, and which as Animists or worshippers of their own tribal gods, and *though the classification is necessarily very arbitrary,* the process can be clearly observed (emphasis added).[13]

Much work has been done on understanding the labelling and understanding of 'castes' and 'tribes' in the colonial context and it is well-recognized that classifications were made so as to provide a rationale for the policies of imposition – political, economic and cultural – that had begun when the British first came into contact with the myriad peoples of India.[14] In this context it has been pertinently pointed out[15] that in the colonial context "these communities were given different appellations and thus most such 'peoples' have come to be known by names they did not recognize themselves, while widely dispersed masses of people were brought under a blanket nomenclature".[16] In fact, today the Indian nation state collapses earlier identities but uses these new terms like 'tribe' to essentially define a politico-administrative category that hardly has any socio-cultural specifications and organic link to cultural practice. Interrogating what we mean by 'tribe' is

---

13 R.V. Russell, and Hiralal, 1916, *Tribes and Castes of Central India and Berar*, p. xi.

14 B. Cohn, 1987, *An Anthropologist Among Historians and Other Essays*, New Delhi: Oxford University Press, pp. 249-50.

15 Arvind Das, 1992, *India Invented: A Nation in the Making*, New Delhi: Manohar, pp. 58-72.

16 Ibid., pp. 58-59.

not however, an irrelevant academic exercise. It is necessary because we need to question certain erroneous stereotypes of 'peoples' that imply that the oldest inhabitants of the land had shallow histories or none at all. Further, the way their names, territories and languages were remembered has hardly any relevance to the way they perceive themselves. The new modern ways of identity formation as rigid and frozen categorizations impede our understanding of the complex nuances of the way in which the distinctions between the so-called 'tribes' and the other social aggregates like the peasant castes were maintained in the past. They have also removed any sensitivity that we may have had to understand the contemporary self-perception of the concerned people by erasing the names that they were known by. Working only within a modern framed concept like ethnicity is beset with debates and tribulations of the present. A pertinent example is the Indian nation-state's dealing with the north-east – the perpetual fear of an erasure of earlier identities looms large for innumerable groups in the region.

There are questions regarding the accuracy of interpretations of a social order totally alien to those who first wrote about it and wanted to understand it. These questions are not only about the colonial state's intentions to control its disparate subjects located in totally fragmented groups, but also about method. In the colonial sociology of knowledge that was thus created, the most important was the factography of the decennial censuses. The zenith of this rampant empiricism was reached in the late nineteenth and early twentieth century. Thus writes anthropologist Simon Charsley,

> One census commissioner after another struggled to discern some order amongst the differently-based groups which might properly be regarded as castes.[17]

---

[17] Simon Charsley, 1996, "'Untouchable': What Is in a Name?", *The Journal of the Royal Anthropological Institute*, **2**: 1-16.

A process that was meant to tidy up India in fact became a Western obsession with caste, leading to the pigeon-holing of the populations of India in each successive census. This then played a crucial role in the institutionalization of new forms of caste.[18] There was basic agreement among most administrators in 1871, that caste should be the basic category to organize the census even though there was no agreement on what caste really was. Even the simple query that asked for the name of a caste to which someone belonged yielded a bewildering variety of responses that caused endless difficulties for the enumerating staff. By the 1871 census, however, the schema of four *varṇa*s on the one hand, plus one unified community of the 'outcastes' on the other, was adopted as representing the divisions of the Hindu community. In 1891 a disturbing feature of enumeration was added: anthropometrical measurements were noted, thus confirming a racial tone in the interpretations of castes.[19]

The 1891 census list of 'vague and indefinite entries' had 2.3 million people.[20] The other problem was listing the definite and indefinite entries in terms of 'social precedence'. By the 1901 census this created havoc because of the measure adopted by Risely to allow castes to petition if they had not been properly listed. They did so by holding meetings, writing petitions and organizing protests. By 1931 caste groups were distributing hand bills to fellow caste members to tell them how to answer the census questions. The result, writes Inden, was "a mountain of petitions and polemical literature concerning caste standing that . . . continues to have its effect to this day."[21] It is worth noting that the above situation resulted in the fact that the British could no longer ignore the political effects of this process in the making of the census and in 1931 they abandoned the use of

---

18 Cohn, op. cit., pp. 224-54.

19 Bandhopadhyaya, op. cit., pp 30.

20 Cohn, op. cit., p. 224.

21 R. Inden, 1990, *Imagining India*, Basil Blackwell, p. 59.

caste for census counting altogether.[22] None the less, new caste identities had already been created to which even today, caste groups return, to find authenticity for their claims to protective discrimination – a policy that has been adopted by the modern Indian state after Independence.

Apart from anthropological and administrative surveys that gave a certain image to the way Indian society should be understood and labelled, we cannot ignore the science of philology. Even late into the twentieth century Richard Lariviere makes a plea for a return to philology so as to give "the fullest possible voice to the views of classical Indians . . . of all social classes . . ." by "carefully and thoroughly editing their texts". And again, his belief was that "hard-core philological work" is "necessary to reconstruct what ancient Indian society must have been like."[23] This attitude impacted both the process of the construction of texts and removed all agency from the people whose texts were being read through these modern methodological avenues. That the very process of the editing and translating of ancient Indian texts on which are based the definitions of 'caste' were concretized by Indologists' and Orientalists, is well-documented. The famous Sacred Books of the East series firmly set the pace for other series to construct texts using scientific philological techniques, a trend that culminated with the monumental critical editions of the *Rāmāyaṇa* and *Mahābhārata*.[24] The projection of a society based on such texts was sometimes seen as stagnant, uncivilized and bereft of any logical thinking by one set of scholars or, as one mystical, spiritual,

---

22 Cohn, op. cit., pp. 249-50.

23 Richard Lariviere, 1994, "Protestants, Orientalists, and Brāhmaṇas: Reconstructing Indian Social History", Gonda Lecture, Gonda Foundation, Netherlands. Accessed online at http://www.hvk.org/articles/0501/12.html on 12 May 2010.

24 Peter van der Veer, 1999, *Monumental Texts: The Critical Edition of India's National Heritage*, pp. 134-55.

mythically and ritually rich and philosophically enlightened by another set of scholars. Orientalists based their views of the so-called Orient on Hegel's notion of Positivism and the dialectics of how civilization is meant to progress within the template of European history. It was thus based on a unitary notion of nature projecting a kind of universalism that came to be accepted uncritically by subsequent generations of scholars both from the West and the East.[25] This Orientalist vision of Indian society tremendously impaired our understanding of the social content of many of the ancient texts as they interpreted their meaning within a frame of reference alien to them – it translated and then commented on these texts with a gaze of retrieving a logic that was inherently absent in them and thus for generations to come, gave solid meanings to social order, ritual and belief that is difficult to unlearn. These ideas came with the package of Western liberal values and these being the more valued ideas of defining the world, a hegemonic approach was perpetuated that allowed little space for the voice inherent in the text to be heard. Its implications for India are that most modernist renderings of ancient Indian society are built on these texts and the constructed meanings that have been generated in modern dictionaries that try hard to systematize the rather fluid and dispersed knowledge that they received from these texts. An example par excellence is that of Monier-William's *Sanskrit–English Dictionary*[26] that then became the basis from which all knowledge about meanings of words began to flow. Scientific 'truth' built on the concept of linear time and the notion of progress, tended to favour a mechanistic view of nature and the material civilization that was built on it. With colonialism the scientific method came to India giving the so-

---

25 R. Inden, 1986, "Orientalist Constructions of India", *Modern Asian Studies*, **20**(3): 401-46.

26 M. Monier-Williams, 1899, *A Sanskrit–English Dictionary*, New Delhi: Munshiram Manoharlal.

called dispassionate observer the right to study and scrutinize the colonized society while imposing new ways of perceiving reality. This view of the world brought into focus a certain way, an ideology, whose underlying premise was the standardization of civilization – the birth of the 'Universal' in India.

Taking the example of subordinate and marginal groups we find that the process of naming in the colonial context had far-reaching consequences for the way the social order came to be understood, which then laid the foundations for modern India's tryst with caste and democracy. Colonial historiography generated a method that equated precision and detail with scientific truth. This was best exemplified in the monumental exercise that was taken up by Risely to collect anthropometrical data on the different ethnic populations of the subcontinent. It thus generated a labelling pattern for social groups which ignored the difference between them, and above all, unconsciously, through a system of ironing out difference, destroyed the sense of self-esteem these groups may have had due to their particular skills and practices that had defined their individual identities in the first place.[27] It was also decidedly different from the multiplicity of collectivities in terms of which people in different contexts were identified in the sources of the ancient and early medieval period.

In tracing the genealogy of the varieties of nomenclature we draw on an article by Simon Charsley that traces the modern origin of the term 'untouchable' and the concept of 'untouchability', after Risely had first introduced it under a schedule entitled "Class VII: Castes Untouchables". We are informed by Charsley that the categorization procedures had been a difficult task since the different committees of the so-called 'native gentlemen' and commissioners from the various regions and localities of the country had in fact found that, at

[27] Charsley, op. cit., pp. 12-13.

the ground level, there was a bewildering variety of 'impure castes', all known by their individual names. They none the less tried to gloss over these differences and brought the question of characterizing them to the forefront of the official discourse. The notion of the 'outcaste' as a so-called fifth *varṇa* came to be deeply entrenched and generalized terms like *pariah, pañcama,* etc. became popular to describe them all. This exercise simultaneously brought into focus the racial question of distinguishing castes based on their Aryan, non-Aryan and aboriginal origins, to explain the endemic differences between the high and low castes, while putting all the 'impure castes' under one umbrella. However, this article further elaborates on how a greater uniformity was achieved when the question of untouchability began to disturb social reformers and nationalists and, therefore, the term 'depressed castes' came to be widely accepted, making the social agenda of their 'upliftment' a special cause. That the lot of these communities had to be improved in a dramatic way was taken up by both M.K. Gandhi and B.R. Ambedkar during the first half of the twentieth century. Charsley discusses at some depth that whereas Gandhi's ambiguity in the use of the term 'untouchable' often suffixing it with 'so-called', became clear in his later adoption of the term *harijan,* Ambedkar vociferously used it to its fullest and exploited its potential to bring out the pathetic condition of these communities so that it would impact the conscience of people, particularly those shaping the future of the country. His endeavours culminated in the 'untouchable' being seen as a 'separate element in the national life of India'. This was a long journey from when Risely had first used it for census purposes. However, in 1921, it is noted that the census took up the classification of these communities under the phrase 'depressed classes'. Since disagreements persisted on the best nomenclature that should be used, 'depressed classes' was replaced in 1935, after several other suggestions were rejected, by an apparently technical term 'scheduled castes'; however, the criteria used to put groups into this category remained their impure status in society.

In tracing this history of the emergence of the term 'untouchable' Charsley argues that it was a modern construction and sees the impact of its use in both positive and negative terms. As an anthropologist he sees this construction as "both an interpretation of the past and the basis for affirmative action in the present". For purposes of raising the question of the ill-treatment of untouchables and drawing in questions of their political and social struggles, unifying them under a single category was a significant achievement. But the issue of an identity based on value that could be asserted with confidence had still to be achieved. Even Ambedkar eventually felt that the cause of the 'upliftment' of untouchables had not been able to provide them a sense of an independent and solid identity, full of confidence that was not necessarily built on earlier notions of their selfhood. Thus his conversion to Buddhism can be seen as a conscious attempt at creating a new positive identity that was rooted in cultural values and not simply born out of a total rejection of the past. The importance of unifying the downtrodden in terms of their caste impurity did not die with Ambedkar.[28] In fact, due to Ambedkar's[29] efforts, in the twenty-first century, "untouchability is no longer what it was. The old questions of ritual pollution are now superseded by a range of social and economic changes. New *dalit* strategies have transformed Indian politics,[30] while not necessarily putting an

---

28 Contursi A. Janet, 1933, "Political Theology: Text and Practice in a Dalit Panther Community", *The Journal of Asian Studies*, **52**(2): 320-39.

29 Edmund, Weber, Hrsg. Von, 1999, "Ambedkar and the Hindu Culture", *Journal of Religious Culture*, **18b**: 1-17.

30 Julia Leslie, 2003, *Authority and Meaning in Indian Religions: Hinduism and the Case of Vālmiki*, Aldershot & Burlington: Ashgate Publishing, pp. 36-37.

end to segregation and exploitation. The colonial historical and ethnographic writing that had searched for a single overarching term in the use of such phrases as 'untouchable', 'outcaste', 'depressed classes' has today come to be replaced more conventionally by the terms *harijan*, 'scheduled castes' and 'scheduled tribes'. The effort to rename continues and currently the most popular terminology that has been accepted is *dalit* or *bahujan* or sometimes, even *dalitbahujan*, which tries to encompass within its scope the oppressed śūdra *jāti*s as well,[31] so bringing under its umbrella a very large segment of the exploited people in Indian society.

The one single problem with the use of these overarching terminologies is that it tends to blank out the existing hierarchies even among the *dalit* groups. Problems related to claiming rights under the affirmative action scheme of the government arise because the really deprived among the *dalit*s have little access to these opportunities. This is an issue that has been brought to the forefront by anthropologists in their contemporary studies of these communities.[32] A debate continues among them on whether those listed under the scheduled-caste category should be seen as totally outside the caste system or whether, among them too, there are caste differences that replicate the *varṇa–jāti* system. In this regard Deliege takes the middle ground to suggest that *dalit*s neither totally reject the system nor fully replicate it. He writes:

> Untouchables are indeed part of Hindu society as their essential economic and ritual roles exemplify, but they are also, and at the same time, excluded from that society, and this marginalization is constantly reassessed through various

[31] Kancha Illaiah, 1995, *Why I Am not a Hindu: A Śūdra Critique of Hindutva Philosophy, Culture and Political Economy*, Hyderabad: Samya; and E. Zelliot, 1992, *From Untouchable to Dalit: Essays on the Ambedkar Movement*, New Delhi: Manohar, pp. vii-ix.

[32] Charsley, op. cit., p. 17.

taboos and discrimination.[33]

If *dalits* are then partially outside the caste system, then in our opinion, they define the critical margin of the *varṇa–jāti* society. In being subordinated and oppressed on the margin they interestingly define the criteria of their inclusion as *jātis* from time to time. Concluding his genealogy of the term 'untouchable' in modern times, Charsley writes:

> . . . what needs to be studied now are the differences in the way the local groups . . . communities of people identifying and naming themselves as members of particular castes within villages, and other larger units, are placed economically, socially, culturally, and politically.[34]

A couple of years ago, while prefacing a discussion on how early Indian society classified marginal and subordinate groups,[35] I thought it pertinent to contrast the early Indian system of naming excluded groups with nomenclatures that emerged in the colonial context, precisely for the reasons that Charsley has raised in the quote above.[36] The making of the *varṇa–jāti* system in pre-modern India was deeply layered in a thought system (so I argued) rooted in ideological underpinnings revolving around a certain notion of history (*itihāsa*) and time (*yuga/kāla*), which was conceived of as multiple – cyclic, linear and at different levels of existence, both mundane and sacred and in different spatial (*loka/deśa*) orders – place, locale, region, country but also with a link to the universe. This was a tendency that provided

---

33 Robert Deliege, 1992, "Replication and Consensus: Untouchability, Caste and Ideology in India", *Man*, N.S., March, **27**(1): 169.

34 Charsley op. cit.

35 Aloka Parasher-Sen, 2006, "Naming and Social Exclusion: The Outcaste and the Outsider", in Patrick Olivelle (ed.) *Between the Empires*, USA: Oxford University Press, pp. 415-55.

36 Aloka Parasher-Sen, 2007, *Subordinate and Marginal Groups in Early India up to 1500 AD*, Delhi: Oxford University Press, 2nd edn., pp. 10-28.

possibilities for generating multiple identities alongside asserting local distinctiveness against a stable understanding of order in society. The attempts to harmonize man and society with the cosmic order were done on a grand scale in the earliest Śruti traditions of India. In an elaborate study it has been pointed out by Brian Smith that the earliest cosmogonies on the origin of the universe that laid out the *varṇa* scheme in fact do not mention the social hierarchy but revolve around all aspects of the natural world. However, ultimately:

> The end result of classification schemes organized around the concept of *varṇa* was that certain humans could present what was an arbitrary social status or status claim as natural and sacred; that is, social hierarchy was presented as inexorably part of the immutable and divinely given order of things.[37]

This ideology of an all-encompassing 'natural world' being classified into *varṇa* came to be deeply entrenched and persuasive, penetrating into all aspects of life in the Hindu universe. It gave an effective epistemological explanation linking the individual to the social and then to the divine and cosmic levels of existence. It was precisely because of this connectedness to an overarching supernatural authority that authors of the later Smṛti traditions effectively legitimized their claims to social and political pre-eminence. Simultaneously, because the whole system was layered with philosophical sanctions and precepts, any escape for ordinary people from it was difficult, if not impossible. To put it succinctly:

> Socio-historic contingencies and natural 'laws' were treated within the same mythico-ritual discourse, and were endowed with the same status of utter facticity and eternal truth. To challenge any part of the system was to challenge all, and a

[37] Brain Smith, 1994, *Classifying the Universe: The Ancient Indian Varṇa System and the Origins of Caste*, Oxford: Oxford University Press, p. 7.

> challenge to any part could be refuted with overpowering arguments.[38]

Notwithstanding these explanations and the apparent solidity of the law and faith in *dharma* as it emerged, it must be stated that the epistemological shifts made by the so-called heterodox sects as early as the sixth century BCE and the later emphasis on *bhakti* as a medium to gain legitimacy, provided space and deviations, however limited, for a questioning of *dharma* and the boundaries defined by it. The most potent forms of questioning emerged from within the Tantric traditions of the early medieval and medieval times, in many parts of the country. Though there was never a complete overthrow of the hierarchical structures, complex levels of domination and subordination emerged, defying the theoretical ordering as presented in the Dharmaśāstra[39] or legal texts. At best the latter provided the fundamental metaphysical raison d'être for legitimizing the existence of the *caturvarṇa* in the hands of the different ruling elites over historical time. The essential point is that though *varṇa* ideology purported to support the undifferentiated idea of the foundation of all life in *dharma*, that is, an innate natural order based on metaphysical understanding of oneness, at the same time, we need to take cognizance of that fact that it could lead to a differentiated understanding of the social reality through the continual formation of *jāti*s without breaking the perennial unified message of the universal order (Sanātana Dharma).[40] Andre Beteille,[41] for instance, has drawn our attention to the writings of Niharranjan Ray and N.K. Bose who, in the 1930s and 1940s, recognizing that the actual divisions of Bengali Hindu society were many, continued to use the term *barṇa* (Bengali for

---

38 Brain Smith, op. cit., pp. 7-8.

39 P.V. Kane, 1936, *History of the Dharmaśāstra*, 5 vols., Poona.

40 Chaturvedi op. cit., pp. 10, 90.

41 Andre Beteille, 1996, "Varṇa and Jāti", *Sociological Bulletin*, March, **45**(1): 15-18.

varṇa) to articulate their views about the nature of historical and contemporary Bengali society. In this usage what they were in fact describing was *jāti*. This perceptive essay on the polemics of the use of the terms *varṇa* and *jāti* in a contemporary Indian situation and how this shift in vocabulary reflects on the representation of caste, points to the essential complexities of defining a dynamic and changing caste society.

Similar vocabulary shifts and the interchangeability of the use of these two terms in the past have also to be recognized. Suvira Jaiswal[42] has given several examples highlighting their interchangeability, as for instance, the reference in the *Aṣṭādhyāyī* of Pāṇini wherein *varṇa* is used twice to describe mixed groups which in later legal literature are known as *jāti*s and the brāhmaṇa too is described with the term *jāti*. She further explains that reflecting on conditions of around the same period, early Buddhist texts frequently use the term *jāti* to describe the brāhmaṇa, kṣatriya, vaiśya, and śūdra groups which in the legal Brāhmanic tradition of the time were clearly known by the term *varṇa*. She concludes that "in the perception of the participant peoples . . . *varṇa* and *jāti* did not constitute two different systems but one. . . ."[43]

Semantics apart, within the larger understanding of the *varṇa* ideology the term *jāti* began to be used as a suffix for those groups that were assigned status at various levels within the system as defined by the Dharmaśāstra tradition, thereby underlining the fact that the *varṇa* structure was not inherently rigid but was in a constant state of flexibility and mobility. Thus some of the earliest legal texts introduce the notion of *varṇasaṁkaraṇa* that then became an inherent part of the explanation on the 'mixture of castes' or *saṁkīrṇa jāti*s.

---

42 Suvira Jaiswal, 1979-80, "Studies in Early Indian Social History: Trends and Possibilities", *Indian Historical Review*, July 1979–January 1980, **IV**(1-2): 1-44.

43 Ibid., pp. 9-10.

When the *varṇa–jāti* system had undoubtedly expanded, later writers on law like Yājñavalkya, interestingly, use the term *varṇa* to describe the so-called mixed castes (*saṁkīrṇa jātis*). This is despite the fact that this law-writer in fact makes a distinction between *varṇa* and *jāti* in two other passages.[44] Though it has often been pointed out that the above explanations of 'mixed unions' merely reflect a normative view of society that was hardly the social reality, this rather artificial adjustment in fact reflected some change in the ideological perception of the legal writers based on their observation of historical circumstances. Aktor gives us one such example of a valid way of looking at how the phenomena worked in the context of everyday practice. He takes the example of some twelfth-thirteenth-century inscriptions that narrate how a conflict between two groups of south Indian artisans (known as *kammalas*) was resolved. It was settled with reference to different Śāstras that dealt with their occupations and their *varṇasaṁkara* status. He writes:

> For a modern reader this use of the system logically presupposes that *varṇasaṁkara* is understood as the past origin of the group. If it referred to individuals descending directly from unequal parents their *varṇasaṁkara* status would not have to be ascertained from Śāstras. Therefore the procedure here was to correlate the traditional work of the two groups with the *varṇasaṁkara* definitions in the Śāstras in order to establish these traditional tasks as more than simple work, but as *adhikāras*.[45]

Here two important points are made. The first is that the past is not looked at in essentialized terms but rather, from how the present should be interpreted and second, it brings to the fore the question of traditional rights that resorted to texts for resolving

44 Suvira Jaiswal, 1979-80, p. 9.

45 Mikeal, Aktor, 1999, "Smritis and Jātis: The Ritualization of Time and the Continuity of the Past", in Daud Ali (ed.) *Invoking the Past: The Uses of History in South Asia*, New Delhi: Oxford University Press, pp. 258-79.

conflict however much they were rooted in local situations.

Reflecting on this issue from within the tradition, Yudhiṣṭhira in the *Mahābhārata* when asked to identify the basis of *varṇa*, confesses his inability to do so since members of every *varṇa* beget children from women of all *varṇas*, creating so many *saṁkīrṇa jātis*.[46] This statement can be understood against the background of the experiences of the Pāṇḍavas during their period of exile, which entailed travel through vast tracts of the plains and forest country, thereby bringing them in contact with different patterns of social organization. The general emphasis in all these texts on the contexuality of *dharma* based on *deśa* (country) and *kāla* (time)[47] has to be seen in the light of the improbability of the unilateral imposition of their system on the varied and complex diversity of the subcontinent. In fact, in all periods of history the origin of *jāti* reflected both a deviation from the theoretical concept of *varṇa* and the rather rigid and artificial explanations of the *varṇa* theory as represented in the literature and inscriptions of different periods. This has to be understood against the backdrop of various, even normative texts, now telling us about the increase in the so-called 'mixed castes'. Discussing the proliferation of castes as noted in the literature of different periods, R.S. Sharma points out that the earliest law books mention only ten to fifteen, whereas sixty-one mixed castes are identified in Manu's law book, a work of the first-second century CE. This number increases to a hundred in the *Brahmavaivarta Purāṇa*. Further the *Viṣṇudharmottara Purāṇa*, a work of about the eighth century CE, states that "thousands of mixed castes are produced as a result of the connection of

46 P.H. Prabhu, 1999, *Hindu Social Organisation: A Study in Socio-Psychological and Ideological Foundations*, Bombay: Popular Prakashan, pp. 138, 309.

47 V.S. Sukthankar et al. (ed.), 1933-36, *Mahābhārata*, 19 vols., Poona: BORI.

vaiśya women with men of lower castes . . . ,".[48] A survey of a variety of literature on the Niṣādas, for instance, has revealed a rather complex process of the acculturation of mixed castes into the *varṇa–jāti* system, as also their geographical distribution and migration over different periods in historical time where some of them were ultimately confined to the status of impure castes according to the *varṇasaṁkaraṇa* theory. Indeed, earliest references reveal that they were in all probability a powerful autochthonous 'tribe' inhabiting areas where the *varṇa–jāti* system was beginning to spread and adapt itself.[49]

A survey of some of the inscriptions of the early medieval period pertaining to the Deccan has indicated how, except for the brāhmaṇa *varṇa* and *cāṇḍāla jāti*, the names of the other *varṇa*s and *jāti*s are hardly mentioned. Social groups are however mentioned, using their administrative, professional, or occupational designations.[50] This pattern of representing social groups was not unique: several studies have shown that regional literary, but particularly inscriptional sources deviate from the Dharmaśāstra terminologies when describing social groups that were trying to adjust to the *varṇa*-oriented society. Most of these rather specific names used to describe ruling elites, professional trading groups, or even the labouring and oppressed social groups conventionally listed by historians under the *varṇa* categories of kṣatriya, vaiśya and śūdra respectively, were in fact, described by their individual identities, either indicated by the region they came from, their official designation in the

---

48 R.S. Sharma, 1981, *Social Change in Early Medieval India (circa AD 50-1200)*, New Delhi: People's Publishing House, pp. 22-23.

49 Ganganatha Jha (tr.), 1998, *Kumārila Bhaṭṭa's Tantravārttika* (A Commentary on *Śābara's Bhāṣya* on the *Pūrvamīmāṁsā Sūtras* of Jaimini), 2 vols., Delhi (repr.), pp. 67-84.

50 Tejaswini Yarlagadda, 1993, "Social Groups and Economic Change Seventh to Thirteenth Century AD", in Aloka Parasher-Sen *Social and Economic History of the Deccan: Some Interpretations*, New Delhi: Manohar, pp. 165-229.

administrative set-up, or their economic and cultural function in society.[51] Interesting local and regional data reveal how, as in the case of the Boyā brāhmaṇa mentioned in the Eastern Cāḷukyan inscriptions, the *varṇa* nomenclature was adapted with the suffix of the name of a war-like tribe called the Boyās, clearly indicating a process of acculturation.[52] The Boyās, like the Niṣādas, Śabaras, etc. were clearly originally peoples outside the fold of the *varṇa–jāti* system.

The above discussion thus outlines the complexity of the way this terminology was used in the varied textual contexts of different periods. Further, it needs to be emphasized that the term *jāti* was also used as a suffix to describe the so-called 'untouchable' groups, not assigned any *varṇa* and sometimes used also to refer to *mleccha* and forest communities who were in any case outside the *varṇa* system as a whole.[53] This does not suggest the breakdown of different identities, but rather, can be understood as a means of dialogue and accommodation in using the same terminology to encapsulate separate identities both within and outside the *varṇa* system. It also suggests a very important trend in ancient and medieval literature of not always clubbing individual generic names of peoples under one overarching terminology. Thus, both inside and outside the *varṇa* system, groups known through their *jāti* nomenclature could be identified in various ways through their occupational, ethnic, linguistic, or regional specificity.

---

51 P.V.P. Parabrahma Sastry, 1996, *Rural Studies in Early Andhra*, Hyderabad: V.R. Publication, pp. 50-56.

52 B.S.L. Hanumantha Rao, 1995, "The Boyas in Medieval Andhra History" in B.S.L. Hanumantha Rao (ed.) *Social Mobility in Medieval Andhra*, Publication No. 155, Hyderabad: Telugu University, pp. 75-98.

53 Aloka Parasher, 1991, *Mlecchas in Early India: A Study in Attitudes Towards Outsiders up to AD 600*, New Delhi: Munshiram Manoharlal, pp. 133-35.

In highlighting these examples, we do not argue that the *varṇāśrama dharma* as a conceptual category had somehow collapsed. On the contrary, it continued to hold sway and its maintenance were most often considered one of the foremost duties of a king.[54] There were, however, several disturbances that had disrupted the functioning of the *varṇa–jāti* system because of pressure from 'foreign' and 'tribal' groups that invaded different parts of the subcontinent from time to time. For most of what has been called the ancient period in Indian history, the success of Buddhism in almost all parts of the subcontinent was seen as a threat to the norms of society upheld by the brāhmaṇas. Thus, periodic attempts at resistance to the system of oppression caused discomfiture to the elite sections in society. This is reflected, for instance, in passages of the Purāṇas and epics that describe the unsettled conditions of what they define as the Kaliyuga. One of the significant characteristics of this age was that it predicted doom because of the collapse of the traditional *varṇāśrama dharma*.[55] The system could not be destroyed as certain foreign rulers, like the Śakas, in a bid to be accepted by the traditional elite, had proclaimed that they would protect the *varṇāśrama dharma* and appease the brāhmaṇa.[56] All that ultimately happened was that foreign invading hordes like the Yavanas, the Śakas, the Pahlavas, and powerful indigenous peoples and tribal groups like the Pauṇḍras, the Kirātas, and the Abhīras succeeded in getting incorporated at the level of the higher caste groups.[57] Various other tribal groups, like the

---

54 Aloka Parasher, op. cit., pp. 126-49.

55 B.N.S. Yadava, 1978-79, "The Accounts of the Kali Age and the Social Transition from Antiquity to the Middle Ages", *Indian Historical Review*, July 1978 – January 1979, **V**(1-2): 31-63.

56 Aloka Parasher-Sen, 1993, "Tribes and Indian Civilization: The Nineteenth Century Intrusion", in Alok Bhalla and Sudhir Chandra (eds.) *Indian Responses to Colonialism in the 19th Century*, New Delhi: Sterling Publishers, pp. 149-74.

57 R.S. Sharma, 1981, *Social Change in Early Medieval India (circa A.D.* →

Niṣādas and the Medās, on the other hand, were incorporated at lower ritual positions.[58] This happened over long periods of historical time. Under these circumstances the system had to undergo change. Further, in the context of the agrarian expansion and the particular economy of the land grant system,[59] early medieval times saw several permutations of the *varṇa–jāti* system in different regions of India.[60] The flexibility of the interchange between these terms *varṇa* and *jāti* continued into early medieval times and was not confined to the elite discourse. Such flexibility in popular usage is reflected in a tenth-century copper-plate inscription from Bengal[61] which refers to a village called Bṛhatchattivaṇṇa, literally meaning a village inhabited by thirty-six *varṇa*s, perhaps meant to describe a village where thirty-six *jāti*s lived. Therefore, the popular perception reflected not two systems but one, so long as hierarchical relations were maintained to define the social organization as a whole.

An important marker and an early consolidated definition in this context is the well-known dictionary, the *Amarakośa*[62] authored by Amarasiṁha during the fifth century CE. In the chapter entitled Śūdravarga (chap. X) Amarasiṁha makes a clear distinction among types of people living on the margins of mainstream society and in subordinate conditions. He first begins with the definition of a śūdra who is conventionally called *jaghanyāja*, or one born from the nether limbs but, in another definition, also describes the śūdra as one born from the mixed marriages of spouses belonging to different castes

← *50-1200)*, New Delhi: People's Publishing House, p. 24.

58 R.S. Sharma, ibid., pp. 24-25.

59 B.D. Chattopadhyaya, 1994, *The Making of Early Medieval India*, New Delhi: Oxford University Press, pp. 22-28.

60 Suvira Jaiswal, op. cit., pp. 24-25.

61 Pushpa Niyogi, 1967, *Brahmanic Settlements in Different Subdivisions of Bengal*, Kolkata: Indian Studies, Past and Present, p. 55.

62 C.D. Deshmukh, 1981, *Amarakośa*, New Delhi: Uppal Publishing House, pp. 111-16.

(referring here to the term *varṇa*). A list of śūdra *jātis* thus formed is then given along with their assigned vocations. This is followed by a list of various artisans and professional groups called 'mixed mixtures'. All these are, however, clearly distinguished in this dictionary from those that are referred to in low and contemptuous (*nīca*) terms, for which ten synonyms are given in the text. Further, for the slave (*dāsa*) eleven equivalents are given and nine synonyms for the *cāṇḍāla*. This is finally followed by the term *mleccha* to describe mainly the hunting tribes – the Kirāta, Śabara, Pulinda, etc. What is important to note is that whereas, at one level, these definitions are distinguished from each other, at another, a certain amount of ambiguity is also perceptible. Thus, for instance, *cāṇḍāla* mentioned as one of the mixed *jātis* in the definition and category of the śūdra, is also independently described to indicate the lowest category, along with the synonymous names of several other groups. Interestingly, here the Niṣāda occurs as a synonym of *cāṇḍāla* whereas, in other early Indian literature Niṣāda is well known as a progenitor of the *mlecchas*. The lexicon differentiates between the *śūdra, dāsa, cāṇḍāla* and *mleccha* in order to articulate the dominant society's concern with separating those lower orders that were members of the fourth *varṇa* from the ritually impure groups, outside it, those that were slaves and finally, those that were culturally identifiable as different communities. Fick,[63] for instance, explains the complexity of the place of the *dāsas* in early Indian society. He clarifies that they could definitely not be categorized as 'castes' and therefore, they were not what he describes as the 'despised castes' who had the adjunct of 'impurity' attached to them but, neither were they the exact equivalents of the slaves known in the classical Greek and

---

[63] Richard Fick, 1972, *The Social Organization in North-East India in Buddha's Time,* tr. S.K. Maitra, repr. Delhi and Varanasi: Indological Book House, p. 307.

Roman tradition.[64] In fact, in the early Buddhist context we are told that among some people like the Yavanas and Kāmbojas there were only two *varṇa*s defined as the *ārya*s and *dāsa*, commonly translated as the master and slave emphasizing thereby their class and occupational position.

The above lexicon clubs all these groups in one chapter and emphasizes their communality in terms of being at the receiving end of society vis-à-vis the dominant and privileged groups, which, on the other hand, are described in three separate chapters in the same dictionary. Another aspect that emerges while examining these definitions is that they are implicitly placed in relation to the *varṇa* system. Thus, śūdras are located at the bottom of this hierarchy but are very much within its ambit. *Cāṇḍāla*s are placed on the critical margins of the *varṇa* society and linked to it in terms of their conscious exclusion from it. Finally, the *mleccha*s are defined totally outside it as the perpetual outsiders and therefore as potential contesters of the *varṇa* ideology. The *Amarakośa* notes that the *mleccha*s are exclusively wild tribes but the term is also commonly used in different kinds of literature to describe foreigners.[65] Finally, the above definition also addresses members clubbed in each of the broad groups by their particular names, which, over time, would now and again become generic names for particular kinds of occupational activity or distinct ethnic characteristics.

Despite the apparently powerful hold and tenacity of the *varṇa* nomenclature, some of the earliest texts also inform us of another categorization of social groups that highlight the intricate details of the groups' cultural and social diversity. This categorization involved description of people within *varṇa* as well as outside it. Bhattacharya points out that, apart from the four classifications, each carrying its own identity, ancient texts

---

64 Richard Fick, op. cit., p 304-05.

65 M. Monier-Williams, 1851, *An English–Sanskrit Dictionary*, New Delhi: Munshiram Manoharlal, repr. 1988, p. 837.

sometimes clubbed together the three upper *varṇa*s as *dvija-jāti*s and contrasted them with the fourth *varṇa*, namely, the śūdras. In other instances all four *varṇa*s were clubbed together and then contrasted with those outside the system, who were referred to by various terms like *antya, antyavāsin*, etc.[66] An unusual early reference in the *Nirukta* of Yāska, a text from about the seventh century BCE, refers to the four *varṇa*s as *jana*. Further, the *jana* are combined with the Niṣāda, an autochthonous tribe, and called the *pañcajana* (five tribes). The latter, of course, were never known as being part of a *varṇa* though in later Dharmaśāstra literature they did emerge as an 'untouchable' caste.[67] They were also well known in the epic literature as the progenitors of the *mleccha* communities. It can be argued that this is reflective of a tendency to explain transitory historical processes that affected all social groups and, therefore, such unusual ways of describing the four *varṇa*s as well as the Niṣādas did not remain permanent or popular. In common perception ancient Indian society was supposedly marked only by the apparently powerful hold and tenacity of addressing groups based on their *varṇa–jāti* nomenclature. This perception has to be revised. Some of the earliest texts also inform us of other categorizations of social groups highlighting intricate details of their cultural and social diversity. This involved descriptions of people who initially stood outside the formal system of a *varṇa*-ordered society, in terms of their ethnic appellations.

To recapitulate: it is important for us to recognize that an

---

[66] S. Bhattacharya, "Political Authority and Brāhmaṇa-Kshatriya Relationship in Early India: An Aspect of the Power Elite Configuration", *Indian Historical Review,* July 1983-January 1984, vol. **X**(1-2: 1-20): 2-3.

[67] V. Jha, 1977, "From Tribe to Untouchable: The Case of the Niṣādas", in R.S. Sharma and V. Jha (eds.) *Indian Society: Historical Probing in Memory of D.D. Kosambi*, New Delhi: People's Publishing House, pp. 67-84.

important landmark in our immediate past had meant that caste had been re-invented and re-incarnated to provide intellectual justifications for its perpetuation in the colonial context. With admissible variations Orientalists and Indologists framed a discourse around definitions of the origins, character and naming of castes and non-castes necessarily bringing in the question of 'race' as a defining character of differentiation. Our current interpretations of both caste and the notions of diversity rest on the constructions that brought into being new nomenclatures to define pre-existing identities as part of a complex historical process. One would concur with Nicholas Dirks when he writes:

> forms of casteism and communalism that continue to work against the imagined community of the nascent nation state have been imagined as well. . . . And they have been imagined with such success that when we think of India, we must now insistently be reminded that *India's post-colonial condition is not its pre-colonial fault* (emphasis added).[68]

However, as has been poignantly articulated:

> pre-colonial forms of knowledge are too often relegated by the scholars of colonialism and nationalism to the happy condition of indeterminacy, diversity, holism – acting as foils for the drama of modernity. Their own conditions of production, internal structures, and agendas for power are too often ignored.[69]

A concern for focusing on pre-modern Indian sensibilities, therefore, needs some emphasis. In contrast to the modern, Kapila Vatsyayan explains:

---

68 Nicholas Dirks, 1992, "Castes of Mind", *Representations*, Winter **37**: 76.

69 Daud Ali (ed.), 1999, *Invoking the Past: The Uses of History in South Asia*, SOAS Studies on South Asia: Understandings and Perspective Series, New Delhi: Oxford University Press, p. 9.

> tradition or *paramparā* at its best connotes a flow, a vertical transmission in time and spatial spread horizontally. It does not constitute a frozen, static object or even a corpus of values and behavioural patterns. When the dynamics of the flow is sustained, we recognize it as a world-view and lifestyle, distinctive and not static. . . .[70]

On the question of which meaning to define 'caste' would dominate at different points in time, it would be apt to conclude with Alice's inquisitive mind:

> "The question is", said Alice, "whether you can make words mean so many different things".
>
> "The question is", said Humpty Dumpty, "which is to be master – that's all".[71]

Furthermore, the modern search for a single overarching term in the use of such phrases as untouchable, outcaste, depressed classes, *harijan*, scheduled caste and scheduled tribe in the colonial context so as to bring under its umbrella a very large segment of the exploited people in Indian society, is unable to effectively capture the vast diversity that lies beneath them and which is graphically engulfed in the historical records. This search in fact led us into the larger domain of how the textual traditions of early India articulated the process of naming that then became part of social memory and cultural practice and that has not totally been erased from the collective psyche even today. The linguistic apparatus adopted in pre-modern times nurtured a certain flexibility to govern everyday practices and the meanings attached to the words used for them that could be

---

70 Kapila Vatsyayan, 2005, "From Interior Landscapes into Cyberspace: Fluidity and Dynamics of Tradition", in Kamala Ganesh and Usha Thakkar (eds.) *Culture and the Making of Identity in Contemporary India* (*The Asiatic Society of Mumbai Bicentenary Volume*), New Delhi: Sage Publications, p. 42.

71 Lewis Carroll, 1998, "From Through the Looking-Glass", in *The Complete Illustrated Works*, Wordsworth edns., p. 184.

made recognizable, repeatable and interpretable within the force of tradition. In this way a more effective way of the preservation of various cultural identities through the recognition of diversity was possible to articulate and maintain on the subcontinent for generations. To quote Certeau

> . . . naming simultaneously posits a linkage and a place. It functions at once as *participation in a system* and *as access to the symbolic*.[72]

Therefore, depending on the context of their use, names have an integrative value or an exclusionary propensity but none the less, in both circumstances, they are written into a system of communication.

Rutherford's view that "identity marks the conjuncture of our past with the social, cultural and economic relations we live within" seems strikingly apt in this context.[73] Questions of identity formation are intrinsically related to the way the past is perceived or written about in historical narratives. The modern craft of history writing in its essential task of retrieving the past each time, with each age and each theoretical framework must necessarily construct new identities. Our overall conclusion suggests that the modern constructions have by and large, given us a distorted prism through which we try and understand hierarchy and social diversity in early India both in terms of its documentation and the interpretations built upon it. The written texts of the dominant culture that were used as 'footnotes' to do so, were embedded in a different conceptualization of time where history and memory were both engrained and entwined into ritual practice locatable in time (*kāla*) and place (*deśa*) as long as customary law and local practice did not go against Śruti as

---

72 Michel de Certeau, 1988, *The Writing of History*, New York: Columbia University Press, p. 262.

73 J. Rutherford (ed.), 1990, *Identity: Community, Culture, Difference*, London: Lawrence & Wishert, p. 19.

canon and Smṛti as tradition. It is true that the texts that have been used above contain only "fragmented history and form" but they always present "an integrated world-view".[74] The aim in this tradition was not to totally wipe out historical reality altogether or, simply supplant it with structures of the mythical, but rather, it was to capture the process of cultural continuity and cultural renewal with interjections, interrogations and insertions possible within the defined limits of *dharma*. This gave a certain distinctiveness to the way traditional India looked at the past and therefore, the need for a sensitive revaluation of the source material we use to write history is urgent. Mikael Aktor has comprehensively argued that in the Smṛti or remembered traditions of early India, the very 'ongoing' production of these texts used the past and asserted 'epistemological authority' but through a 'flexible source'. He views this method as one of "creative preservations" and an "ongoing literary production. . . . The practical function of this process was to establish a flexible source of epistemological authority. The arguments of the day in the living debate which has been the heart of traditional Indian intellectualism were not in themselves authoritative; they had to be substantiated by texts which, on the one side, were relevant to present arguments and, on the other, had a status as being related to the normative past. *Smriti*s functioned as such texts."[75] Aktor also argues that the making of Smṛtis and more importantly, the Nītiśāstra, often located locally, was also continually making new *jāti*s and this gave society a continuous way to look at their past in terms of changes in the present. Thus, rather than seeing the texts as part of an unchanging, monolithic

[74] Wendy Doniger, 1992, "Rationalizing the Irrational Other: 'Orientalism' and the Laws of Manu", in *New Literary History*, **23**: 25-43.

[75] Mikeal Aktor, 1999, "Smritis and Jātis: The Ritualization of Time and the Continuity of the Past" in Daud Ali (ed.) *Invoking the Past: The Uses of History in South Asia*, New Delhi: Oxford University Press, pp. 258-79.

discourse of power one needs to recognize the presence of an organism that provided symbiotic spaces that were often tenuous and that the so-called centre of power was constantly negotiating with social groups.

The textual traditions – Śāstra and Bhāṣya taken together – later articulated these fundamental ideas into their interpretations of classifying social groups from time to time. The result is that even today there are many oral traditions available to contemporary scholarship that have now begun to throw up new versions for understanding selfhood of different, especially subordinate and marginal, social groups inverting in many cases the textual Brāhmanical version. Categorizing, translating and fixing people in 'castes' that began with modern ways of perceiving reality on the subcontinent resulted in closures that went hand in hand with arbitrariness, power and knowledge control in grappling with the Indian social reality. It so fixed populations into silo moulds that today, as Julia Leslie[76] has argued, everybody seeks textual authority to confirm apparently unchanging identities doomed to either artificial heroic pasts or perpetual states of victimhood. But the production and nature of pre-colonial knowledge are relegated to amnesia at best.

DISCUSSION

Tripathi

Aloka has raised the question of hierarchy, diversity and difference in our own tradition. I am wondering whether it's a question of shifting the very idea of hierarchy, difference and diversity to a core which is not the philosophical supposition of a basic, foundationally Advaitic position. In such a frame how can diversity, hierarchy and difference be central? Is it not an import from the West that we are imposing and making central to the entire issue? Indeed here lies the role of the translator,

---

[76] Leslie, op. cit., p. 2.

whether from the West or India. It is not the case that hierarchy, diversity and differentiation constitute the core questions of the traditional Indian mind. The core is something different and what we are doing is superimposing the modern interpretation on our own understanding and on our own view of life.

Aloka

Very briefly my response to that is that I do not suggest that hierarchy, etc. is at the core of the understanding. The core of the understanding is to create an order, a universal order. Now handling hierarchy, difference and diversity is a constant endeavour. And what modernity has told us is that it is indeed a constant. At some point of time somebody said that this is how things are going to be. Hierarchy was constantly redefined and so were 'difference' and diversity. There was a kind of dialectical relationship between them. But that idea of an original order, that balance, I should say, had to be maintained.

I would juxtapose your question with the three levels of the cosmic, the divine and the human. It was at the human level that the actual, pragmatic problem of handling differences arose because people were not closeted in one space. They were constantly expanding in time and space. So even the *smṛitikāra*s refer to *deśa kāla* – in place and time. As historians we only look at time and do not bother about space. This world particularly is a spatial thing – a constant flow – and that is why history is a problematic term to use: we should rather use *paramparā* or some alternative of how this tradition handled the question of not making difference its central core.

8

The Case of Nāṭyaśāstra of Bharata and Its Commentary Abhinavabhārati

K.D. Tripathi

Experiences of Rendering Sanskrit Texts/Categories of Indian Thought in a Trans-Cultural Context: Present and Past

IT is not that Sanskrit texts are being translated and categories of Indian thought are being rendered in a transcultural context in the present era for the first time. Nor is it the case that all the translations done in the transcultural context in our times or all the interpretations of the Indian thought categories made are prejudiced. Yet, why do we feel we have to approach this issue from the angle of the 'politics of translation' at the very outset, especially when it comes to translating, interpreting texts in the English language or, in any of the modern European languages? Apparently, the reason is that the study of India in our times is predominantly made as the West obliges us to study India. This is not the case only with the studies made by the people belonging to a culture different from that of India; it happens even with those who are born in or who belong to India as has been rightly pointed by S.N. Balagangadhara in his learned presentation:

> We look at the world the way West looks at it. We do not even know whether the World would look different, if looked at our way. . . . When Indian anthropologists, psychologists or

> sociologists do their anthropology, psychology or sociology, the West is really talking to itself.[1]

The problem in fact possesses even greater dimensions, for we have mostly forgotten our own language of thought and the methodology of exploring our own thought-tradition, hence of approaching other traditions. What is being suggested here is that had we been familiar with our own thought, language and the methodology that we employed in our own traditional disciplines, we could have approached non-Indian traditions with the insights available from our own.

Moreover, the question remains: who are these 'we' figuring in the formulations of Balagangadhara and such other similar presentations? The answer may be that these are the intellectuals and the people who form a dominant part of the Indian middle class which arose gradually as a result of our contact with British colonialism and the rest of the Western world. It is also true that the population of such a middle class is on the increase and its impact on the rest of the Indian people – the peasant and the workers, the traditional Indian intellectuals and the common folk – is a formidable one. Hence, the observations and the resultant emphatic declarations of a few scholars that India is on the verge of losing her memory may possess a great measure of truth. However, it remains to be determined whether this is true for all Indians or whether it arises from the Western sense of its cultural and civilizational superiority on the one hand and consequent declarations made by Western intellectuals starting from Hegel down to Heidegger and Husserl that India and the entire non-Western world is destined to be completely Westernized, on the other. The genesis of this predominantly modern approach towards India lies in the triumphant mood of the Western thought which appears to be engrossed with the idea of the unipolarity of the world. A shift from the relatively

---

[1] S.N. Balagangadhara, 2011, *Comparative Studies and the Explanatory Problem, A Methodological Essay* in this volume, p. 61.

tolerant to the mostly intolerant attitude on this matter has taken place in our times.

This appears to be a major reason why the discourse of rendering the Indian classical categories in the English language begins with the discourse on 'Orientalism'. In contrast to this, it is noteworthy that our past witnessed the rendering of Sanskrit texts in transcultural contexts in a more congenial and liberal atmosphere.

Sanskrit narrative texts were translated into 'Pahalavī', Syriac as well as into Arabic and through them into most of the modern European languages. This happened with Indian philosophical texts as well. There was a successful model of translation available in Tibetan and Chinese. This model neither altered the cultural spirit of the original nor that of the language in which the translation was done.

The success, authenticity and aptness of this model can be surmised by the fact that there are instances of the restoration of the original from the translation, where the original was lost.

Not only the narratives and philosophical texts, but scientific texts like *Caraka Saṁhitā* were also translated into Persian and Arabic in tenth century CE.[2] It is a well-known fact that Indians freely interacted with the Greeks and the Arabs in the realm of astronomy as well as astrology. The cultural identity of the translated text was never compromised.

Therefore, while we are engaged in rendering the text or interpreting the categories of thought of a given culture in its own context, it is the question of intentionality which is foremost. One has to be especially cautious in the context of transcultural renderings of the texts or interpreting the categories of thought from one culture to another.

The value of such enterprises has to be determined in terms

2 Priyavrata Sharma, 1981, *Caraka Saṁhitā*, Inroduction, Varanasi: Chaukhambha Orentalia, p. xxiii.

of their ultimate purpose. It must be clear to the translator/interpreter, whether he/she is engaged in such an exercise for the purpose of assimilating it into the culture of translating language or to forge a meaningful dialogue on an equal footing. When these questions are clear in our minds, then one's cultural needs may be responded to satisfactorily and cultural distances may be bridged to a great measure. Consequently, a satisfactory translation/interpretation may be made for a better understanding of the original. We may learn a lot from Tibet, China, Persia and the Arabs in this direction.

The above considerations notwithstanding, certain core thought categories may remain untranslatable. For resolving this problem, a suitable methodology may be evolved. Such methodologies have been evolved in the past as well as in our present times. In order to arrive at such a methodology, we have to understand first the intrinsic nature of the classical Sanskrit categories occurring in the text to be translated and the context in which they emerged. Once the nature of the text has been understood, the translation may be made without committing any violence to the language of the translated text and the context in which such a text has emerged. Then one may be free to interpret them in keeping with one's respective cultural needs.

The Problem of Texts

The non-availability of properly and critically edited texts poses a problem in offering an authentic and good translation. *Nāṭyaśāstra* (hereafter *NŚ*) and *Abhinavabhāratī* (hereafter *Abhi. Bhā*) belong to the class of Śāstric texts which have a different nature from that of the epic texts – the *Rāmāyaṇa* and the *Mahābhārata*. The *Rāmāyaṇa* and the *Mahābhārata*, although composed by an author seminally drawing heavily on earlier oral traditions, have a narrational character; they have retained their oral character too. The epics have been extremely popular in the vast space in which they have attained somewhat gigantic proportions and have attracted divergent readings as well as departures from the original narrative content due to various reasons which need not be discussed here. On the other hand, there are the Purāṇic texts which share their oral nature with the epics as well as their encyclopaedic character with the great epic the *Mahābhārata* together with their own specific Purāṇic character defined as *pañca-lakṣaṇa* (five traits) namely: *sarga* (manifestation of the Universe or creation), *ratisarga* (dissolution), *vaṁśa* (genealogy), *manvantara* (the era of a particular Manu) and *vaṁśānucarita* (the deeds of one particular genealogical line). Purāṇic texts are also basically narrational and deeply rooted in the orality of the tradition. The nucleus written form has been expanded due to their assimilative character with the intense desire of transmitting orally all knowledge, all related cosmogonic and cosmological myths, relevant geography, all allied legends and history, all relevant thoughts, social development and behaviour, and so on.

On the other hand, there are Śāstric texts which are different from the extremely popular literary works like those of Kālidāsa which are available with their bewildering variants and versions. This variety is of course due to their immense popularity which resulted in innumerable variant readings inserted in the poetry and variations in the plays. This was in turn due to their being a valuable part of vibrant recitative as well as performative traditions which remained constantly growing for centuries throughout this vast land.

Although equally widely read throughout the country, Śāstric texts have been deeply rooted in their regulated form in spite of originating in an oral tradition, i.e. Śruti, i.e. the Veda and Vedāṅgas. Besides, the Śāstras represent the systematization of the thought-tradition and its growth within a well-defined structure of *sūtra* (lit. 'thread') the text composed in aphoristic style couched in cryptic language marked by brevity and precision, *vārttika* and *bhāṣya*. (*Vārttika* is form of text explaining what is unsaid or imperfectly said. Its main function is supplying omissions. *Bhāṣya* is a further investigation of both *sūtra* and *vārttika* almost word by word, offering comments of its own and unfolding the implicit concept.) Structurally, a 'Śāstra' may be seen as *uddeśa* (mentioning or specifying the subject matter to be enunciated), *lakṣaṇa* (definition or accurate description of the subject in hand) and *parīkṣā* (investigation) which is another term for *bhāṣya*. The tradition develops with the commentaries or the successive flow of expositions and interpretations. As a result, the Śāstric tradition could not tolerate the variation which might have disrupted its strict *sampradāya* (school of thought). This is the reason why Śāstric texts are free from such an immense variety of versions or staggering variant-readings. No instance of southern, northern, western and eastern versions can be cited of the Śāstric texts as we come across in the case of the Epics and Kālidāsan texts.

However, the *NŚ* of Bharata belongs to a separate category of Śāstra which is not simply theoretical, but which belongs to the realm of practice also, a practice which has been constantly creative, innovative and wedded simultaneously to the principles of continuity and change. It is predominantly a *prayoga śāstra*. However, it is different from the category of *prayoga śāstra* such as *mimāṁsā* which systematizes and carries forward the practice aspect of Vedic ritualistic tradition of *śrautā yāga* (sacrificial portion). Although *mimāṁsā* has been a model for *prayoga śāstra*, it adhered more to the principle of continuity due to its strict Vedic theological character. Changes and growth might have occurred in the realm of ritual practice also but they could be seen within well-defined and more regulated limits of the ritual tradition.

Thus, *NŚ* belongs to the category of text which has developed its different versions and variations of readings due to the growth and innovative character of the theatre, dance and music. Interestingly, a great degree of uniformity of the Śāstra has been maintained in all its versions. It is neither heterogeneous nor homogeneous, but is rather a unified text of unitary character, which has expanded as its vibrant and growing practice blossomed into its different regional forms and styles. This development necessitated the emergence of regional Śāstric texts. The constant "inflow and outflow" as well as 'centrifugal' and 'centripetal' growth of the *NŚ*, to borrow a phrase from Kapila Vatsyayan,[3] has given to the text a very different nature among all the texts which belong to the *prayoga śāstra* category.

The only surviving commentary on the *NŚ* available today is the *Abhi.Bhā* of Abhinavagupta (eleventh century CE), the great master hailing from Kashmir. It is significant that the manuscript of this commentary has been discovered in Kerala on the southern shore of the country. It most probably reached Kerala in the lifetime of Abhinavagupta wherefrom it travelled to modern Tamil Nadu and the *karaṇa*s and *aṅgahāra*s as described in the *NŚ* and the *Abhi.Bhā*. Here these were carved out on the walls of temples in different places of modern Tamil Nadu.

The *NŚ* is the source text of classical Indian aesthetics and theory of art. No authentic meaning of the *NŚ* can be ascertained unless we go deeper and examine the *Abhi.Bhā*, the commentary thereon. It is remarkable that the later tradition of commentators as well as authors of a number of original texts follow Abhinavagupta. The authentic meaning of the text and the concepts forming the core of the text can be determined by going deeper and examining the extant tradition of *prayoga*, particularly in the realm of music, dance and theatre. In the absence of critically edited texts and their properly translated versions done from the performative perspective and the interpretation/translation of the categories/terms, the understanding of classical Indian theory of arts and aesthetics has remained a difficult task.

---

3 Kapila Vatsyayan, 2003, *Bharata: The Nāṭyaśāstra*, New Delhi: Sahitya Akademi.

However, the project of translation could not wait for the critically edited texts for two reasons. First, although the different versions of the *NŚ* text mostly vary in the given order of chapters as well as in the total number of the chapters in different editions, this variation of the sequence as well as the number of the chapters can be explained satisfactorily. This is also the case with the inflated or deflated size of some of the chapters. Likewise, it appears that although the variations of the readings are important, the translation work may start afresh now after nearly 150 years of the modern study of the *NŚ* and more than fifty years of the study of the *Abhi.Bhā* after its publication. Of course, some new and authenticated readings after the preparation of a critical edition, may open some new dimensions of some of the core concepts. However, our understanding of the core concepts of Indian classical theory of art and aesthetics can be explored even with the available texts, for now.

As far as the text of *Abhi.Bhā* is concerned, it has been edited on the basis of only one manuscript with profuse lacuna as well as misplaced portions, corrupt readings and so on. Moreover, while editing the text, Kavi[4] has filled the lacuna in his own language here and there without giving any hint, where he does so. Thus, understanding the *Abhi.Bhā* and understanding of the *NŚ* through this sole old available commentary is also a formidable challenges. Moreover, except for some of the portions and fragments, no translation of the total commentary is available in any language. Its translation in Hindi by Madhusudana Shastri from the first to the twenty-seventh chapter which follows the text edited by Kavi, has been published from Banaras Hindu University in three volumes. However, it serves a very limited purpose, for it has been done by a scholar of

---

4 Ramakrishna Kavi, *Nāṭyaśāstra* with *Abhinavabhāratī* in four volumes in Gaekwad's Oriental Series. Vol. I, appeared in 1926, Vol. II in 1934, vol. III in 1954 and vol. IV in 1964 published from Oriental Institute, Baroda, India.

Sanskrit poetics who was, it appears, not conversant with the theory or practice dimensions of traditional theatre, dance, music, sculpture and architecture. In spite of the difficulty and problems, remarkable work has been done by a number of scholars towards the understanding of the theatre, dance and music tradition as delineated in the *NŚ* and as gleaned from the *Abhi.Bhā* and the post-Abhinava tradition. Besides, a huge amount of work has been done on the issues related to classical Sanskrit poetics. A lot more can be done by the inner collation of the *Abhi.Bhā* -text and the available text can be improved to a large extent. Thus the non-availability of any translation of the complete text, although causing immense difficulty, can be solved to a great extent. However, the properly edited and translated complete text of the *Abhi. Bhā* would be a very valuable exercise and could immensely improve our understanding of the classical, pre-medieval, medieval and post-medieval traditional theatre, dance and music as well as Indian theory of art. Whatever translation has been carried out before the completion of Kavi's edition of the *NŚ* with the *Abhi.Bhā* may be updated now and a project of bringing out the critically edited *NŚ* as well as the properly edited *Abhi.Bhā* may be taken up simultaneously.

Manmohan Ghosh is a pioneer scholar who took the lead in translating the *NŚ* into the English language (*The Nature of Translation and the Emerging Problems*). He prepared his own text of the *NŚ* for translation in order to solve the problems for the reader caused by the different editions of the texts then available. The question was: which edition to rely on for translation? Editions published from France during the last quarter of nineteenth century were not complete, though the *Kāvyamālā* edition published from Bombay by the end of nineteenth century was complete. There was another edition published from Varanasi exactly after the first quarter of twentieth century which was complete. The second edition of

Kāvyamālā was also made available by his time. The Gaekwad edition also appeared in its first volume in 1926 and the second and third volumes were published in 1934 and 1954 respectively. They were available to Manmohan Ghosh, but this edition was not complete at the time of his translation. Besides, complete editions were replete with variant readings and variations in the sequence and the expanse of the different chapters of the text. Ghosh resolved these problems by evolving his own version of the *NŚ* on the basis of his study of the text without using any new and fresh manuscript material and offered his English translation to his readers. The Gaekwad edition was complete with its fourth volume in 1964. However, Ghosh did not see this last volume consisting of most important chapters of the text from the twenty-eight chapter to the end. He could not benefit by the excellent commentary which is the prime source of understanding of the abstruse core categories of the text. Ghosh had to encounter the challenge of rendering such culture-specific categories as *veda, śāstra, loka, nāṭya, rasa, bhāva, bhāvānukīrtana, abhinaya, dharmi, vṛtti, pravṛtti, svara, ātodya, gāna, gāndharva, raṅga* and the terminologies and concepts allied to these core categories.

His problem about culturally-specific categories remains almost unresolved even today. However, he could have explained and interpreted some of them by taking recourse to the *Abhi.Bhā.* Similarly, he could have taken help from the uninterrupted chain of the later texts and on *nāṭya, nṛtta, nṛtya, gāna, ātodya* and other allied art forms as well as the commentaries like those of Kallinātha and others. Besides, there has been an unbroken tradition of *prayoga* (practice). This tradition of *prayoga* has preserved some of the concepts despite enormous changes in practice in course of time. One can access the original concept by carefully analysing the process of change and offer the correct rendering of the text as well as its unhindered journey in all its practical aspects.

However, this could not happen. In order to make my point clear, I may cite an instance.

The *NŚ* defines *abhinaya* in terms of its three components which form its core content, namely *śākhā*, *nṛtta* and *aṅkura*.

> *asya śākhā ca nṛttañca tathā aṅkura eva ca* ।
> *vatūnyabhinayasyeha vijñeyñni prayoktṛbhiḥ* ॥
>
> *āṅgikastu bhavecchākhā aṅkuraḥ sūcanā bhavet* ।
> *aṅgahāravinișpannaṁ nṛttaṁ tu karaṇāśrayaṁ* ॥
> – *NŚ*, chap. 8, śls. 14-15

Ghosh translated the verses as follows:

> Producers of plays should reckon the *śākhā*, dance (*nṛtta*) and the *aṅkura* as the three aspects of histrionic representation. The gestures are called *śākhā*, pantomiming through them is the *aṅkura* and that which is based on the *karaṇa*s and consists of *aṅgahāra*s is called *nṛtta*.[5]

Out of many terms and categories we may select only four for our consideration – *abhinaya, āṅgika, śākhā* and *aṅkura*.

Abhinaya has been translated by Ghosh as 'histrionic representation', *āṅgika* by 'gestures', *śākhā* by 'gesture' and *aṅkura* by 'pantomiming'.

Ghosh takes recourse to readily available categories of Western dance and theatric terminology and renders these basic categories of Indian tradition in their terms. This method is unable to give their full and correct idea. *Abhinaya* cannot be simply 'histrionic representation'; it is much more than that. It is a means of 'registering', the special conventional gesture employed in *nāṭya*, integrating in it elements of *laya* (rhythm), *tāla* (beat), *svara* (notes of musical scale), *āhārya* (dress, make-up, props, etc. which are not essential components of the performer

---

5 Manmohan Ghosh (ed. & tr.), 2007, *Nāṭyaśāstra*, repr., Varanasi: Chowkhamba Sanskrit Series Office, vol. I, p. 152.

like his body, voice and mind, but are added [lit. 'brought near'] and, hence form the completeness of the *abhinaya*) and much else, for it is a category of performing art form emerging in a holistic frame of tradition.

Likewise *śākhā* is not simply gesture; it is very different and requires scholars as Abhinavagupta and Kapila Vatsyayan, ancient and modern ones, to make it intelligible to a modern reader. Both the scholars view this entire corporeal *abhinaya* in terms of body as a trunk and major and minor limbs in terms of its branches as has been defined in the chapter on *sāmānyābhinaya*.

The case of *aṅkura* is much more complex. Bharata himself defines it in terms of another allied concept *sūcā* or *sūcanā*, which has also been elaborated in the chapter on *sāmānyābhinaya*.

The correct meaning of the term and the whole concept of *sūcā* and *aṅkura* are still vibrantly present in different Indian classical dance forms and especially elaborated in the only living Sanskrit theatre tradition of Kerala, namely 'Kudiāṭṭam'. The concept of *aṅkura* is not confined to *nāṭya*: it pervades even art forms such as music and to a large extent paintings as well as sculpture and architecture. *Sūcā* is initial and indicatory to the corporeal manifestation of the inner abstract *bhāva* on the face and the body before one speaks and utters the word. Ghosh fails miserably in translating the verse defining *aṅkura* in the 20th chapter. The text reads:

> *hṛdayastho nirvacanairaṅgahinayaḥ kṛto nipuṇasādhyaḥ* ।
> *sūcevotpattikṛto vijñeyastvaṅkurābhinayañ* ॥
> — *NŚ*, chap. XXIV, śl 44, Ghosh's Text, vol. I, p. 173

Ghosh's translation is:

> When one skilfully represents by Gestures in the manner of *sūcā* and having the same source as the feeling which one has in one's own heart, it is called the representation of *aṅkura*.[6]

---

[6] Manmohan Ghosh, op. cit., p. 445.

Ghosh misses the meaning of the term *utpattikr̥ta*. He also ignores the most significant word *nirvacanai* 'done without uttering the text' (the meaning of which is expressed through *āṅgika* [corporeal] *abhinaya*).

The *aṅkura* (lit. 'sprout') is a specific kind of *āṅgikasāmānyābhinaya*. Like the *sūcā* it is performed by resorting to *utpatti* (generation). In other words it is a form of imaginatively performed generative and elaborate *abhinaya* which shoots forth successfully like a chain of sprouts. It is also done taking recourse to *āṅgika abhinaya* only without uttering the word implicit with multilayered meanings which are every time one by one made explicit by the artist without utterance. This process is still vibrantly present in a Kudiāṭṭam performance.

This same process may be experienced in musical renderings in its *alāpa* portion when a *rāga* is gradually expanded and elaborated. Again this process may be seen to a certain extent, in elaborative dimensions of classical and folk Indian paintings, sculptures and architecture.

It may be pointed out that a term *upaja* derived from *utpatti* is still prevalent in the north Indian Hindustani music circles and the term *aṅkura* is used to express the idea of the generation of very imaginative and innovative ways of rendering vocal or instrumental music. It is known to Indian logicians who also used this as a defining term when a new argument or point shoots forth during the debate.

It is clear that the idea of *aṅkura* is a still living one in not only the spaces of the arts, but of thought also. Thus, while rendering the text in the English language or any other language of another cultural background, one has to be fully aware of the tradition in which the specific text has emerged.

It becomes all the more important when one tries one's hands on the texts of Indian arts and aesthetics which have preserved their tradition in a vibrant dimension.

Rendering of *Abhi.Bhā* is an even more challenging task, for it not only carries forward the Nāṭyaśāstric tradition in its theory and practice, but has also given a new dimension to Indian aesthetic thought by attaining new heights in terms of the culmination of Āgamic metaphysics, spiritual and ritual practice as well as social vision. Abhinavagupta is a unique master who is credited with having clearer insight into Indian thought and practice in its entirety. This enables him to successfully integrate the apparently divergent streams into a unified Śāstra. *Abhi.Bhā* also begins the trend to approach a *prayoga śāstra* with the clear vision of method of exposition of such a Śāstra. His perception of the Śāstric tradition or *āmnāya* (tradition), the relationship between the knowledge as 'Veda and Śāstra', underlines the need for incorporating variant readings of the text wherever necessary and explaining the structure of the Śāstra, the hermeneutics it needs for unfolding its meaning, the need to demonstrate the inner consistency of the text by the exposition of the implicit, and resolving the apparent contradictions by offering solutions for them. Abhinavagupta is fond of elaborate discussion, yet never forgets to offer a brief summary of the discussion at the end. He introduces the subject matter in hand which occurs in the text, discusses in detail and summarizes it closely following the text. He demonstrates the application of the principle by citing the targets, wherever they are applicable. The *Abhi.Bhā* begins with these perceptions and clearly states the principles of the hermeneutic approach:

> *upādeyasya saṁpāthastadanyasya pratīkaṁ* ।
> *sphuṭavyākhyā, virodhānāṁ parihāraḥ supūrṇatā* ॥
>
> *lakṣyānusaraṇaṁ sliṣṭavyaktavyāṅśavivecanaṁ* ।
> *saṅgatiḥ paunaruktyānāṁ samādhānasamākulaṁ* ।
> *saṅgrahascetyayaṁ vyākhyāprakāo 'tra samāśritaḥ* ॥
>
> — *Abhi.Bhā*, *NŚ*, Nagar edn., 2003, vol. 1, p. 2

He is so committed to show the unity of the Śāstric text,

that he never fails in showing inner connections word after word, sentence after sentence, chapter after chapter. The final culmination is the unity of Śāstra as one great sentence (*mahāvākyā*).

His prose is of a piece with the best Sanskrit prose, loaded with meaning still astonishingly leaning towards the principle of clarity and lucidity. However, it is always necessary to be attentive to his metaphysical, ontological and epistemic positions presented in a most compact language with the intense desire to exhaust all the meanings. The meaning must arise from the given words only, therefore, his insistence on understanding through etymology based on its roots and based as well on syllabic formations. He is only satisfied when he combines the principles of theory with instances of its clear application in practice.

Unfortunately, full advantage of the commentary and its later tradition has not been taken in the translation of this great work. The difficulty is that to translate the *NŚ* or the *Abhi.Bhā*, one needs another Bharata or Abhinavagupta, which is almost impossible today. Piecemeal efforts at translating the texts in portions would also not work, for they would lack in uniformity. Only a committed team of scholars can do the job in our times.

Another dimension of the problem in rendering the categories of the Indian theory of arts and aesthetics in the English language lies in the fact that we need a team of scholars equally conversant with the Western theories of the arts. Only then can we discover the correspondences in the Western tradition of theory and practice. Fortunately some models are available in the works of A.K. Coomaraswamy[7] and the works

---

7 Anand K. Coomaraswamy, (i) 1995, *The Transformation of Nature in Art*, ed. Kapila Vatsyayan, New Delhi: Indira Gandhi National Centre for the Arts and Sterling Publishers.
(ii) 1957, *The Dance of Śiva*, rev. 14th edn., New York: The Navodaya Press.

of M. Hiriyanna,[8] K.C. Bhattacharya[9] and Kapila Vatsyayan.[10]

Anand Coomaraswamy was searching for the nearest possible correspondences of Indian aesthetic categories in the core categories available in Chinese and other Asian traditions on one hand and the corresponding categories in the pre-renaissance tradition of Europe especially in the works of M. Eckhart. He has successfully rendered the core categories in the English language which appear to be quite authentic from the Indian Śāstric viewpoint on one hand and may be intelligible to the Western reader on the other. He also offered a model of translation in his *Mirror of Gesture* by assimilating the visual sources available in Indian paintings and sculpture in order to make the concept more intelligible. This was certainly a right approach and was readily followed in Kavi's edition of the *NŚ*. Thus Coomaraswamy is a path-breaker who sets a model for future scholarship.

Hiriyanna does it by understanding these categories in the light of Advaita Vedānta and searches for parallels in early modern Western philosophy.

K.C. Bhattacharya discovers his way, taking recourse to a deeper philosophical analysis for making the central category of *rasa* intelligible to the Western frame of mind.

Kapila Vatsyayan has assimilated all these approaches in her effort to render these categories intelligible to the modern reader; she has enlarged the area of exploration further by integrating

---

8 M. Hiriyanna, 1954, *Art Experience*, Mysore: Kaivalya Publishers.

9 K.C. Bhattacharya, 2011, *Concept of Rasa: Indian Philosophy in English*, ed. Nalini Bhushan and Jay L. Garfield, New York: Oxford University Press.

10 Kapila Vatsyayan, (i) 1983, *The Square and the Circle of Indian Arts*, New Delhi: Roli Books International.

(ii) 2007, *Classical Indian Dance in Literature & Arts*, New Delhi: Sangeet Natak Akademi.

into it the studies of V.S. Agrawal.[11] She has rendered singular service to the cause of the furtherance of understanding and making them intelligible to the modern reader by going deeper into the ideational background of Indian aesthetics and its philosophical and fundamental principles. This augurs well for further work in the field of Indian arts and aesthetics in general and the spaces of theatre, dance and music in particular.

RESPONSE

Kapila Vatsyayan

Prof. Tripathi has raised some very fundamental questions, giving examples from his own experience of the past twenty-five years. What he has presented is the historiography of the editing of the *Nāṭyaśāstra*, which is important in terms of the manuscripts especially for those of us who have been engaged in making what are called 'critical editions', a category which is in itself a question mark. Some of us have raised this question as to what constitutes an authentic text and what is today termed as a 'critical edition'. For the last two days we have been talking about *the text:* what is that text and which are the manuscripts on which the published text is being discussed.

The next question is about authenticity. There is some kind of distancing if not rupture between those who have put their noses into the leaves of unpublished materials, made collations, brought them out as 'critical editions' and faced the nitty-gritty problems of selecting particular words from variants available in different manuscripts, and those others who understandably work on published texts.

As regards *Abhinavabhāratī*, perhaps we should shift our attention to Dachigam. I happen to be a Kashmiri and I know

---

11 V.S. Agrawal (i) 2003, *Indian Art*, Varanasi: Prithvi Prakashan. (ii) 2003, *Studies in Indian Arts*, 2nd edn., Varanasi: Vishwavidyalaya Prakashan.

where Abhinavagupta lived along with all the people you have mentioned. I wondered what they were doing at those heights, talking about such things. Dachigam today is under the Army, and last year I got special permission to spend three days and nights there. Those were rare people, people in time, physical linear time, and one has to experience that ambience to empathize with what they were doing.

I just want to raise these two questions because if I ask the rhetorical question, what were they doing there, the next question would be, what happened to the *Abhinavabhāratī* the written text: when was it written, when was it located, where was it located? As most of you know, after a lapse of many centuries a written text of *Abhinavabhāratī* was located in Kerala, the manuscript being in the Grantha script. We have then to go by the written text in Grantha, attributed to Abhinavagupta, but cannot say that this manuscript was the original writing of Abhinavagupta. Needless to state, there are a host of questions which have not been raised and are not normally raised.

DISCUSSION

Aloka

Tripathi ji after listening to you it occurs to me that the central question remains: how do we in a contemporary context put together a textual tradition? And when Kapila ji raises this whole question of dating, of genealogy, of where to locate the text and so forth, then it would seem that the living traditions should be the beginning point and only after them the texts. Is that what you are suggesting? Would that be viable?

For example there are a variety of *jāti*s and these constitute a living tradition; despite the processes of homogenization of identities, they continue to exist in the social system. So the way this adaptation is taking place and what has survived as a living tradition should also be taken into account.

Kapila Vatsyayan

When you talk about living traditions, all I am saying is that this is something that we have to define. Tripathi ji is naturally talking about this technical term called *prayoga* in the theatrical space.

Aloka: Intervenes

lakin āp ne yeh kahā thā ki yahāṅ se śuru karte haiṅ kyoṅki yeh abhi hai hamāre pāss – śāstroṅ ne bhi śuru kiyā thā: ab hum ko kyā karnā chāhiye? (But you said that we should start from here because these living traditions are still with us: the Śāstras themselves have their origin in practice: which is the right approach?)

Tripathi

If we identify our contemporary theatre with modern theatre and also post-modern theatre then if you ask me about the relevance of the text, I would say that as early as 1892 Craig observed that the future of theatre will lie in Asia, in India. We have already reached the dead-end of modern theatre and speak of the 'death of theatre' in post-modern terms. The question regarding technology remains at the core of the entire discourse, be it film, TV or video which are all considered genuine art forms. In the light of these facts, what is the relevance of traditional Indian theatre and the text related to it?

Moreover some have now come to the conclusion that this theatre is not dead: so aver people like Richard Shechnev, Peter Brooke and Eugenio Barba. They come to India and different regions of Asia and Africa to derive a new language for their creativity. Here lies the relevance of traditional Indian theatre as well as the text which is deeply rooted in *Nāṭyaśāstra*. But what do we mean by our contemporaneity? What do we mean by our modernity? I am reminded of Habib Tanvir who took up this challenge as early as the 1950s. He was educated abroad and in the search for his own identity he came to India and started work with the tribals of Chhattisgarh. This is the answer. Habib Tanvir is a modern theatre man, that is his answer.

P.K. Mukhopadhyay

The dilemma is with our living tradition. I have found that with theatre art forms in Kerala also the performers display no knowledge of the texts. They learn from their own continuing tradition but are unable to relate themselves consciously to the text. On the other hand, theoreticians are relating their performances to those traditions, but it may be asked as to whether we are interpreting those traditions in a particular way because we already have this textual knowledge and try to substantiate our reading of the text with the tradition. The concept *aṅkura* is not confined to Nyāya Śāstra.

Tripathi

I would like to point out how the text has reached the artist. For example, I was looking for something in the living tradition and to my surprise came across *aṅkura stutpathi* where *aṅkura* has been defined in terms of generation. *Aṅkura* is that variety of *abhinaya* which arises from a generative process. For example when I was listening to north Indian classical music, members of the audience exclaimed *wāh kyā upaj kā gāna hai* 'How beautifully this music develops'. So whether they identify it with the *Nāṭyaśāstra* or not, the Śāstra is linked to it – this is how I understand it.

9

The Death of Language
An Afterword

Wagish Shukla

THE Sanskrit words for language do not relate it to the 'tongue'. More correctly, the 'mouth' is merely a mediator in the Indian conceptualization of language. We speak, but 'speech' – *bhāṣā* or *vāk* or *vāṇī*, etc. – has a trans-physiological status. Language, as understood in the West, is merely a corporealization of this existence which is free from actual representation. The actual representation may be a vocal representation or a scriptal representation; it may be a dynamic print on the space–time, an inscription on the cosmos, in fact, the cosmos itself. If we examine one single word *vān*, from which *vāṇī* derives and look at some other derivatives thereof, we find that *vāṇa* means 'musical instrument' as well as 'arrow', *vānija* means 'commerce' and *vāninī* means 'actress/dancer'. This is in addition to the well-known meaning of *vāṇī* as 'sound' or 'language' and the not so well-known meaning of the same word as 'price'. It is not irrelevant, I think, to recall that contemporary linguistics has to make major theoretical adjustments if it wants to consider drum-signalling as a language; in fact, the written language is itself a major problem area for the theoretical formulations in linguistics. In terms of the theoretical range itself, therefore, certain conclusions implicit in the Indian visualization of language are still in the process of being accommodated by the Western visualization.

To recapitulate: the Indian concept of the exteriorization of language is embodied in the following:

1. The performative act of dancing and acting and the production of rhythmic sounds through musical instruments. This is what I have called a 'dynamic imprint on space–time' above. This is not a retrievable record; it is more in the nature of an archiving in a non-traceable crypt. But it does not perish. Let us note here that *vāṇa-śabda* means 'sound of the lute' as well as 'the whizz of an arrow'.
2. The performative act of speaking and writing.
3. The performative use of commercial traffic. We may relevantly draw attention to the fact that the word 'interpret' derives from *pratium* meaning 'price' and signifies 'to fix a price by common accord'. This is the social aspect of language, relating *vāṇī* and *vāṇija*, the two meanings of *vāṇī*, one as language, and the other as price.

Language is fascist, as Roland Barthes once said, because it forces us to seek a meaning for every grammatically constructed sentence. I would expand this by saying that fascism is actually a consequence of the very conditions that are involved in the *praxis* of language as a public institution, in the coercive deployment of words to communicate a meaning. But this fascist hold is broken by asking: communication with whom? As the Mīmāṁsā thinkers assert, the gods do not reside outside the hymn. I do not think it can ever be convincingly demonstrated that there is meaning outside the word. When two persons speak with each other, they create an instant pidgin, a vulgate. This vulgate, for which I shall re-purpose the word *apabhraṁśa*, is characterized by the fact that its usages are not to be derived by the rules of the primal language but by the rules of communication that generates the *apabhraṁśa*. Thus, when a poet writes a poem, her language is grammaticated by the requirements of poetic communication. Nobody can argue that T.S. Eliot wrote everyday English but nobody can deny that he wrote his poetry in English.

To recapitulate: language is performative. I could have said, perhaps should have said, 'representative'. However, I believe that in the Indian mind representative acts are actually performative. A sculpture is a performance. A painting is a performance. There is no ideal 'Truth' with a capital T which is to be represented; it is the performance through which truth manifests itself. I must emphasize here that my use of 'performance' here is distinct from, and is indeed in opposition to the Chomskyan use of 'performance'. When Chomsky speaks of the 'competence/performance' binary in linguistics, he wants to assert that there is an 'innate capacity' of language in all human beings, a faculty called 'competence', whereas there is an actual *praxis* called 'performance'. My use of 'performance' is related more to creativity, the capacity to generate things new, what is called *pratibhā* or *śakti* in Sanskrit literary theory. By 'performance' I mean this creativity. Someone could say that there is a Chomskyan notion of 'creativity' as well. I cannot enter the finer details of the differential here and will prefer to close this part by saying that while there are common points underlying my use of 'performativity' and Chomskyan 'creativity', my use of 'performativity' should be understood as closer to artisticity. Here again, I could be accused of excluding what is known as 'everyday' or 'ordinary' use of language. However, my contention is precisely that there is no such thing as an 'everyday use of language' in the Indian philosophy of language sciences.

This should not go unsupported and I will supply my argument. I have noticed that all the Indian words that relate to language, poetry, drama and other such activities also carry a meaning which is directed towards violence. Let me briefly point out some of these words:

1. *Śabda*, which means 'word' and is the core on which grammar concentrates, derives from 'sap' which means 'to curse'.
2. *Nāṭya*, which means 'dance/drama' and is the core on which literary theory concentrates, derives from *naṭ* which means (a) 'to act', (b) 'to dance', and (c) 'to hurt', 'to kill'.

3. *Vāṇ*, some of whose derivatives and meanings we have mentioned above, incarnates as *vāṇ* and in this form it gives rise to a series of words which derive their meanings from its significations such as 'to love', 'to conquer', and 'to injure' 'to kill'; the basic signification 'to sound', is of course retained.

In some places, I have taken up this point with other words like *ānanda* and *rasa*. Essentially, the import is that violence is at the root of language use and that communication is a kind of injury. This is of course not an injury to anybody else – for there is no communication with anybody else at this level of identity marking. Every speaker creates a listener in her own image and speaks to herself when she speaks to this other. But it is an injury all the same.

Language is the practice of death, a mactating knife dividing the language performer in two parts – the speaker and the listener.

The word 'mactating' in the above sentence is not exactly a well-known English word and I insert an interlude here to explicate it. I have taken the idea from Emile Benveniste. He posits this word in the context of sacrifice and asserts that the word 'libation' should be related to the situation when the material offering is liquid, say melted butter, and that when this offering is solid, such as an animal, it should be called 'mactation', which is rooted in the Latin verb *mactare*, meaning 'to sacrifice an animal'. Benveniste's account is not quite complete here because when he says that this is confined to Latin and survives in the Spanish *matar*, meaning 'to kill', he is obviously not taking into account the verb *matamataya* used by Bhavabhūti in exactly this sense of sacramental killing in his *Uttara-Rāmacarita*, or, for that matter, the word *matak*, which means 'dead body'. Incidentally, the word *mactare* also means 'to exalt' which is in complete accord with the basic concept that the sacrificed animal is exalted out of its earthly existence into a heavenly one.

To end the interlude and return to my story, the mactating knife of language manifests itself in a trinity: the speech act, the speaker and the listener. This trinity is the accessible and analysable face of language, the object of linguistic science. The mactating knife, i.e. language, is non-substantive, the specter in the spectrum which eludes the spectrograph. Mirza Ghalib asked a fundamental question:

> The spectation, the spectator, and the spectated are in reality one!
>
> I'm in a fix; how do we account for spectrology?

Therefore there is no everyday use: every time a language performance takes place, it is a non-substantive *Dionysia*, a hollow celebration of the death of God, the punishments of man and the hideous caricatures of existence on earth. The performance takes place on an absent centre around which the satiric disfigurement which is called 'meaning', and the masked and booted actors who are called 'words', dance into the demented pastiche known as *syntagmata*.

We will be speaking about the death of this practice of death in our times. The metaphorical equation of the language performance locus with *Dionysia*, which I have proposed above, thus entails that the proposition of the death of language is to be isomorphed to Karl Jasper's proposition of the death of tragedy. It may even be taken as an extension of this particular thesis. This extension is obtained by isomorphing the tragedy – the practice of death which language performance is – to the following metaphorical equation given in *Śrīmadbhāgavatam* (XI.10.12.1):

> The teacher (= speaker) is the first *araṇi* (that is, the lower wood-piece from Premna Spinosa) and the student (= listener) is the second (that is, the upper) *araṇi*. By attrition, the two kindle the fire of discourse. This conjunction is the source of pleasure.
>
> And this fire then burns the qualificata that span this illusion

> which is the causality of the universe. When the qualificata perish in this fire, the fire of discourse itself perishes exactly as any fire does due to lack of fuel.

And let us note that *araṇi* also means 'pain', and thus the source of pleasure – the discourse, the knowledge, the language – is being posited as the conjunction of two pain statements as if the language game follows a cancellative logic in which two negatives add up to a positive. But this normative choice of labels – negative for pain, positive for pleasure – is invalidated by the passage itself. The fire is the source of pleasure, consuming the qualificata and in turn, being consumed by their consumer energy. The cancellative logic extends the arithmetic of this consumer culture: two negatives add up to a positive vanishing into zero.

Language is the practice of death in this sense. It is in this sense that it is the performance of tragedy. When this performance ceases to be *Dionysiac* and succumbs to the Apollonian evangelization mouthing the True, the Good, and the Beautiful, the death of tragedy – that is, the death of the practice of death – occurs.

Our times have clocked in at the zenith of the Apollonian evangelization graph with only the postmodern speculum keeping in a possible de-Apollonianization. This article is an afterword to this death of the practice of death. But we must first say something about writing.

Writing, says Lakshmana Deshikendra in his *Śāradā-Tilaka*, is the body of language: 'I home myself in the goddess named language who morphs as writing.' This must be immediately differentiated from the allegedly Aristotelian position of modern linguistics which traces writing as a secondary representation: a code which encodes the spoken sounds which themselves form a code.

The *Śāradā-Tilaka* position picturizes the alphabet as a tree; the branches are constituted by earth, the leaves by water and so on. The Pāṇinian alphabet arranged as a list of forty-two letters is collocated into a matrix of nine subdivisions, each subdivision a cluster of the representatives of the five elements – the second subdivision does not contain the letter for earth and the ninth subdivision does not contain the letters for earth and water; so the arithmetic is consistent. The point is: all corporeality, the cosmos as we know it or can know it, is a piece of writing: the representation as a tree paints the letters for the empty space as the fruits of this tree. To put it in another way: there are no fruits in this cosmic system.

The *lipitaru* (tree of writing) therefore, is a philosophical painting and represents the well-known Vedāntic thesis that the world is unreal like a painting on a canvas. In other words, the cosmos we have before us is merely a representation. But a representation of what? Is there a reality out there which this cosmos represents as a painting?

In the Indian system, we find two answers which are actually two versions of the same answer. The first one, which I shall call the 'mild version', is given as follows:

> I bow to Śiva, the one to be lauded by all the arts, who paints this painting, the world, on a no-canvas with no tools.

I call it a 'mild version' because the painter, Śiva, has not been explicitly negated. I have taken this verse from *Setubandha*, the commentary by Bhāskararāya on *Yoginī-Hṛdayam*; the precise reference is the commentary on the verse 50 in chapter. 1. Another commentary on the same book, *Dīpikā* by Amritananda Yogi, quotes a verse that can be called a 'milder version'.

> Śiva who paints by the stylus of his desire for this painting, the world, on himself as canvas, is the only watcher of the result and is pleased.

This version is milder because here the canvas and the stylus are not negated; they are identified with the painter. But if we combine the two verses given by the two commentators, we see that the painter is indeed negated, because if the canvas and the stylus are identical with the painter and the canvas and the stylus are negated, then it follows that the painter is also negated. This conclusion is what I shall call the 'strong version'.

Let us also note that the original verse, *Yoginī-Hṛdayam* I.50, whose commentaries have been referred to, uses the word *ullekha* for painting which means (a) writing, (b) painting and (c) quotation.

I now want to quote from this work:

1. The reader is the space on which all the quotations that make up a writing are inscribed without any of them being lost; a text's unity lies not in its origin but in its destination.
2. Writing is now linked to sacrifice and to the sacrifice of life itself. . . . Where a work had the duty of creating immortality, it now attains the right to kill, to become the murderer of its author.
3. Representation is death itself which may be immediately transformed into the following: death is [only] representation.

The metaphor of death, repeatedly used in the above quotations, forces one conclusion: writing erases the writer. But the reader is still supposed to exist; to use the words of Roland Barthes, the unity of a text lies in its destination through the origin being voided out of relevance. But I have argued above, on the basis of Indian intellectual authority, that there is no destination either. I will give just one more reference in this connection; on this reference I have expatiated elsewhere. Bharata Muni in his *Nāṭyaśāstra* talks about the architecture of the Hall of Performance for a play. As a spectator enters it, from the entrance to the centre a series of deaths awaits her. This series of deaths destroys all identity markers that constitute her: the geographical space, the historical time, the psychological power that could enable her to associate with the actors or the plot in the play. This is catharsis at its extreme and it works with retrospective effect: you are purged of everything that constitutes you before you approach the text. You are an empty space, with the defining dimensions of length, breadth and height, together with the arrow of time, collapsed into a dimensionless singularity, a black hole in which all mathematical equations, on which the structure of space–time rests, fail. The quotations that make up the bricolage known as writing – Roland Barthes' 'text' – are to be collapsed into this black hole.

Language use is non-chronic, non-topic. The endless debates in linguistics about diachrony and synchrony, about its dispersal and change and variation over time and space, are constructs so that the academic industry can go on but there are no inference engines.

In writing, the writer and the reader are not the only ones who are extinguished. As Mirza Ghalib astutely notes in one of his Persian verses:

> I wish you would weigh it that the manifestation of the pen and the writing is exactly the stake and the rope for the hanging of meaning.

Yet the meaning is also extinguished. Writing turns language into an object to be stored and retrieved, to be examined at one's convenience. As a physical construct, it carries no self-destructing gene. So the first thing it does is to kill speech and the speaker. The question is no longer, 'what does the speaker mean?' The question is, 'what do the words mean?' Not, let us note, 'what does the writer mean?'. Modern linguistics started in the late eighteenth century of the Christian era when William Jones noted that several Sanskrit words corresponded to words in European languages, suggesting a common origin. When Pāṇinian grammar became known to the West, its positions as understood were restructured in the basic axiomatics of linguistics. The primacy of speech over writing and of synchrony over diachrony is one such holy cow of modern linguistics. Scholars have only now begun to question such readings of Indian grammatical positions.

I will not deal with the question of chronological precedence here. However let us note that the dating mechanism of Western scholarship was, at least until recently, severely constrained by a constructed Biblical chronology which put the date of the creation of the universe at 4004 BCE and, if I recall correctly, of the Tower of Babel accident sometime around 3500 BCE. A similar commitment to placing the cradle of civilization in what is called the Near East makes it impossible for anything of significance to be non-Semitic in origin. Thus the Phoenician inscriptions were deciphered by assuming that the Phoenician language must have been akin to Hebrew. This assumption is generally omitted in the accounts of the deciphering of this language. Then this writing system is supposed to have been passed on to the Greeks and to India, and the sequence assumes that writing is a superposition in India.

When Tulsīdās wrote his *Rāmacaritamānasa*, he went to Raskhan and orally transmitted the epic to him for three years. He did not just hand over the manuscript to Raskhan. And the oral transmission for the purpose of communication is also dispensable, because when Guṇāḍhya wrote his *Bṛhatkathā*, he read out six volumes of the seven-volume work to himself in a jungle with no human population.

You do not need a partner to play the language game. You recite the Vedas orally, but 'orally' does not describe it completely because the hand has to move in space at the same time. The tactile accompanies the oral. And let us not forget that the Vedic literature is heard: not written or read or composed. To play the language game, you do not need a partner but the game has to be played orally, visually and tactually. These do not support each other; they erase each other.

Lipi comes from the root *lip* (to smear). In particular, it means 'to smear the tip of an arrow with poison', so that *liptaka* means 'poisoned arrow'. And let us not forget that there are at least five kinds of *lipis* in the Indian conceptualization. To quote from the *Vārāhī-Tantra*:

> There are five kinds of scripts. The performing arts constitute a script. The representational arts constitute a script. The literary arts constitute a script. The verbal arts constitute a script. And when worms eat into paper, this constitutes a script.

This last, the script produced by the worm eating into paper, is the basic script on which all other scripts expatiate. Let me quote from Māgha to explicate the idea:

> The Creator was accused of being no writer. It was said that His creation of Lakṣmī, the goddess with the ultimate beauty, was as if a worm had eaten into paper to shape a letter and the Creator had claimed credit for being the writer of this literary masterpiece. So the Creator created all these most beautiful women in the city of Dvārakā, each one jealous of the beauty of others and thus proved completely beyond doubt that He was indeed the author of the literature known as Lakṣmī.

All the literary exercises that we entertain, the scriptal acts that have been listed in the verse quoted above from *Vārāhī-Tantra*, are no more than exercises in mimesis, a mimesis of one basic vermiculation, one basic textual cut made quite unintentionally into the absent canvas somewhere some time, eating away a part. Every time a letter is traced, an anti-environmental attack is launched and an incision by the poison-tipped arrow, which is called the pen, is completed in the cosmic body realized as the body of the individual. Of course there is the 'pleasure of literature', the pleasure that the writer and reader feel when they approach literature. I have elsewhere commented on the words in Indian literary theory which are used to describe this joy and in particular pointed out that *nirvṛtti*, the word that Mammaṭa uses for this pleasure, directly means 'death'. I wish to comment on one particular mode of *nirvr̥tti* using a verse by Māgha.

Nirvr̥tti is of course the same as *nirvāṇa*, which is now an established entry in the English lexicon. It means 'death'. It also means 'pleasure', and there is little doubt in my mind that the high position this word occupies in the Buddhist system is inspired by this word-play. Māgha is using the same word-play, locating it into a different sphere:

> These waterfalls in the hills of Raivataka, from a height dash themselves onto stones and bounce back to the heavens providing the comfort of cool to the *apsaras* whose body-temperatures are high due to sexual arousal. In this they are like those men who commit ritual suicide by dropping to their death from a mountain peak and spiritedly fall upon these sexually aroused *apsaras* propelling their bodies to orgasm [*nirvāṇa*].

By the writing act, every author commits ritual suicide and leaps into an orgy of pleasure with the reader as partner. The verbal root *likh* (to write), also means to unite sexually with a female, as attested by Nīlakaṇṭha in his commentary on the *Mahābhārata*.

*****

We have walked through the killing fields of language in the above paragraphs. The death of the author, the death of the reader and the death of meaning have been mentioned and commented upon. I have used references and citations from India as well as the West. The basic difference between these two sources of ideas needs to be briefly examined.

The examination can begin by looking into the labels 'India' and 'West'. As classificatory labels, they are misleading if read as geographical markers. The purchase of the nub of the matter is obtained by replacing 'Indian' by 'pagan' and 'Western' by 'revelatory'. These are not exactly religious brand names. For instance, Plato is mostly revelatory but it is not the case that he is never pagan. In an exactly religious classification, he is a pagan. But the India/West classification is not quite vacuous either because the Indian mind is the only pagan mind that has survived, and on available evidence, it is also the only one that has carried the pagan logic to its extreme ends.

What is this pagan logic? Quite simply, it is the sense of the tragic. This is of course not a new suggestion. Thus Karl Jaspers has argued that tragedy is not possible in a Christian universe. More recently, in the context of the Islamic universe, the following observation has been made:

> With the Muslim poets, life became directed by God's own hand. God, for purposes of His own, willed man to be or not to be. The tragic end of destiny was blunted and the once living and poignant tradition became a flat convention.

However, I think that it is the observations made by Nietzsche that go to the core of the problem. As is well known, he divided the Greek vision into two categories: the Dionysian, which may be roughly called 'wild', and the Apollonian, which may be roughly called 'harmonious'. The Greeks, Nietzsche argued, were basically Dionysian. So there was no logic and no beauty in their possession; they had to create them. Science and art were thus forced upon human kind and were performative, not representational, using the terminology I have employed in some earlier paragraphs in this piece. This Dionysian vision has been called Asiatic by Nietzsche; we know that the reason for this terminology is that the God Dionysus came to Greece from India. The Dionysian is thus the same as Indian. This Indian mind which I have called pagan to essentialize the point out of geopolitical associations, has to earn its solutions: there are no revelations that provide these solutions. When pagans created gods, they created them as linguistic units, not as solutions. As our Mīmāṁsā thinkers insist, there are no gods outside the particular *mantras* in which they are invoked. There is no Dionysus outside the Dionysia. Which is why the Vedas are authorless: *apauruṣeya* – nobody, in particular no god – has created them.

Language is the only possession that a pagan has and all the struggles must consist of reordering its units, for want of a better description. There remains the question, of course, whether this possession is given to the pagan, but I do not think it is a problem to answer it. It is quite clear that language is given to a pagan in the same sense in which existence is given to her. If there is any logic or beauty in language, if there is any meaning in it, it is consequent and proportionate to the effort the pagan has to put towards defining and codifying things. But definition and codification are Apollonian acts and we must look at the apparent contrast that confronts us here.

Response

Navjyoti Singh

The main point that Prof. Shukla is making appears to be that language as we know in modern times is morbid; it is a dead matter.

A few questions come to mind. One is the circularity entailed by the worm eating into the surface on which a script is inscribed. By its performance, the worm creates a new script. But language, in the view being discussed, is itself performative rather than referential. So a circularity surfaces in the grammar of the two scripts – that of the worm and the one it eats into.

The question is: is there a higher or alternatively an even more basic script from which all others get derived? Can this circularity thus get voided?

There is another issue which I wish to raise. There are, in certain traditions, oral inscriptions; not like the written externalized graphic ones but sonic inscriptions, dating from antiquity as for instance the inscriptions of the Veda. So we need to ask: what is the status of the Veda and what is the script of its inscription? Somewhere the Sanātana tradition is vitally dependent on this Vedic inscription which is inscribed orally in the mind of the Vedapanthīs. And that has been a main anchor of the Sanātana tradition. How would you relate the idea of paganism to the oral inscriptions of the Veda?

Discussion

Shukla

Basically we have to get out of certain usages. For example death is not morbidity. I mean it is not related to morbidity. Unfortunately every language carries a load. I have used the word 'death' because I am writing in English. But if I were to write in Hindi or in Sanskrit, I would have used *mr̥tyu*. To understand what *mr̥tyu* is, one must read the *Śatpatha Brāhmaṇa* which is a well-known and easily available Vedic document: it will say that in the centre of the sun there is *mr̥tyu*. So the sun which is a symbol of life-giving forces, has at its centre *mr̥tyu*. *Mr̥tyu* does not have morbidity, death has. What can I do? I am writing in English. There is no word for *mr̥tyu*. So these are certain limitations and these are also illustrative of the problems that are being discussed.

Navjyoti Singh

. . . *maraṇa* and *mr̥tyu* have the same etymology.

Shukla

Yes but *maraṇa* also has the same connotation. There is a poem by Nirala in which he says: *de mujhe mahā maraṇ*. ['Give me a mighty death' ed.]. If you read *Śrīmad Bhāgavat* you find the same meaning. The moment Kaṁsa is killed people will throw flowers on the one who is killing – why? The reason is that Kaṁsa got *mokṣa* immediately on being killed, sooner that the *gopī*s did or for that matter anybody. Why? Because he was thinking of Kr̥ṣṇa twenty-four hours in the day. There was no time at which he was not thinking of Kr̥ṣṇa whether he was asleep or awake. Therefore he got instant *sāyujyam*. There is no concept of death, it is always *sāyujyam pūje maheśam*. When one worships Durgā, one worships Mahiṣāsura also. Why? Because he is identified with the goddess. So it is the merger of one identity into another: the word I have used for *sāyujyam* is 'transformation'. But anyway, let us accept that I, at least, am not using the word 'death' in the sense in which we relate it to morbidity: I am using it as an English alternative for the word *mṛtyu*.

So if there is one finite life from birth to death and after that there is no concept of anything which is either, then of course death is a terrible thing because you are either going to be eternally condemned or you are going to be in heaven. This is what I meant by saying that if you follow a few precepts you will get 'A' grade and if you don't you have failed the examination and you have to face all the consequences. But this is a closed science. You already know what is to be done. The path is laid down in the Bible, in the Koran. Follow this and you will get well – that is certain. But for the pagan, life is just another name/thing in the minds of people.

Why is there a theory of *punarjanma*? No Indian thinker has ever rejected this theory, whether he be a Buddhist or Jaina or whatever. They all accept *punarjanma* because this is characteristic of the Indian way.

I should explain in what sense I am using the word here – the Veda and the pagan system. Unfortunately the word 'pagan' – (I have been deliberately using it in my articles) originally meant 'vulgar'. . . . So what are the words that have come out of it? 'Villain' is one. Ironically, the 'Urb' which constitutes the Urban, the hallmark of the post-pagan West, is also derived from it.

But note that the 'Urb' is the hallmark that keeps people out. Exclusivity is the idea here and because of that, some are saved. That is why it creates a closed science. Everything is known and you do not have to walk out of the 'Urb' into the wilderness and meet strangers. So 'pagan' is a word I am deliberately using.

But let us look to the Veda. What is Veda in our conception? We are always talking about its date. Now for people who do not believe in dates (such as me) and who are willing to accept quite easily that Veda is *apauruṣeya,* it hardly matters. So the Veda in our system, in our understanding is not authored. So in some sense at least, the death of the author had already occurred in Vedic times.

The Veda is not an authored book, the *Bhagavad-Gītā* is. In the non-pagan systems there is simply nothing without an author. The Bible is not merely the Word, it is the Word of God. It is a received work. In order to get something, to revive something, there has to be a sender and there has to be a receiver. Now this Veda simply exists. Vyās has given so many alternative meanings of the Veda. There are at least nine ways of interpreting it. One of them is *aitihāsika* (historical). So as he said, one can find so many things in the Veda but is the searching technology sufficient to characterize the text, to exhaust its meaning? That which I am calling the pagan system says that there is always something which is beyond one's question and answers. And this is a crucial difference. It is not a closed science (if we prefer to use fashionable and contemporary terminology), it is open but not in the sense that you can add to it but in the sense that it possesses an open architecture. It is not possible to access this through language. So there is always something beyond the practical use of language, this *vaikharī* (spoken) language. It is not only a question of one language not being translatable into another, or one culture not being understood in terms of another. There is always something even about us which cannot be accessed through language. I realize that this needs much more support than I can provide here.

Balagangadhara

It is broadly accepted that one of the most important functions of language is to describe the world outside it. If I make the following proposal, how would you react? Could it be the case that when it comes to the Indian systems, they all (whether it is Advaita Vedānta, Yoga Vāsiṣṭha or Viśiṣṭa Advaita) are teaching one to act, to live in a particular way? In other words, they are not saying what there is in the world but are manuals in a manner of speaking. Of course in order to understand a manual you need reference points in the world. So when they say for example that when the Buddha argued for *anātman* or Śaṅkara spoke about *ātman*, one way of interpreting, which is what most Indian philosophers have done, is that they attribute doctrines to them and say this is a description of the world. But actually they were not describing the world. Buddha does not say *ātman* exists or does not exist or whatever. Śaṅkara is not saying *ātman* exists because that would be a description of our world. So what a *guru* does in our tradition, which is what the *updeśa* is, is to teach one not to look at these as descriptions of the world; he teaches one how to transform them into a way of living. So *Yoga Vāsiṣṭha* does not tell you what the world is like. That can be said in one sentence. Why then does this man have to write so much? It is to help you go on in a certain way and then say that this is not a description of the world. Would you accept that?

Shukla

Yes I would accept that for the very simple reason that the mundane conclusion, the end conclusion of Vasiṣṭha is that Rāma, who was not interested in the world, became interested in the world. Just as Arjuna was not willing to fight but after the Gītā *upadeśa* he agreed to fight. Note that he did not become willing to fight but he agreed to fight.

Balagangadhara

He acted.

Shukla

You are certainly quite right.

10

The History of Indian Materialism

Ramkrishna Bhattacharya

THERE are two ways of reading philosophy: philosophical-doctrinal and historical-textcritical. The first approach does not pay much attention to the growth and development of a philosophical system and treats the doctrine as a whole. The second approach, on the other hand, studies a philosophical system from its inception through further developments till it ceases to grow or stops at a state when it is still growing. The two approaches should be considered complementary, not contradictory. I propose to follow the second approach in order to get a more comprehensive view of a system.

The history of materialism in India is much older than the Cārvāka, also known as Lokāyata. Two doctrines, *bhūta* and *svabhāva*, are mentioned in the *Śvetāśvatara Upaniṣad* 1.2 (not later than third century BCE). Both the names are associated with the later developments of materialism. In the early centuries of the Common Era there were several pre-Cārvāka materialist views in south India as mentioned in the old Tamil epics such as the *Maṇimēkalai*.

The word Cārvāka is a proper name borrowed from the *Mahābhārata* but seems to serve as a nickname of the adherents of the Lokāyata system. All Cārvākas were not unanimous in their approach to the relation of the body and consciousness: some believed that consciousness *arises* out of the combination of earth, water, fire and air whereas some others held the view that the consciousness is only *manifested* out of these elements.[1] Unlike the pre-Cārvāka materialists, the Cārvākas did not rule out inference as a whole as an instrument of cognition; they admitted inference in so far as it was based on perception rather than any word of the scriptures. Thus the doctrinal aspects of the Cārvāka/Lokāyata are more complex and richer in content than the textbooks of Indian philosophy represent them to be. For one thing the pre-Cārvāka materialists used to believe in the existence of five elements (ether or space, *vyoma* or *śūnya*, in addition to the four mentioned above). But the Cārvākas admitted only four elements presumably because space was not perceivable by the senses.

The word 'cārvāka' as the name or nickname of a system of philosophy as also of its followers is *not* encountered before the eighth century CE. The other name, Lokāyata, in the Buddhist tradition (Pāli and Sanskrit, Mahāyāna and Hīnayāna) *does not* mean materialism: it signifies Vitaṇḍāśāstra, the art of disputation. By the eighth century the two names, Cārvāka and Lokāyata, along with another, Bārhaspatya (relating to Bṛhaspati, the mythical *guru* of the gods) are used interchangeably to signify materialism. Another oft-used term, *nāstika*, means the denier of the other-world but also the defiler of the Veda. In the first sense the Cārvākas alone are to be called so, but the same word is employed against the Buddhists and the Jainas in the second sense. The names mentioned by the opponents of materialism, such as Dehātmavāda, Bhūtacaitanyavāda, Tajjīva-taccharīravāda and the like, are used mainly to suggest the Cārvāka/Lokāyata.

There was at least one base (*mūla*) text of the Cārvākas, a collection of aphorisms (*sūtra*s) attributed to Purandara. There were several commentaries, no fewer than five, on this or some other base text. They were composed by Aviddhakarṇa,

---

1 Kamalaśīla, 1981, *Tattvasaṁgrahapañjikā*, Varanasi: Bauddhabharati, pp. 633-34.

Udbhaṭabhaṭṭa (Bhaṭṭodbhaṭa), Kambalāśvatara, Purandara, and Bhāvivikta. Extracts from the commentaries of the first four are found in the works of the Brāhmanical, Buddhist and Jain opponents of materialism. There are reasons to believe that there were other commentators of the *Cārvāka-Sūtra* too.

In the present state of our knowledge it is impossible to be definite about the origin and growth of the Cārvāka/Lokāyata. However, it can be asserted that it was a living philosophy from the eighth century to twelfth century CE after which this system seems to have disappeared without leaving any trace. The reason for this sudden disappearance is not known. It is nevertheless certain that when Sāyaṇa-Mādhava compiled his digest of all philosophies *Sarva-Darśana-Saṁgraha* in the fourteenth century CE, he had no Cārvāka/Lokāyata text to quote from, or even refer to.

The earliest known materialist (rather proto-materialist) is Ajita Kesakambala, a senior contemporary of the Buddha (sixth/fifth century BCE). After a long gap, in the early Common Era we have the mention of three materialist schools in the Tamil epic, *Maṇimēkalai* (between the fourth century and the seventh century CE). It is only in the eighth century CE that Kamalaśīla quotes a few Cārvāka aphorisms verbatim in his commentary on the *Tattvasaṁgraha*,[2] a polemical work written by his preceptor, Śāntarakṣita. In several Brāhmanical, Buddhist and Jaina works (written between the eighth century and the twelfth century CE) more such aphorisms are quoted. They are concerned mostly with the following issues:

a. The first cause (*jagat-kāraṇa*);

b. the relation of consciousness to matter;

c. the nature of the spirit or self or soul (*ātman*);

---

[2] For a collection of such aphorisms and other fragments, see R. Bhattacharya, 2009, *Studies on the Carvaka/Lokayata*, Firenze (Florence): Societa Editrice Florentina, pp. 69-104.

d. rebirth and the other-world (*paraloka*);

e. efficacy of the performance of sacrificial rites (*yajña*); and

f. the valid instrument(s) of cognition (*pramāṇa*).

All the items mentioned above were controversial. A sharp line was thus drawn between idealism and materialism on both ontological and epistemological grounds. It is evident that the Cārvāka/Lokāyata epistemology was tailor-made to defend its ontological positions.

Since our knowledge of materialism in India is derived wholly from the works of its opponents, it is difficult to be certain about the social and ethical outlook of the materialists. The charge of hedonism brought against the Cārvāka/Lokāyata appears to have no basis, for no aphorism is quoted by the antagonists which is the case when they try to refute other views of the Cārvākas. The one verse found at the end of the *Sarva-Darśana-Saṁgraha* (*SDS*), chap. 1, which urges people to drink clarified butter even by incurring debt (*ṛṇaṁ kṛtvā ghṛtaṁ pibet*) is a gross distortion of the original reading of the half-line, "nothing is beyond the ken of death" (*nāsti mṛtyor agocaraḥ*).[3] The first reading is found in only one instance in the *SDS*; in thirteen other occurrences of this verse there is no mention of either borrowing or of clarified butter. Amusingly enough, in the *SDS*, the original version is quoted first at the beginning of the chapter but at the end the distorted version is offered. If Kṛṣṇamiśra and Śrīharṣa are to be believed, the Cārvākas were opposed to gender discrimination and casteism (see the *Prabodha-Candrodaya*, Act 2 verse 18 and the *Naiṣadhacarita*, canto 17, verses 40, 42, and 58).

A few verses of doubtful origin have been attributed to the Cārvākas in several compendia and digests of philosophy. Some of them oppose animal sacrifice and flesh-eating and may be of Buddhist and/or Jaina origin. Other verses that deny the alleged

3 For a detailed study see Bhattacharya, op. cit., pp. 201-06.

result achieved by performing post-mortem rites may genuinely reflect the materialist view. The thrust is no doubt anti-Vedic, or rather against the religious acts ordained by the canonical law-books, the Dharmaśāstras. But it is doubtful whether such an attitude was the focus of the materialist tradition in India. More probably the anti-religious attitude was the logical corollary of its epistemology and ontology.

At least one parable, the parable of the wolf's footprint,[4] is of pre-Cārvāka origin, as it is alluded to in the *Mahābhārata* (*Mbh*) (critical edition, 12.132.2; vulgate edition, 12.134.2). The parable was supposed to teach that a moral inference unsupported by perception may lead to wrong conclusions. The parable, however, has been widely used both by the Buddhists and the Jainas to represent the Cārvāka view. Some other verses (such as *viśeṣe 'nugamābhāvāt sāmānye siddhasādhanāt*, etc. 'No concomitance being possible in the case of the particular and there being the charge of "proving the proved" in the case of the universal', etc.)[5] representing the epistemological position of the Cārvākas may reflect the view of one or the other Cārvāka philosopher but such versified versions appear to have been composed by their critics while representing the opponent's view (*pūrvapakṣa*); they may not be verbatim quotations.

The verses attributed to the Cārvākas, in any case, could not have been the pivot of the Cārvāka system. Like many other philosophical systems in India, the Cārvāka/Lokāyata too developed along the line of a base text followed by its commentaries and sub-commentaries. The verses are mere popular sayings (*ābhāṇaka* and *lokagāthā*) passing from mouth to mouth, generation after generation till they were written down.

There are, however, reasons to believe that the pre-Cārvāka materialist views too were orally transmitted.

---

4 For a detailed study see Bhattacharya, op. cit., pp. 175-86.

5 For all the variants of the verse see ibid., p. 86.

The epistemological position was not stated clearly and unambiguously: only the ontological views were declared, mostly in terms of a series of negations, such as: there is no soul without the body, no after-life and no after-world, no merit in performing sacrificial rites and in paying gifts to brāhmaṇas, etc. The epistemological grounds of these views were first formulated by the school that came to be known first as the Lokāyata (and then as the Cārvāka) somewhere around the sixth century CE. To search for any unbroken thread from Ajita Kesakambala to Bhaṭṭodbhaṭa (the last known commentator) will not bear fruit, for there is so much of temporal gap and so many missing links between the proto-materialist ideas and the base text (as well as the commentaries thereon) which came to replace all earlier materialist views. Purandara is said to have been the author of a *sūtra*-work as well as of a *vṛtti* (exposition) most probably an auto-commentary. There are other commentators like Aviddhakarṇa who may have been Naiyāyikas writing commentaries on the *Cārvāka-Sūtra* without being converted to materialism.

There is no way of knowing whether the materialists had a large following in either south India or elsewhere. Nevertheless, materialism as a system of philosophy was considered a formidable adversary by all the orthodox (Vedic) schools, such as Vedānta and Nyāya-Vaiśeṣika, as well as by the heterodox (anti-Vedic) schools, such as the Buddhist and the Jaina. In the centuries of great debate, between the eighth century and the twelfth century, the Cārvāka/Lokāyata has been criticized, slandered and ridiculed not only in the philosophical literature but also in poetry and drama. This is an indication of the great weight and potential worth of materialism in the Indian philosophical tradition.

What is urgently needed now is a philosophical map and a time-chart, however tentative it may be, to locate and ascertain where and when so many philosophical systems in India arose and spread to other regions, at which points of time. A particular variety of Śaivite philosophy originated in Kashmir; the Pāśupata doctrine owes its birth to south India and Navya-Nyāya spread from Mithilā to the Navadvīpa region of south Bengal as late as the fifteenth century. Prābhākara Mīmāṁsā, which was predominant in Rāḍha (a part of southern Bengal) at least in the tenth century, thus lost its ground. Similar instances will be found in other parts of India too. Kāśī (Varanasi) was long known to be the place of confluence of all philosophical systems, at least the pro-Vedic ones. Buddhist philosophy flourished mainly in upper India, although there were adherents in south India as well. Jaina philosophy had its centre in west India, particularly in Gujarat and Rajasthan. Only when the map is drawn and the time-chart is prepared shall we be able to envisage the whole philosophical scene properly.

Lastly a few words about Jayarāśi Bhaṭṭa's *Tattvopaplavasiṁha*. The work has been claimed to be the only surviving text of the Cārvāka/Lokāyata but the very nature of the work goes against such a claim. That Jayarāśi was not a materialist but a nihilist is amply clear from the last sentence of his book:

> When all the principles are upset (*upapluta*) then all [human] practices are to be understood as happening without any judgement.

Unlike Nāgārjuna or Śrīharṣa, Jayarāśi had no system of philosophy either to establish or to uphold. In his case it was all refutation, and refutation for refutation's sake. The only principle he sets out to upset is the validity of all-known instruments of cognition, such as perception, inference and word. Mrinal Kanti Gangopadhyaya has pointed out[6] that

---

6 M.K. Gangopadhyaya, 1998, *Mukhabandha* (Introduction) to *Jayarāśibhaṭṭer Saṁśayavāda* (a Bangla translation of the *Tattvopaplavasiṁha*, chap. 1 by Dilip Kumar Mohanta), Kalikata: Sanskrita Pustak Bhandar, pp. ix-xiii.

Jayarāśi's position is diametrically opposite to Vātsyāyana's: the latter is intent on establishing the principle of four *prakāras*, namely, *pramāṇa, pramātā, prameya* and *pramiti*. Once *pramāṇa* is established, the other three are automatically accepted (Introduction to his commentary on the *Nyāya-Sūtra*). Jayarāśi, on the other hand, not only questions (as a sceptic does) but seeks to *upset* the very concept of *pramāṇa* itself. In this sense he was a nihilist par excellence. In fact, Gangopadhyaya has rightly said that Jayarāśi was affiliated neither to the Cārvāka/ Lokāyata nor to Śūnyavāda or Māyāvāda: he had a doctrine of his own, namely, Tattvopaplavavāda. As there are Māyāvāda, Vijñānavāda, Śūnyavāda, etc. so is Tattvopaplavavāda, a particular type of approach or philosophy. His Jaina opponents mentioned this along with other *vādas*.

Jayarāśi's reference to Bṛhaspati as *bhagavān* does not confirm his affiliation to Bṛhaspati's system. Śrīharṣa the Advaita Vedāntin too uses the same term, *bhagavān suraguru*. Would that make Śrīharṣa a Cārvāka?[7]

It may also be noted that Jayarāśi is prized more in Europe and Japan than in India. He has been criticized and presented everywhere in the Jaina works as a *tattvopaplavavādin*, never as a Cārvāka. Those who have criticized him have also sought to refute the Cārvāka/Lokāyata. Erich Frauwallner too never considered the *Tattvopaplavasiṁha* to be a Cārvāka work.[8]

Elli Franco's translation of and notes on the *Tattvopaplavasiṁha* are indeed excellent, but his view of Jayarāśi as a kind of *lokāyatika* and his polemics against Chattopadhyaya[9] have not found favour even in the West. Karel Werner in his review

---

7 Śrīharṣa, (n.d.), *Khaṇḍanakhaṇḍa Khādyam*, Varanasi: Chowkhamba, p. 26.

8 S.N. Dasgupta, 1973, *History of Indian Philosophy*, vol. 2, Delhi: Motilal Banarsidass, pp. 256-57.

9 E. Franco, 1994, Preface to *Perception, Knowledge and Disbelief*, 2nd edn., Delhi: Motilal Banarsidass, pp. XI-XIII.

of Franco's book, proposes to steer a middle way between Chattopadhyaya and Franco;[10] earlier still, Walter Ruben and K.K. Dixit pointed out many a flaw in assuming Jayarāśi as a Cārvāka.[11] Chattopadhyaya was too modest to include his views on the *Tattvopaplavasiṁha* in the anthology, Cārvāka/ Lokāyata, edited by him. He had in fact written two articles in Bangla in 1963,[12] refuting the notion that the *Tattvopaplavasiṁha* was a materialist philosophical text (as A.L. Basham had once called it).[13] Chattopadhyaya reiterated his opposition to this misconception in his three popular books in Bangla and English.[14] Franco was apparently unaware of Basham's claim and therefore unhesitatingly declared in the preface to the second edition of his *Perception, Knowledge and Disbelief* that "no one ever claimed that Jayarāśi was a materialist" (pp. XII-XIII).

Basham was not alone in making this regrettable mistake. Those who work on the basis of secondary sources have all followed suit and represented the *Tattvopaplavasiṁha* as a Cārvāka *materialist work*. They even ignore the fact that Franco, along with Sanghvi and Parikh, label him cautiously

---

10 K. Werner, 1995, Review of Franco, E., *Bulletin of the School of Oriental and African Studies*, **58**(3): 578.

11 D. Chattopadhyaya, and M.K. Gangopadhyaya (eds.) 1990, *Cārvāka/ Lokāyata*, New Delhi: Indian Council of Philosophical Research, pp. 505-30.

12 D. Chattopadhyaya, 2010, *Saṅghaṁ Śaraṇaṁ Gacchāmi Ityādi Agranthita Racanā*, Kolkata: Ababhas, pp. 74-84.

13 A.L. Basham, 1954, *Wonder That Was India*, New York: Grove Press, p. 297. In a later edition, *Wonder That Was India,* Calcutta: Rupa & Co., 1973, p. 300, Basham however revised the statement: Instead of "one materialist philosophical text" he wrote "one anti-religious philosophical text".

14 D. Chattopadhyaya, 1964, *Indian Philosophy*, New Delhi: People's Publishing House, pp. 221-23 n4; 1989, *In Defence of Materialism in Ancient India,* New Delhi: People's Publishing, pp. 36-41; 1987, *Bhārate Vastuvād Prasaṅge*, Calcutta: Anushtup, pp. 33-39.

as representing "a minority (*ekadeśa*) within the Lokāyata school" and admit that "Jayarāśi rejected some of the traditional Lokāyata doctrines and interpreted some of the *sūtra*s of Bṛhaspati as reflecting opinions which are not Bṛhaspati's own". The very notion of a *non-materialist* Lokāyata as proposed by Sanghvi and others is alien to the Indian philosophical scenario. The Cārvāka/Lokāyata has been referred to by all ancient and medieval philosophers in India as a materialist system; no one speaks of such a non-materialist school.[15]

RESPONSE

Wagish Shukla

Let us try to examine a few points thrown up by this paper. Why is this Lokāyata a brāhmaṇa? Because the brāhmaṇa happens to be the main opponent. But perhaps also because in this context the brāhmaṇa believes in a kind of argumentative frame for all humans which is not available in any system which has to assert something which is describable as Tattvopaplavavāda or rather the Pramāṇopaplavavāda. Let us try to trace the origin of these positions. In the first place there are obviously two different things which may have been one in origin but where the system developed in two directions. According to Śrīharṣa there are three groups of people that can be bracketed in, *lokāytika*, *śūnyavādī* and somewhat surprisingly Śaṅkara's Vedānta. Now all of them are certainly not *nāstika*. One might say that the *lokāyate* are *nāstika*, that *śūnyavādī*s are *nāstika* in a different sense, but Śaṅkarācārya was not a *nāstika*. Nor in the intellectual history of India is this bracketing by Śrīharṣa an isolated comment. This seems to be a widely accepted bracketing because we do find Vyāḍya, a Jain scholar of the eighth century

---

15 Franco once told me in a letter (Hamburg, 20 July 1997) that if I could accept both Buddhist idealists and Buddhist realists, why could I not accept the sceptic *lokāyatika*s and materialist *lokāyatika*s? This is inference by analogy which is always doubtful.

or so – he precedes Śrīharṣa – also bracketed the *śūnyavādī, tattvopaplavavādī* and the *brahmavādī* together. Now, there may be many *brahmavādī* systems but presumably if somebody qualifies to be called a *brahmavādī,* he or she would accept *brahma satyam*. Then the basic question is, what is being denied? Etymologically, *satya* here is derived from *sat*. So, they are all *pramāṇopaplavavādī* according to at least two persons yet one of them is an adherent of Advaita Vedānta, namely Śrīharṣa. He is a well-known *vedāntin* and he destroys all the *pramāṇa*s just like Jayarāśi Bhaṭṭa does. Nevertheless, he has to assert something also. And that assertion is that there happens to be something which may or may not be accessible via argument.

What I am trying to say is that mere negativism, while it can be used in a limited sense as the denial of arguments, in this case what is being denied is perception, which is not nihilism. Are they not trying to assert something positive? I suggest that what these people are trying to say is: look here, don't be arrogant, do not think the linguistic techniques that you are devising are going to capture the truth. In particular do not be terrorized by the tyranny of truth, which your language has created by its definitions and consequent deliberation.

Now let us come to a crucial question. What is the difference between this Tattvopaplavavāda and the Cārvāka? When it comes to the acceptance of the *pramāṇa*s there are roughly, perhaps inaccurately, four divisions in the Indian style. One is the *indriyādhipatya*, that proposes that unless something can be grasped by an *indrī*, it is not a *pramāṇa*. So, for those Cārvākas who accept *pratyakṣa* as a *pramāṇa* and deny all others one can say yes, theirs is an *indriyādhipatya* position. Then there is *anīndriya adhipatya*. This is the position of the Śaṅkara Vedānta, where nothing is a *pramāṇa* unless it is either *āgama* or *antaḥkaraṇa*, or rather *citta*. And finally we have the Āgamapatya Mīmāṁsā which admits only Āgama nothing else. So, if it comes to classification and categorization we may say that Cārvāka happens to belong to the *indriyādhipatya* but this categorization again will be limited to the *pratyakṣavādī* interpretation which accepts only knowledge from the senses. The Vedāntic position is very strongly against this, when it says that the *indriyas* are not only incompetent but positively misleading.

There are in fact very few people in India's intellectual history who ultimately do not accept that discourse has limitations. Some have been aggressive about it, like Nāgārjuna or like Jayarāśi. Śrīharṣa has not been so aggressive. But I am unable to locate a single individual, at least amongst the major intellectual stalwarts who claim that what they are saying is enough to describe the world. Sure there is a way to describe the world, and they are suggesting a method, but they do not claim adequacy for it.

Surely this position cannot be described as materialism.

DISCUSSION

Mullick

In closing this very fruitful session I would like to draw your attention in the context of the translational problem to the description of this view as materialism. Look at the richness of the field, the argumentation and the very fine points that have been raised. Because we say that the Cārvākas or Indian materialists do not represent the real tradition, probably because of its contrast to idealism we have set it aside. This is again because of the Western method of carving up philosophical stances and schools. If one claims that no one can show that there is a soul or anything at all for that matter, then one is dubbed a materialist.